Richard M. Alderman
"The People's Lawyer™"

KNOW YOUR RIGHTS!™

NINTH EDITION

Answers to Texans' Everyday Legal Questions

LONE STAR BOOKS

Guilford, Connecticut
Helena, Montana

LONE STAR BOOKS

An imprint of Globe Pequot
Distributed by NATIONAL BOOK NETWORK

British Library Cataloguing in Publication Information available

Library of Congress Cataloging-in-Publication Data

Names: Alderman, Richard M., author.
Title: Know your rights! : answers to Texans' everyday legal questions / Richard M. Alderman.
Description: Ninth edition. | Guilford, Connecticut ; Helena, Montana : Lone Star Books, [2018] | Includes index.
Identifiers: LCCN 2017036578 (print) | LCCN 2017039876 (ebook) | ISBN 9781493030460 (e-book) | ISBN 9781493030453 (pbk.)
Subjects: LCSH: Law—Texas—Popular works.
Classification: LCC KFT1281 (ebook) | LCC KFT1281 .A37 2018 (print) | DDC 349.764—dc23
LC record available at https://lccn.loc.gov/2017036578

♾️™ The paper used in this publication meets the minimum requirements of American National Standard for Information Sciences—Permanence of Paper for Printed Library Materials, ANSI/NISO Z39.48-1992.

Printed in the United States of America

KNOW YOUR RIGHTS! ™

YOUR

RIGHTS! ™

NINTH EDITION

For my grandparents

CONTENTS

CHAPTER 4

Contracts, 39

CHAPTER 5

Credit Cards, 54

CHAPTER 6
Debt Collection, 70

CHAPTER 7
Divorce, Marriage & Child Custody, 104

CHAPTER 8
Door-to-Door Sales, 132

CHAPTER 9
Employment, 135

CHAPTER 10

False & Deceptive Acts, 150

CHAPTER 11

Immigration, 171

CHAPTER 12

Landlord & Tenant Rights, 185

CHAPTER 13
Lawyers, 213

CHAPTER 14
Mail-Order, Telephone & Online Sales, 216

CHAPTER 15
Miscellaneous Problems, 222

PREFACE TO THE FIRST EDITION

You may not think about it, but nearly every day you have to know the law. Not only must lawyers make decisions based on knowledge of the law, but people like yourself must apply basic legal principles in daily life. And if you do not know the law, you are making decisions partially uninformed.

The Texas and federal legislatures have passed scores of laws designed to protect you in your everyday transactions. Most of these laws are considered self-regulating. This means the laws are supposed to work because you know about them, and your knowledge keeps merchants from trying to violate the laws. The breakdown in this system is apparent: Because most people do not know their legal rights, the laws often do not work.

This book is designed to ensure that our laws do work by helping you learn about them. The book covers a wide variety of topics ranging from credit card rights, to landlord-tenant relations, to the legal aspects of warranties and wills. The choice of topics and the format of the book are based on my personal experience as "The People's Lawyer™" for a Houston television station.

As "The People's Lawyer™," I have received thousands of letters about the most common legal problems. This mail has led me to two conclusions: First, many of you share the same everyday legal problems to which you do not know the answers; and second, there is no readily available source of information. This book was written to address both problems.

But this book is not designed to make you a lawyer, nor is it meant to encourage lawsuits. Instead, it is designed to make you aware of the choices and rights you have under the law. Whether you are dealing with a store that will not replace a damaged television set, a neighbor whose barking dog keeps you awake all night, or perhaps a landlord who deducts too much from your security deposit, you must know your legal rights to reach a fair, equitable solution.

Once someone knows you know your rights, he is usually quick to try to work something out. Compromise and settlement—not litigation—should be the goals of any legal system. They are the goals of this book.

Richard M. Alderman
"The People's Lawyer™"

PREFACE TO THE NINTH EDITION

As I noted in the original preface to this book, my goal in writing *Know Your Rights!*™ was to help everyday people understand the law, enabling them to better stand up for their rights. The book has been even more successful than I imagined. Now, more than thirty years after its initial publication, I find I must again update the book to keep up with the increasing number of legal questions I have received and the changes made to the law by the courts and legislature.

The format of this edition remains the same. What has changed is the coverage. In the first edition, I discussed what I believed to be the most common legal questions people had. In subsequent editions, I added several new chapters and expanded many of the existing ones. For example, chapters discussing divorce, immigration law, and employment were all added. In this edition, I have expanded the coverage of nearly every chapter and updated answers to comply with current law.

As you might expect, some of the material in earlier editions has become out of date or incorrect because of action by the courts and legislature. A problem with any book about law is keeping it current. With the publication of this edition, you now have the most up-to-date information available. It is unavoidable, however, to prevent even this edition from being dated. The material is based on the law as it exists in June 2017. To track any changes in the law and stay current with new developments, visit my website, www.peopleslawyer.net, and subscribe to my free Consumer Alert Newsletter.

Those of you who are buying this book to replace your eighth edition already know how valuable a resource it can be. If this is your first purchase, let me emphasize what I said in the first edition. *Once someone knows you know your legal rights, he is usually quick to try to work something out.* I hope you find this book one of the best investments you have ever made.

Richard M. Alderman
"The People's Lawyer™"

KNOW YOUR RIGHTS!™

NINTH EDITION

CHAPTER 1

Applying for Credit

For nearly all of us, credit is an essential part of life. Our homes, our cars, and much of our personal property are purchased on credit. Just imagine what it would be like if we had to pay for everything with cash. Yes, America is truly a land of consumer credit; together we owe almost four trillion dollars.

Because of the importance of obtaining credit, Congress has passed three laws to protect people who are trying to get it:

1. The **Equal Credit Opportunity Act** ensures that all credit applicants start off on the same foot by prohibiting discrimination based on color, age, sex, race, or marital status.

2. The **Truth in Lending Law** protects individuals from paying too much for credit by requiring that all relevant information be disclosed before a contract is signed and, more importantly, that the information be provided in an understandable manner. In other words, you must be given enough information to permit you to shop around for credit.

3. The **Fair Credit Reporting Act** requires that you have a full opportunity to find out what information is in your credit report. It also gives you the right to have any errors that might exist in that information corrected.

When you apply for credit, you should know the law. You should also know what factors are important in obtaining credit and what information your creditors cannot use to deny you credit. As you will discover in the following letters, there are legal solutions for some of the more common problems you may experience while trying to obtain credit. For copies of all the relevant laws, as well as updates on any amendments, go to my website, www.peopleslawyer.net.

What is the CFPB?
"The new federal Consumer Financial Protection Bureau."

Dear Mr. Alderman:
I have been told that there is a new federal agency that protects consumers. What is its name and how do I make contact?

You are correct. There is a new federal agency designed exclusively to protect consumers. The Consumer Financial Protection Bureau (CFPB) was created after the 2008 financial crisis to protect consumers. Following problems in Congress, it finally began work in 2011. The CFPB provides a single point of accountability for enforcing federal consumer financial laws and protecting consumers in the financial marketplace. Before, that responsibility was divided among several agencies. Today, it's the primary focus of the CFPB. Here is a list of some of the things included in the work of the Bureau:

- Rooting out unfair, deceptive, or abusive acts or practices by writing rules, supervising companies, and enforcing the law
- Enforcing laws that outlaw discrimination in consumer finance
- Taking consumer complaints
- Enhancing financial education
- Researching the consumer experience of using financial products
- Monitoring financial markets for new risks to consumers

Since the CFPB began its work, it has returned almost $12 billion to consumers. In 2016 it revealed that Wells Fargo employees had opened two million phony accounts without consumer permission, resulting in a fine of $100 million. You may obtain more information about the CFPB, and view its numerous consumer resources at www.consumerfinance.gov.

Note: At the time this book was written, Congress and the President were considering ways to severely restrict or eliminate the CFPB. One way to stay current with developments in this area, as well as with consumer rights in general, is to subscribe to my free Consumer Alert Newsletter at www.peopleslawyer.net.

Why can't I get credit?
"You must be told why."

Dear Mr. Alderman:
I need your help. I can't figure out why no one will give me credit. I have applied for two credit cards, and both times I was turned down.

I have a good job, and I have never had financial problems. What can I do to get credit?

If you have been turned down for credit and have not been told why, someone has violated the law. Under the Equal Credit Opportunity Act, you must be notified of the decision within 30 days after your application was completed. *If credit is denied, you must be notified in writing. The notification must explain the specific reasons for the denial or inform you that you may request a full explanation.*

If you are denied credit, be sure to find out why. In your case, reread the letter you received and see if it tells you who to contact for an explanation. If it does not, write the creditor and demand to know the specific reasons it denied you credit. You also should consider filing a complaint with the Federal Trade Commission (FTC), www.ftc.gov, and with the Consumer Financial Protection Bureau (CFPB), www.consumerfinance.gov/complaint.

After you find out why you were denied credit, you can take steps to correct the problem. It may be that the creditor thinks you have asked for too much money or that you have not been employed or lived in the community long enough. Once you know why, you can discuss these reasons with the creditor and attempt to work it out. Sometimes you will discover the creditor simply had incorrect information. As you will see in the next letter, credit reports may be wrong, and when they are, you can correct them.

How do I get a copy of my credit report?
"There are three credit bureaus."

Dear Mr. Alderman:
I have had problems getting credit because of prior debt problems. I have had a good credit history for the past eight years, and I now want to make sure that my credit report is accurate and that the negative information has been removed. How do I get a copy of my report?

You are correct in wanting to obtain a copy of your credit report. It is very important to periodically review your credit report to make sure it is accurate and complete. There are three major credit bureaus and each probably maintains a file on you. You may request a copy of your report from each agency. Here are contact data for each agency:

- Equifax: (800) 525-6285; www.equifax.com
- Experian: (888) 397-3742; www.experian.com
- TransUnion: (800) 680-7289; www.transunion.com

How much does a copy of my credit report cost?
"You get one copy a year for free."

Dear Mr. Alderman:
I know it is important to review my credit report. I was wondering,
how much does it cost to get a copy of my report? I see ads all the
time for a "free credit report." Is there usually a charge?

In the past, credit bureaus charged for a copy of your credit report unless you had recently been turned down for credit. The companies advertising "free credit reports" provided the report for free, but also tried to get you to purchase their other services. Under a change in the law, however, every credit bureau now must give you a copy of your report for free once every twelve months. I strongly suggest you take advantage of this free service and review your report to make sure there are no errors or problems with identity theft. The best way to ensure the accuracy of your reports is to get one report every four months. For example, you may get a free report from Equifax in January, Experian in May, and TransUnion in September. For your free copy, go to www.annualcreditreport.com.

My identity was stolen. What should I do?
"Here are the steps to follow."

Dear Mr. Alderman:
I just discovered that someone in California stole my identity and
opened new accounts in my name. I found out when I was rejected for
a credit card due to unpaid accounts I didn't even know existed. What
should I do? Am I going to be liable for all these bills?

How can someone steal your identity? Identity theft occurs when someone uses your personal information such as your name, Social Security number, credit card number, or other identifying information without your permission to commit fraud or other crimes. The thief actually lives as you, at another address, opening new accounts and incurring bills in your name. As you have discovered, you usually don't find out about this until he stops paying the bills, and it goes on your credit report.

Identity theft is a serious crime. People whose identities have been stolen can spend months or years—and their hard-earned money—cleaning up the mess thieves have made of their good name and credit record. In the meantime, victims may lose job opportunities, be refused loans, education, housing, or cars, or even get arrested for crimes they didn't commit.

Here is what you should do to start cleaning up the mess the thief has made with your credit.

Immediately contact the fraud departments of any one of the three major credit bureaus and place a "fraud alert" on your credit file. The fraud alert requests creditors to contact you before opening any new accounts or making any changes to your existing accounts. As soon as the credit bureau confirms your fraud alert, the other two credit bureaus will be automatically notified to place fraud alerts, and all three credit reports will be sent to you free of charge.

Then, read the reports carefully and close the accounts that you know or believe have been tampered with or opened fraudulently. Use the ID Theft Affidavit, available from the Federal Trade Commission, when disputing new unauthorized accounts.

File a police report! Get a copy of the report to submit to your creditors and others that may require proof of the crime.

File your complaint with the Federal Trade Commission. The FTC maintains a database of identity theft cases used by law enforcement agencies for investigations. Filing a complaint also helps the FTC learn more about identity theft and the victim's problems. The FTC website is www .consumer.gov/idtheft. You also should visit the website for the Consumer Financial Protection Bureau (CFPB). The CFPB is a government agency created after the 2008 financial crisis to protect consumers. The Bureau enforces the consumer credit law, creates tools to assist consumers, answers common questions, and provides tips that help consumers navigate their financial choices and shop for the deal that works best for them.

The bottom line is that although it may take some time to clean up the problems caused by the identity thief, you should not have any liability. Under the law, you are not liable for any credit extended in your name without your authorization. Your credit report also should be cleaned up so that there is no reference to the fraudulent account.

What is "phishing"?
"Don't let it catch you."

Dear Mr. Alderman:

I just received an email notice from a bank telling me my account has been suspended. It was very official looking. There was a link for me to reactivate the account. I don't even have an account at that bank. What kind of a scam is this?

It probably is what is called "phishing." Phishing involves sending official-looking emails, usually with the official logo of a company, telling you that there is trouble with an account. There are phishing emails that appear to be sent from eBay, Paypal, and numerous banks and credit card companies. They all have one thing in common—they are an attempt to get your personal information for purposes of identity theft.

In most cases, the phishing email will tell you that there are problems with your account or that it has been suspended. There will be a link for you to click to "reactivate" or "update" your account. Clicking on the link probably will do two things. It may install a worm on your computer, and it probably will take you to a very official-looking site that asks you for information about your account.

The bottom line is simple—NEVER give out ANY personal information in response to an email, PERIOD! If you receive an email you think may be legitimate, do not click on the link. Call the business involved or go directly to their website. Don't get caught by identity theft phishing. For more information about phishing, visit the FTC website at www.consumer.ftc.gov/articles/0003-phishing.

How can I stop identity theft?
"You can't stop it, but you can stop it from happening a second time."

Dear Mr. Alderman:
I have read so much about identity theft that I am really afraid it will happen to me. I try to protect my personal information but I know it is impossible to keep everything private. Is there any law I can use to prevent a thief from stealing my identity?

There is no law that completely stops identity theft. Although we have passed some laws making it harder to steal a person's identity and punishing identity theft with stricter penalties, all of us are still at risk of being victims of this crime. No matter how careful you are, and regardless of whether you avoid all the "phishing" emails, a thief may still steal your identity.

There is a way, however, to make sure it doesn't happen a second time.

Texas has a law allowing people who have been victims of identity theft to place a "security freeze" on their credit information, prohibiting access without express consent. A security freeze effectively prevents further identity theft by requiring that the consumer expressly consent to dissemination of information in his or her credit report. Any consumer filing a security freeze will be provided with a personal identification number that must be provided to the credit bureau each time an application for credit is made.

A security freeze will protect your credit from identity thieves; however, it will also make obtaining new credit more difficult. For this reason, I do not recommend that you use a security freeze unless you rarely apply for new credit and are not in a hurry when you do. Texas law provides that credit bureaus can't charge you more than $10 to put a freeze on your credit. It also requires that one credit bureau must honor a security freeze placed on a consumer's credit by another credit bureau. Here is information about how to file a security freeze:

Equifax
Phone: (800) 685-1111
Address: Equifax Security Freeze, P.O. Box 105788, Atlanta, Georgia 30348
What You Need to Do: Mail a certified request letter and payment, with a copy of your ID and a valid police report, investigative report or complaint, as well as complete address, date of birth, and Social Security number. For more information or to place a freeze online go to www.freeze.equifax.com.
Cost: $10, free for ID theft victims

Experian
Phone: (888) 397-3742
Address: Experian Security Freeze, P.O. Box 9554, Allen, TX 75013
What You Need to Do: Mail a certified letter with your full name, including middle initial; current address and two proofs of address (utility bill, bank statement, driver's license); Social Security number; date of birth. You must also send a valid police report, investigative report, or complaint. For more information or to place a freeze online, go to www.experian.com/freeze/center.html.
Cost: $10, free for ID theft victims

TransUnion
Phone: (888) 909-8872
Address: TransUnion Security Freeze, P.O. Box 6790, Fullerton, CA 92834
What You Need to Do: Send a certified letter and include your name, address, Social Security number, and credit card number with expiration date to pay for service. You must also send a valid police report, investigative report, or complaint. For more information or to place a freeze online, go to www.transunion.com/credit-freeze/place-credit-freeze.
Cost: $10, free for ID theft victims

What can I do if my credit report is wrong?
"You have rights."

Dear Mr. Alderman:

I was just refused a credit card. I was told the reason was that I had missed several payments on my motor home . . . but I don't even own a motor home. When I asked where the company obtained this information, I was told it was in my credit report. What should I do? I am sure all my creditors believe I am living in a motor home I'm not paying for.

A law protects you from having inaccurate information in your credit report. It is called the Fair Credit Reporting Act. This law protects you from inaccurate reporting of credit information by giving you the right to find out what is in your report and allowing you to require that the reporting agency correct any errors. Because of the importance of having an accurate and up-to-date credit file, I suggest you contact the credit reporting agency immediately and assert your rights under this law.

The Fair Credit Reporting Act applies to any "consumer reporting agency." The most common type of consumer reporting agency is the credit bureau. Information gathered by a credit bureau, called a "consumer report," is sold to creditors, employers, insurance companies, and other businesses for the purpose of evaluating your creditworthiness. If you are denied credit because of information contained in such a report, the creditor must give you the name and address of the credit reporting agency. I assume that, in your case, the creditor supplied you with this information.

The next step is to contact the credit reporting agency and request a full report of the information in your file. Under the law, the agency must provide you with a copy of the report within forty-five days. If you have been denied credit, you must be given a copy at no charge. A new law enacted in 2005 also allows you to get one free copy of your report from each agency once a year.

Under the law, the credit reporting agency must tell you about every piece of information it has concerning you. You also must be told the names of everyone who has been given a copy of the report within the past two years for employment purposes or the past year for any other purpose.

If you disagree with any of the information, you have the right to demand that the agency reinvestigate the items in question. The credit bureau must promptly reinvestigate. If the new investigation reveals an error, the agency must, at your request, send a corrected version of the report to everyone who received the old report within the past six months.

In your case, demand that the credit bureau reinvestigate. If the credit bureau discovers you do not own a motor home, you may require the bureau to renotify your creditors and give them a copy of the accurate report. Sometimes, though, the credit bureau will stand by its original report.

For example, a creditor may have reported that a consumer was late in paying some bills. The consumer paid late only because he did not receive the bills on time. The credit bureau may refuse to change the report because the creditor still says the consumer paid late. If this happens, you have the right to include a brief statement containing your version of why you paid late. This statement will become part of your file and will be sent whenever a creditor requests a credit report.

You should also be aware that there is a time limit on how long credit information can be reported by a consumer reporting agency. Generally, after seven years information is considered obsolete and may not be reported. However, a few exceptions to this rule exist:

- Bankruptcy information can be reported for up to 10 years.
- No time limit exists for information reported for a prospective job with a salary of more than $75,000.
- No time limit exists for information reported on more than $150,000 worth of credit or life insurance.

If you have ever applied for a charge account, a personal loan, insurance, or a job, someone probably has a file on you. This file might contain any information that creditors use to determine your creditworthiness. Everything, including how quickly you pay your bills, whether you have ever filed bankruptcy, and whether you have ever been sued, may be written into your credit report.

Because a good credit report is so important, it would be a good idea to check your file before a problem arises. It is quite easy to call or go online to get a copy of your report:

- Experian, (888) 397-3742, www.experian.com
- Equifax Credit Services, (800) 685-1111, www.equifax.com
- TransUnion, (800) 888-4213, www.transunion.com

You also may get a free copy of your credit report from each of the three bureaus once a year at, www.annualcreditreport.com, or call (877) 322-8228.

Does the seven-year reporting period begin anew when the account is reassigned?
"No."

Dear Mr. Alderman:

Seven years ago I had some financial problems that resulted in negative information on my credit report. I know that after seven years such information may not be reported. I looked forward to having a clean report. Now a different debt collector has contacted me and told me that it purchased my account. The company said that if I don't pay, this will be considered a new debt and the seven years will start all over again. Is this correct? I worked too hard to have my credit ruined for another seven years.

What the company told you is incorrect. The seven-year period is based on the date the account is first written off or placed for collection. The assignment of the account to a new debt collector does not restart the clock. Hopefully, the company will not take any steps to "re-age" the information. If it does, let the credit bureau know that it is the same account and that the information has become obsolete.

How can my ex-spouse's debts appear on my credit report?
"They were your debts as well."

Dear Mr. Alderman:

My former common-law husband and I bought a car and financed it through his credit union. He was the buyer. I just cosigned the note. After he missed two payments, they repossessed the car. They asked me to pay, but I told them that as far as I was concerned this was his debt. Now they have put this on my credit report. Can they do this?

Basically the answer is yes. As I discuss in Chapter 4, cosigning a note is a very serious undertaking. You are agreeing to the same obligation as the other person. If he doesn't pay, you have to. If there is a default, it is your default as well. The information will appear on both your credit report and his.

Remember, you have the right to add your own statement to your credit report explaining information contained in it. You may want to add a brief statement indicating that this is your ex-husband's debt.

How can I shop for credit?
"Truth in Lending."

Dear Mr. Alderman:
I am in the market for a new car. I know it's important to get the best
interest rate, but it is all so confusing. There are all kinds of ads with
different rates, and every time I call to ask about interest, they tell me
about the APR. What is an APR? How can I compare interest rates as
well as price? It seems that you can't find out the interest rate until
after you buy something.

Creditors used to be free to confuse consumers by using all sorts of language when they loaned you money. Interest rates could be quoted as "add on," "discount," or "simple." Terms of an agreement, such as down payment, total price, and penalties, could be hidden throughout the contract, and it would take a lawyer to figure them all out.

But under a law known as the Truth in Lending Act (TILA), all this has changed. Under this federal law, creditors must use standard language to disclose terms and must let you see a completed copy of the contract before you sign. *The purpose of the TILA is to let you compare rates and shop around.*

Under the law, if you went to three different car dealers, they would each have to provide substantially similar disclosures so you could compare how much you would pay and at what interest rate. The Truth in Lending Act requires that all borrowers receive written disclosures about important terms of credit *before* they are legally bound to pay the loan. These important terms include:

- *Annual Percentage Rate:* the APR is the cost of credit expressed as a yearly rate in a percentage;
- *Finance Charge:* the cost of credit expressed as a dollar amount (this is the total amount of interest and certain fees you will pay over the life of the loan if you make every payment when due);
- *Amount Financed:* the dollar amount of credit provided to you (this is normally the amount you are borrowing);
- *Total of Payments:* the sum of all the payments that you will have made at the end of the loan (this includes repayment of the principal amount of the loan plus all of the finance charges);
- *Lenders must also disclose* other important terms such as the number of payments, the monthly payment, late fees, whether you can prepay your loan without a penalty, and other important terms.

A credit sales contract should be written in standard language and should clearly reveal all costs involved in the contract.

Big Wheel Auto   Alice Green

ANNUAL PERCENTAGE RATE The cost of your credit as a yearly rate.	FINANCE CHARGE The dollar amount the credit will cost you.	Amount Financed The amount of credit provided to you or on your behalf	Total of Payments The amount you will have paid after you have made all payments as scheduled	Total Sale Price The total cost of your purchase on credit, including your downpayment of $ _1500 —_
14.84 %	$1496.80	$6107.50	$7604.30	$9129.30

You have the right to receive at this time an itemization of the Amount Financed.
☐ I want an itemization.   ☒ I do not want an itemization.

Your payment schedule will be:

Number of Payments	Amount of Payments	When Payments Are Due
36	$211.23	Monthly beginning 6-1-17

Insurance
Credit life insurance and credit disability insurance are not required to obtain credit and will not be provided unless you sign and agree to pay the additional cost.

Type	Premium		Signature
Credit Life	$120 —	I want credit life insurance.	_alice Green_ Signature
Credit Disability		I want credit disability insurance.	Signature
Credit Life and Disability		I want credit life and disability insurance.	Signature

Security: You are giving a security interest in:
☒ the goods being purchased.
☐ _____.

Filing fees $ _12.50_   Non-filing insurance $ _____

Late Charge: If a payment is late, you will be charged $10.

Prepayment: If you pay off early, you
☒ may   ☐ will not   have to pay a penalty.
☒ may   ☐ will not   be entitled to a refund of part of the finance charge

See your contract documents for any additional information about nonpayment, default, any required repayment in full before the scheduled date, and prepayment refunds and penalties.

I have received a copy of this statement.
alice Green   _5-1-17_
Signature   Date

_____
e means an estimate

Note that under the law, "interest rates" must be disclosed as an annual percentage rate (APR). This is a mathematical formula that lets you compare rates, no matter how creditors compute them. Why should you compare? A difference of only a few percentage points in the financing of a car could save you hundreds of dollars.

If you believe your lender has not complied with the Truth in Lending Act, you may file a complaint with the Consumer Financial Protection Bureau, www.consumerfinance.gov/complaint.

Are credit laws different for women?
"No! Equal credit opportunity exists under the law."

Dear Mr. Alderman:

I am a divorced twenty-six-year-old woman. I have worked for the past five years as the manager of a small baking company, and I think I make a good salary. The other day I went to my bank to borrow some money for a home improvement loan. The bank refused to give me the loan and told me a single person with two children might get married, leave town, and not pay back the loan. Even though I assured the loan officers this would not happen, they insisted I get a cosigner. This doesn't seem fair. I know that one of my male employees who makes less than I do just obtained a loan at this bank. Can they do this?

It is difficult to tell if you have been illegally discriminated against, based on your brief letter. However, a law that protects people from credit discrimination does exist. If after reading this you believe you have been the subject of discrimination, I urge you to contact the appropriate federal agency and file a complaint.

Because of the importance of credit in today's society, Congress has enacted the Equal Credit Opportunity Act. *This law prohibits discrimination against an applicant for credit on the basis of sex, marital status, race, color, religion, national origin, or age.* The law does not ensure that any one person will be given credit, but it does require that the same standard of creditworthiness be applied to all applicants.

Under the Equal Credit Opportunity Act, a creditor may not turn you down for credit just because you are a woman or single. To protect you from such discrimination the law specifically limits what a creditor may do when you apply for credit:

- A creditor *may not* ask your sex on a credit application—with one exception. If you apply for a loan to buy or build a home, a creditor is required to ask your sex to provide the federal government with information to monitor compliance with the act. You do not have to answer the question.

- You *do not* have to choose a courtesy title (Miss, Ms., Mrs.) on a credit form.

- A creditor *may not* request your marital status on an application for an individual, unsecured account (a bank credit card or an overdraft checking account, for example), unless you live in a community property state (Texas is a community property state) or rely on property located in a community property state to support your application.

- A creditor *may* request your marital status in all other cases. But you can only be asked whether you are married, unmarried, or separated (unmarried includes single, divorced, or widowed).

To make sure you are treated fairly once you apply, the creditor may not do certain things when deciding whether you are creditworthy. Specifically, the creditor:

- *may not* refuse to consider your income because you are a married woman, even if your income is from part-time employment.

- *may not* ask about your birth control practices or your plans to have children. A creditor may not assume that you will have children or that your income will be interrupted to do so.

- *may not* refuse to consider reliable alimony, child support, or separate maintenance payments. However, you don't have to disclose such income unless you want to in order to improve your chances of getting credit.

- *may not* consider whether you have a telephone listing in your own name, because this would discriminate against married women.

- *may not* consider your sex as a factor in deciding whether you are a good credit risk.

- *may not* use your marital status to discriminate against you.

But some closely related questions are permitted. To estimate your expenses, a creditor may ask how many children you have, their ages, and the cost of caring for them (including your obligations to pay alimony, child support, or maintenance). A creditor may ask how regularly you receive your alimony payments or whether they are made under court order, for purposes of determining whether these payments are a dependable source of income. You also may be asked whether there is a telephone in your home.

Finally, a Texas creditor may consider your marital status because, under the laws of this state, there may be differences in the property rights of married and unmarried people. Such differences may affect the creditor's ability to collect if you default.

The law says a woman has the right to her own credit if she is creditworthy. A creditor may not stall you on an application and must inform you why credit was denied. If you are not given an explanation, you are entitled to request specific reasons for the denial.

If you are denied credit, find out why. If you have been discriminated against, the law allows you actual damages plus a penalty.

What happens when I turn 65?
"Don't worry."

Dear Mr. Alderman:
I am 64 years young, and I have no intention of retiring. I hope to stay at my present job for at least another ten years. I am worried that it will become harder for me to get credit now that I am approaching what many think of as retirement age. I have even heard some companies will cancel your charge cards if they discover you have reached age 65. Is this legal? It shouldn't be; I am just as financially responsible as I ever was.

The same law that protects the woman who wrote the previous letter from sex discrimination protects you from discrimination based on your age. *The Equal Credit Opportunity Act makes it illegal to discriminate against an applicant for credit based on his or her age.* The law does not prohibit a creditor from considering your age, nor does it guarantee that you will obtain credit. It simply prohibits a creditor from using age as an arbitrary basis for denying or decreasing credit if you otherwise qualify.

In your case, the creditor cannot arbitrarily cancel your credit cards just because you turned 65. This would violate the Equal Credit Opportunity Act. However, if you retired at 65 and your income substantially decreased, this fact could be a sufficient basis for a creditor to deny or limit credit. *The law is clear that a creditor cannot require you to reapply, change the terms of your account, or close your account just because you have reached a certain age.*

I must emphasize, though, that age can be a factor in extension of credit. For example, if you are age 62 and you apply for a thirty-year house mortgage, the bank can consider the fact that your retirement income will be less than you presently earn and that your earning potential will decrease.

If you were denied the loan based on these considerations, the creditor would not be violating the law.

So how do you determine why you were denied credit? Under the law a creditor must notify you within thirty days of its action and give you specific reasons for its denial or tell you how to get an explanation. You have the same rights if the creditor closes your account. If after you receive this information you think the real reason was age discrimination, you have the right individually to sue for damages, or you can seek the assistance of a federal agency. The Equal Credit Opportunity Act is enforced by the Consumer Finance Protection Bureau (www.consumerfinance.gov) and the Federal Trade Commission (www.consumer.ftc.gov).

What about these credit repair services?
"Be careful."

Dear Mr. Alderman:
I saw an ad for a credit repair service that guaranteed it would fix my bad credit. I called, and the company wants $2,000. My credit is so bad that it seems worth it. I just want to make sure this is all legal. Is it?

Based on what you said, it may not be. Because of the flood of complaints concerning companies offering to fix bad credit reports, the Texas Legislature and Congress enacted laws to try to limit abuse. The new laws do not permit payment in advance. Additionally, companies must post bonds to protect you in the event you are misled or deceived. Credit repair services are not allowed to charge for getting you credit that's available to the general public or to misrepresent what they can do. The company also must have available a copy of its registration statement that lists any litigation or unresolved complaints against the company. If you sign a contract for services, you can cancel that contract within three days. Finally, any violation of the Texas law, called the Credit Service Organization Act, also violates the Deceptive Trade Practices Act.

The bottom line: The Fair Credit Reporting Act, discussed above, gives you the right to require that your credit file be complete and accurate. There is no way anyone can have accurate but negative information removed from your file. In my opinion, anything the credit repair service can do, you probably can do for yourself for a lot less money. In no event, however, should you ever be required to pay in advance for repair services.

The credit card company didn't tell me how high
the interest rate was. Is that legal?
"No."

Dear Mr. Alderman:
Not too long ago, I got a slick offer in the mail for a new credit card.
It guaranteed me a high line of credit and no annual fee. It sounded
like too good a deal to pass up, so I signed up. The first month, I paid
half my bill, expecting to pay the other half, with interest of course,
the following month. I couldn't believe it when the bill arrived. I was
charged 24 percent interest! Is this legal? How come I was never told
that in exchange for no annual fee, I was going to pay a ridiculous
interest rate?

Under the law, what the company has done is illegal. Credit card companies must disclose all of the important terms, including the interest rate.

Under a federal law called the Fair Credit Accountability Responsibility and Disclosure Act (CARD Act), banks and department stores are required to disclose key financial terms of their credit cards in all their solicitations. This allows you as a consumer to shop around for the best rate, instead of being misled into accepting a high rate by a slick promotion. This law applies to bank cards, department store cards, and other charge cards, such as Visa, Mastercard, American Express, and Diners Club. The law states that solicitation mailings must "clearly and conspicuously" disclose key financial terms, such as interest rates, fees, grace periods, minimum finance charges, purchase transaction charges, and balance computation methods. You also must get this information when your account is about to be renewed for another year.

This law is designed to let you shop around for the best rate when you get a credit card. You will be surprised how much money you can save by getting a card with an 8 percent interest rate instead of an 18 percent interest rate. But read all of the terms carefully. Sometimes that low rate is just an "introductory rate" that may be substantially raised in the future.

To file a complaint under this law, or to obtain more information, contact the CFPB at www.consumerfinance.gov.

CHAPTER 2

Bankruptcy

It is hard to pick up a newspaper or watch television these days without reading that someone or some company has filed bankruptcy. Bankruptcy has become a common way for both businesses and individuals to deal with the problem of excessive debt. Bankruptcy is also one of the most misunderstood areas of law.

Unlike most of the laws discussed in this book, the Bankruptcy Code is a federal, not a state, law. Although many associate the term bankruptcy with failure, it is often just the opposite, a way for a company or individual to continue in business and ultimately be successful.

Basically, there are two very different types of bankruptcy. The more common form of bankruptcy, governed by Chapter 7 of the Bankruptcy Code, allows a debtor to just throw in the towel and give up all "nonexempt" property in exchange for a discharge from most debts. After this type of bankruptcy, the debtor usually owes no money and can start over again free of debt. A Chapter 7 bankruptcy is designed to give you a fresh start.

The second form of bankruptcy, governed by Chapters 11 and 13 of the Code, provides a meaningful opportunity for an individual or company to get more time to pay off its debts. Unlike a Chapter 7, the debtor does not throw in the towel; he gets more time to work things out. Many businesses, such as Continental Airlines, General Motors, Schlotzsky's and Toys "R" Us, have successfully used this form of bankruptcy to get their affairs in order and continue operating. Chapter 13 allows an individual to do the same thing.

Because bankruptcy is such a complicated area of law, this chapter will only discuss the basics, and not in very much detail. It is strongly recommended that anyone thinking about bankruptcy consult with an attorney who specializes in this area. The Texas State Bar certifies bankruptcy attorneys, and you should look for one who is "board certified" in bankruptcy or consumer bankruptcy, whichever is more appropriate. Also note that on April 19, 2005, President Bush signed into law a bill substantially overhauling our country's bankruptcy laws. This law went into effect six months after it was signed. The law substantially changes bankruptcy and makes it more difficult for consumers to discharge their debts.

What is bankruptcy?
"There are two types."

Dear Mr. Alderman:
I just read that the company that was supposed to remodel my house filed for bankruptcy. Yesterday, the workers showed up to do the job. I told them I didn't want a bankrupt company working on my house, and they told me we had a contract. The thing I don't understand is how all these companies are still in business if they filed for bankruptcy. I always thought when you filed for bankruptcy you had to sell everything. Am I wrong? Why would a business file bankruptcy and then stay in business?

You are not entirely wrong because two very different types of bankruptcy exist. Under the Bankruptcy Code, a business or a person can either file to liquidate assets, pay creditors what is owed, and start all over, or the Bankruptcy Code can help the business or person reorganize financial affairs so it or he can stay in business and try to pay off the debts. In the first type of bankruptcy, known as a Chapter 7 bankruptcy, a company usually goes out of business. This is what most people think of when they hear the word "bankruptcy." But in the second, known as Chapter 11 for a company and Chapter 13 for an individual, the business continues to operate. Most of the bankruptcies you hear about are Chapter 11 bankruptcies, designed to give a company time to pay off its creditors and make a fresh start.

So what happens when someone or some business files bankruptcy? First, bankruptcy is controlled by federal law, and all bankruptcies are filed in a special federal court. When an individual debtor (that is what a business or a person is called upon filing bankruptcy) files for a Chapter 7 bankruptcy, he or she agrees to give up all "nonexempt assets" in exchange for a discharge from his or her debts. In Texas this usually means an individual gives up everything except his home and about $50,000 worth of personal property in exchange for the release from his debts. (To learn more about exemptions, review Chapter 6.) The creditors split whatever money is left. All creditors must stop collection efforts, and in most cases the money is divided pro rata, based on the amount of the debt. *After Chapter 7 bankruptcy, the debtor usually doesn't owe any money to anyone.* Of course, if you had liens on your property—for example, your house—you would either have to continue to pay or lose the property. And some debts, primarily taxes, are still owed even after bankruptcy.

When a corporation files a Chapter 7 bankruptcy, it usually gives up everything and goes out of business. The creditors split whatever there is and that is the end of it. The corporation no longer exists, and the debts are considered satisfied.

But under the other type of bankruptcy, a company (or individual) may use the bankruptcy court to get time to reorganize its affairs and try to work things out. Two bankruptcy proceedings let you do this: a Chapter 11 and a Chapter 13. They are very similar. Under either, once the debtor files, all the creditors have to stop trying to collect and wait for the debtor to propose a payment plan to attempt to pay everyone back. Basically what happens is the bankruptcy court gives the debtor protection from hungry creditors, while the debtor tries to figure out how to work things out. The main difference between Chapters 11 and 13 is that Chapter 11 is for any-one—corporations and individuals—while Chapter 13 is only available to people with regular incomes. A Chapter 13 is sometimes called a wage-earner proceeding. Chapter 13 is the type of bankruptcy you may see in newspaper advertisements with headlines such as "Stop Creditor Harass-ment . . . File for Protection Under the Federal Bankruptcy Laws."

To get back to your question: If the company is still in business it must have filed a Chapter 11—or if it is a sole proprietorship, a Chapter 13. This means the company has the right to continue in business, and in fact, its contract with you is still enforceable. I suggest you let them finish the work. If you trusted the company before, there is no reason to trust it less now.

Bankruptcy has taken on a new significance lately, and changes to the law have made it more complicated. With the assistance of the Bankruptcy Code, debtors can gain valuable time to try to remedy their financial affairs. But bankruptcy laws are very complex, and some attorneys specialize only in bankruptcy. *If you are considering bankruptcy, make sure you consult with a specialist. Look for an attorney who is board-certified in consumer bankruptcy by the Texas Board of Legal Specialization.*

What happens when I file?
"That depends . . ."

Dear Mr. Alderman:
I really can't believe I'm writing you this letter, but I need your advice. For twenty years I have been a hardworking citizen, and I've never even been late on my payments. I own a house, with a mort-gage, of course, and two cars. My wife and two children have most of the things they need. Now I am suddenly in trouble.

About six months ago my employer told me I had to take a sub-stantial cut in pay or be fired. Any job is better than none, so I agreed to work for less. The following week, we discovered my wife needed surgery. The bills are already more than $13,000, and my insurance only covers a very small amount. I am behind in all my other bills, and the credit card companies are beginning to hound me.

I would like to pay off what I owe, but I don't see how I can do it. Everyone wants to be paid at the same time. I never thought bank-ruptcy was right—a man should pay his bills—but now it seems to be all that is left. What would happen if I filed for bankruptcy?

First, as I pointed out in above, you should know two different types of bankruptcy exist. In your case, as an individual with a steady income, the choices are a Chapter 7 or a Chapter 13. I will tell you about each in order.

If you file a Chapter 7, all your creditors must stop trying to collect, you lose all your nonexempt property, and you start all over again, usually not owing anyone a cent. The purpose of a Chapter 7 is to free you of debt and let you begin fresh. In exchange for being free of your debt, you have to give up nonexempt assets. In Texas this means a family can keep its home and up to $100,000 of personal property. If you have anything else, it goes to your creditors. After you file bankruptcy, your creditors share whatever money is left. After the bankruptcy is over, your creditors cannot try to col-lect anything from you. The only significant exception to this would be the bank or finance company that loaned you money to buy your house or car. Because they have a lien on your property, you either have to give it up to pay off the lien, or agree to continue paying after the bankruptcy. Another exception is money owed for taxes, student loans, or alimony. These debts usually must still be paid even after bankruptcy.

A Chapter 7 bankruptcy is a serious matter, and you should discuss your particular case with an attorney. If you feel you are so hopelessly in debt that the only way to get going again is to clear up all your bills, Chapter 7 may be the thing for you.

But if what you think you need is just more time to work things out with your creditors, you should consider a Chapter 13. In simple terms, a Chap-ter 13 is a court-supervised repayment plan requiring all your creditors to leave you alone and let you pay them off over a longer period of time, usually three to five years. *The first benefit you get from filing a Chapter 13 is all your creditors must immediately stop trying to collect.* All harass-ing calls, letters, and even lawsuits must stop, and everything goes to the bankruptcy court to be worked out. After you file a Chapter 13, the next step is to come up with a plan to pay everyone back. Usually what you try to do is pay all your creditors less than you are paying now but over a longer period of time. *You should consider a Chapter 13 only if you think that with additional time you will be able to pay everyone off.* If you know that even with extra time you are still too much in debt to pay everyone what you owe them, use a Chapter 7, not a Chapter 13.

To file bankruptcy you will need the assistance of an attorney. Talk with him or her before you file, and make sure all your options are considered.

One more thought: Some organizations help consumers restructure their debt without the need for bankruptcy. These groups are usually called "consumer credit counseling services," and one of them might be able to give you the assistance you need.

There are many credit counseling agencies throughout the state of Texas. They usually don't charge, or charge a very small fee, for their help. If you contact a credit counselor be sure to ask questions and learn about the company before signing any agreement or paying any money. Unfortunately, not all credit counseling agencies are the same, and some may do little more than cost you money. Reputable credit counselors either don't charge or charge a very small fee for their services. One I recommend is Money Management International at (866) 889-9347 or www.moneymanagement.org.

Do I still have the option of filing a Chapter 7 or a Chapter 13? "Not necessarily, there is a 'means test.'"

Dear Mr. Alderman:
I know that the Bankruptcy Act was amended. Do I still have the option of filing either a Chapter 7 or a Chapter 13 under the current law?

Under the current version of the bankruptcy law, a debtor does not always have the option of filing a Chapter 7 or a Chapter 13. The trustee or any creditor may bring a motion in bankruptcy court asking the court to dismiss a Chapter 7 and require the debtor to file a Chapter 13.

To determine whether the debtor may choose between a Chapter 7 and 13, the court employs what is called a "means test." Basically, the test looks at the debtor's income in the six months before the debtor filed for bankruptcy. It then compares this number to the median family income in Texas. If the debtor's income is over the median, he or she will be required by the court to file a Chapter 13.

The means test can be complicated to apply. Be sure to discuss this with your bankruptcy attorney before you file.

Must I do anything before filing bankruptcy?
"You must receive credit counseling."

Dear Mr. Alderman:
I have been told that under the bankruptcy law I must get some form
of counseling before I file. What does the law require me to do? Who
has to pay for this counseling?

Under the bankruptcy law, an individual may not file for bankruptcy unless
he or she has received counseling from an approved nonprofit budget and
credit counseling service prior to filing a bankruptcy petition. The debtor
must pay the costs of the counseling. Counseling may be waived, however, if the U.S. trustee or bankruptcy administrator determines that such a
service is not reasonably available to the individual in the district where he
or she lives. A person who does not receive a waiver or the required debt
counseling is ineligible to file bankruptcy. For a list of approved credit
counseling agencies, visit the U.S. Department of Justice website at www
.justice.gov, and search for "credit counseling agencies."

Can I still keep my home if I file bankruptcy?
"It depends."

Dear Mr. Alderman:
I was told that if I file bankruptcy I get to keep my house, regardless
of value, because under Texas law it is exempt. Is this still true under
the current bankruptcy law?

Under the bankruptcy law, you generally get to keep any property that
is exempt under Texas law. This means that you usually may keep all of
your exempt property discussed in Chapter 6, even after your debts are
discharged in bankruptcy. Under the new law, however, there are some
exceptions to this general rule when it comes to your homestead.

To prevent people from fraudulently taking advantage of liberal state
exemption statutes, the law provides several exceptions to the general
rules regarding homestead exemptions. First, you must have been a resident of Texas for at least two years before filing for bankruptcy to use the
Texas exemption statute. In other words, a person cannot move to Texas
from a state with a smaller homestead exemption and immediately use
Texas law to protect a valuable homestead.

The new law also puts caps on the amount of the exemption when you
have not lived in the house for very long. Under the current law, you may

not use the state homestead exemption to protect property acquired within 40 months (3.3 years) of filing that exceeds $160,375 in value, unless the value in excess of that amount resulted from a transfer of residences within the same state. In other words, assuming you have lived in Texas for the past two years, if the equity in your home is under $160,375, you will be able to keep your home as exempt property. On the other hand, if the equity is in excess of $160,375, you will lose the excess in bankruptcy, unless you have owned the home for more than 1,215 days, or the excess value in the house resulted from the sale of another house in Texas that you bought at least 40 months before you filed.

How often can I file a bankruptcy?
"Generally, every eight years."

Dear Mr. Alderman:
I filed a Chapter 7 bankruptcy five years ago. Unfortunately, I recently lost my job and health insurance and again find myself heavily in debt. Can I file bankruptcy again? How long must I wait?

Under prior law, a debtor could file a Chapter 7 bankruptcy and receive a discharge every six years. That time period has been changed under the current law. Now you may not receive a discharge in a Chapter 7 bankruptcy if you received a Chapter 7 or 11 discharge within eight years of the new filing.

If you want to file a Chapter 13, you cannot receive a discharge if you received a Chapter 7 or 11 discharge within the period of four years preceding the date of your order for relief. If you previously filed a Chapter 13, you basically must wait two years to file another one.

What happens when someone else files?
"You may be out of luck!"

Dear Mr. Alderman:
I bought a house for more than $70,000 from a local builder, Johnson Builders, Inc. The house was never finished properly, and I had problems from the day I moved in. I was finally forced to hire a lawyer, who sued under the Texas Deceptive Trade Practices Act. We won! The court awarded me $36,000, but the builder never paid, and now he has filed bankruptcy and gone out of business. What happens next? Am I ever going to get my money? I have since heard he is back in business, using a different name. Can he do this?

Unfortunately, I don't have any good news for you. If the builder, a corporation, has filed a Chapter 7 bankruptcy, he will be discharged from all his debts, including the money he owes you, and all you get is a pro rata share of his nonexempt assets. What all this legal jargon means is the builder doesn't owe you anything and you get to share whatever extra money he had when he filed bankruptcy.

To make sure you do get whatever is coming, you should file a "proof of claim" with the bankruptcy court. Because you are one of the builder's creditors (someone he owes money to), you should receive notice from the court of how and where to file your claim. Once you file this claim form with the bankruptcy court, you will be included in any settlements and get whatever money you are entitled to. But don't expect to receive much. On the average in bankruptcy, creditors receive only a few cents on the dollar. I should point out that if you are not listed with the court—an unlikely event because of the amount of money you are owed—you are not affected by the bankruptcy.

After the builder has filed bankruptcy he has the right to go back into whatever business he wants, under whatever name he wants. The purpose of bankruptcy is to clear up your debts and get a "fresh start." The builder is now free of his business debts and can begin all over. This may not be the way you would want the system to work, and it is often unfair to people like you, but bankruptcy is becoming a more and more popular alternative for people who find they just have to get out from under their debts and see no other way to do it.

From your letter it appears that the builder filed a Chapter 7 bankruptcy—the type designed to liquidate his assets. However, if the builder filed a Chapter 11, you stand a better chance of being paid, but you should have your attorney help you collect.

Will bankruptcy clear up my student loans?
"Probably not."

Dear Mr. Alderman:
I recently graduated from college. I owe more than $25,000 in student loans, in addition to my other bills. I am having trouble making ends meet, and I am considering filing bankruptcy. How will this affect my student loans?

In the past, some student loans were discharged in bankruptcy, based on the age of the loan. Today, however, most student loans are "nondischargeable." That means that even after you file bankruptcy you will still owe your student loans.

If you have student loans you can't pay, you are probably going to have to consider alternatives other than bankruptcy. Many government-backed student loans and school loans backed by nonprofit agencies are not discharged in a bankruptcy, unless they represent a "substantial hardship"—and this is very difficult to prove.

To have a student loan discharged, you generally have to show three things:

1. You can't keep up with your payment schedule;

2. Your future inability to pay, and that your financial situation is permanent;

3. You've made a good-faith effort to pay.

Good-faith efforts include being as fully employed as you can be, being upfront with the lender, and presenting evidence that when you had money you made payments. What courts don't like to see is that you were fully employed and didn't pay, or used your money for other, "frivolous" items. It is the most difficult to prove substantial hardship when you first come out of school, primarily because you don't have any history of not repaying the loans.

Can a farmer file bankruptcy?
"Yes. There is a special law."

Dear Mr. Alderman:
I am a small farmer who, like most others, is having problems making ends meet. The other day I heard there was some special bankruptcy law for farmers. Is this true? If it is, can you tell me about it?

Because of the special hardships faced by farmers, Congress enacted a bankruptcy provision just for them, as well as for fishermen. The law, called Chapter 12, can help stave off liquidations and give the farmer or fisherman more flexibility than ever before.

Chapter 12 is a special section of the Bankruptcy Act just for family farmers or fishermen with a regular income. These are individuals with debts of not more than $4,153,150 if they are farmers or $1,924,550 if they are fishermen (as of April 2016). Corporate and partnership farmers also qualify if one family owns the corporation or partnership.

If you qualify as a family farmer under this law, you can file a petition that immediately stops all your creditors from taking any action. This is similar to what happens in a Chapter 13; however, Chapter 12 gives you more leeway to determine how your debts will be handled.

The bottom line is Chapter 12 gives farmers and fishermen the flexibility needed to rearrange their debts and at the same time continue in business. If you are having serious financial problems, I suggest you speak with an attorney about filing a Chapter 12.

What happens if my ex-spouse files bankruptcy?
"You may be out of luck."

Dear Mr. Alderman:
I was divorced two years ago. In the decree, my husband agreed to make the payments on our car and I got to keep it. He just filed bankruptcy. The bank says I owe the money for my car payments. The bank says because we both signed the note, I still owe the money. Is this right? Doesn't the divorce decree take priority over the note we signed?

The divorce decree is between you and your ex-husband. The bank that loaned you the money to buy the car is not affected by the decree. In other words, if you owed the money before the divorce, you still owe it. If your husband does not make the payments as ordered by the decree, you must pay the lender. If you do not pay, the bank will be precluded from going after your husband because of the bankruptcy, but it may pursue a claim against you. One way to avoid this problem is to deal with it in the divorce and have the responsible spouse refinance in his or her own name.

Can I keep things I inherit right after filing bankruptcy?
"Property inherited within 180 days after filing usually belongs to your estate."

Dear Mr. Alderman:
I filed bankruptcy a few months ago. My father died and left me his ranch property. My lawyer says that the property will be sold and the proceeds will go to my creditors. I thought that after you file bankruptcy you got a fresh start.

As mentioned above, the main purpose of bankruptcy is to get you out from under excessive debt and give you a fresh start. But bankruptcy is also designed to be fair to creditors and allow them to divide your assets. As a general rule, after you file bankruptcy you no longer owe most of your debts, and you can keep your exempt property. Anything you acquired after you file—for example, additional income—is not part of your bankruptcy estate and does not go to your creditors. There is, however, a major exception. The drafters of the law were worried that people might file bankruptcy right before they inherited property as a way of protecting that property from creditors. To avoid this, the law says that any property you inherit within 180 days of filing becomes part of your bankruptcy estate and goes to your creditors. If you filed "a few months ago," you are probably within the 180 days and what your attorney told you is correct.

CHAPTER 3

Banks & Banking

For most businesses, checks are considered the same as cash. When you go into a store and the clerk asks, "Cash or charge?," you say cash if you are using a check.

Although bank checking accounts are not as popular as they once were, many people still have a checking account and write checks as a means of payment. And most of us know the benefits of using a check instead of cash: You have a record of your transactions, and if the check is lost or stolen, you will not bear the loss the way you would if it had been cash.

Banks handle billions of checks each year and transfer untold amounts of money between accounts. For most of us these transfers go smoothly, and we have little need to know or use our legal rights against a bank. But we do have substantial legal rights.* When something goes wrong you may find that the bank, not you, has to pay.

A thief has been using my checks. Do I have to pay?
"Not unless it was your fault."

Dear Mr. Alderman:
About two weeks ago my purse was stolen in the parking lot of the supermarket. I immediately reported it to the police and then went home and made a list of everything in my wallet. I remembered how important you said it was to notify everyone as soon as possible, so I contacted all my credit card companies. I also called the bank and was told to come in, close the account, and open a new one. The next day I did that and learned the thief had written three checks to himself, signed my name, and cashed them that morning. The bank told me I was responsible for these checks because the forgery was so good there was no way for the bank to know. This doesn't seem right. Before I go and ask to see the manager of the bank, I would like to know what you think. What are my legal rights?

---

* To keep current with the rapidly developing law that regulates banks and protects your rights, visit www.peopleslawyer.net.

Under the law, a bank generally has no right to pay checks on which your signature was forged, and if it does it must credit your account or be responsible for damages. A bank may only pay a check that is "properly payable," and checks with forged signatures are not properly payable. In simple terms, properly payable means in accordance with your instructions; and you did not tell the bank to pay that check—the thief did.

A few exceptions to this rule do exist, but none seems to apply in your case. For example, if your negligence was what made the thief's forgery possible—let's say you carelessly left a signature stamp in a public place—then the bank may not have to pay. Also, if you wait too long to report the forgery, and because of that the bank suffers a loss, you can't complain to the bank.

Basically, the law is straightforward: A bank may not take your money to pay a check on which your signature is forged. Your account must be credited and it is up to the bank either to bear the loss or find the thief and try to collect. If your bankers still refuse to give your money back, take them to justice court or see a lawyer.

P.S.: If your check is stolen, quickly report the loss to the bank. But there is no need to pay the bank for a stop-payment order. As I just explained, it is the bank's loss if it pays.

My check was signed by someone other than the person I gave it to. Do I still have to pay?
"Probably not. . . . You are entitled to the signature you asked for."

Dear Mr. Alderman:
I owed my next-door neighbor $150 for a fence we put up. I gave him a check, which he put in his desk. When he went to cash it he realized it had been stolen. My neighbor asked me to give him another check, but I am worried about what will happen if the thief cashes or deposits my old check. What are my legal rights if the thief forges my friend's name and my bank pays the check?

Under the law, a bank that pays a check with a forged endorsement has no right to take your money to cover the check. If it does, you have the right to require the bank to credit your account.

For example, suppose your check was made out to Bob Neighbor. The thief turns over the check and endorses it "Bob Neighbor pay to Tom Thief." Thief then takes the check to his bank and deposits it by signing "Tom Thief." His bank gives him credit for the check and sends it to your bank. Because your bank has no way of knowing the signatures are not genuine, it will probably pay the check and debit your account. When you get your statement you discover the check has a forged signature. In the meantime, Thief has taken his money and gone.

According to the law, once you show the bank the endorsement is forged, it must credit your account. The bank then has the right to get the money back from the other bank, and that bank must try to recover from the thief.

What you should do now is contact your bank and ask if the check has been paid. If the check has been paid, explain what happened and ask the bank to credit your account. The bank probably will want you to prove your neighbor didn't endorse the check and may ask for him to sign an affidavit to that effect. Once the bank is certain the signature is a forgery, it will probably credit your account. If it does not, you have the legal right to compel the bank to do so.

If the check has not been paid, the bank will probably ask you to put in a stop-payment order. This will ensure the check is not paid, and while it may cost a little money it will avoid a dispute with the bank.

As for your neighbor, once you get your money back from the bank, or put in a stop payment order, you may give him another check. Your obligation to pay him still exists.

As I said in the answer above, a bank may take money from your account only to pay checks that are properly payable. Checks with forged endorsements are not properly payable, and the bank has no legal right to take your money to pay them.

How can I be responsible on a forged signature?
"The law imposes time limits within which you must act."

Dear Mr. Alderman:
I run a small business. I discovered my signature had been forged on one of my checks. I contacted my bankers and asked that they credit my account. They told me that because it happened more than one year ago, I was responsible for the loss. I thought I read that a person has no liability based on a forged signature. Who is right?

You are both right. A person has no liability on a check that has a forged signature. For example, if someone steals your check and forges your signature, you have no liability on that instrument. If your bank pays the check, you have the right to have the bank credit your account. In other words, when a bank pays a check with a customer's forged signature, the bank must bear the loss.

All laws, however, have time limits within which rights must be asserted. For example, if you were injured in a car wreck, you have the right to sue the person who caused the accident. The lawsuit must be commenced, however, within two years. If you were to wait longer than that, your claim would be barred. We call these time limits "statutes of limitation."

Our banking laws also have time periods within which claims must be asserted. Under the law, you must notify the bank of the forged signature within one year. If you wait longer than that, you are precluded from asserting a claim. Your agreement with the bank may also impose an even shorter period for you to report a forgery once you become aware of it.

Knowing your rights is important. Asserting them in a timely manner is essential.

How do I stop payment on a check?
"In Texas, it must be in writing."

Dear Mr. Alderman:

Hello again. I am the same person who wrote you before about the check I gave my next-door neighbor that was lost or stolen. I called the bank and was told I had to stop payment. I said to go ahead and was told I would have to come down to the bank to do it in writing. The bank also told me I would have to pay a fee if payment was stopped. Is this the law, or is my bank just making things difficult? You know how inconvenient it is to go to a bank during the middle of the day.

In most states a customer can stop payment over the telephone. Under Texas law, though, an oral stop-payment notice is not binding on the bank. This means the bank may let you stop payment over the phone but is not obligated to do so. As a practical matter most banks will only honor a written stop-payment order.

As to whether your bank may charge you for putting in a stop-payment order, the answer is probably yes. Although at least one state attorney general (Michigan's) has stated that stop-payment orders are part of the obligation owed a customer and that an additional fee may not be charged, there has been no similar ruling in Texas. *I suggest you consider the cost of stop-payment orders when you shop for a bank. The cost can vary greatly between banks.*

The store charged me $35 for a check that bounced. Is this legal?
"Probably not."

Dear Mr. Alderman:
The other day I bought a CD at my local record shop. It cost $15.95. I paid for it with a check. Unfortunately, I don't balance my checkbook

*as well as I should, and the check bounced. The store called me
and told me I owed $15.95 for the check and $35 for the fact that it
bounced. When I went to pay, the clerk showed me a sign over the
cash register that said All Returned Checks Will Be Charged $35! Is
this legal? Thirty-five dollars is a lot of money.*

Based on what you say, the store probably acted unlawfully. Under the
law a store may charge you a bounced check fee, but only up to $30. The
store properly posted notice that it would charge a fee for returned checks.
Because the amount is more than $30, however, the store acted unlawfully.
You may want to file a complaint with the Texas Department of Banking
(www.dob.texas.gov).

Can my bank charge $40 for a $2 overdraft?
"Be careful, overdraft fees are unregulated."

*Dear Mr. Alderman:
I have a new debit card. I know I should monitor my account carefully, but sometimes I don't. I recently made three small purchases
when I didn't have enough money in my account. The first purchase
put me $2 over my balance; the next two were for less than $5 each.
The total amount I was over my balance was about $12. The bank
paid the full amount, but as a result, I was charged $40 for each
overdraft, a total of $120! This must be usury. Is it legal?*

First, let me emphasize something you said—it is very important you carefully monitor your account to avoid any overdrafts. Whether it is a checking account, a credit card, or a debit card, the best way to avoid overdraft
fees is to never spend more than you have.

That said, I agree the overdraft fees charged by most financial institutions are outrageous, but there is no limit to how much the bank may
charge. The amount, which can range from $20 to $40, is a matter of private contract between you and the bank. This applies to overdraft payments on a check or a debit card. I suggest you speak with the bank about
waiving the fees in this case, and shop around for a more affordable card.
There also is some good news for avoiding similar problems in the future.

Many financial institutions give customers "free" overdraft protection
when the account is opened. Even if you didn't ask for it, the bank or credit
card company provides this service, which allows them to let you exceed
your limit in exchange for a substantial fee. Effective July 1, 2010, however,
the law changed. Under a Federal Reserve Board rule, financial institutions
must give consumers a notice that explains the overdraft policy, and that

allows the consumer to "opt in" to the program. Most consumers do not want overdraft protection for things like ATM and one-time debit card transactions, and would prefer that the card be rejected. For example, do you really want that $5 cup of coffee when the balance in your account is $4, given the overdraft fee is $35? On the other hand, many consumers do like protection when it comes to checks that are used for things like rent and to pay bills. The new rule allows you to make intelligent choices and not be stuck with what usually turns out to be a very expensive convenience.

The bottom line is to carefully monitor your account balances, review the available overdraft programs and fees, and be sure to "opt in" to only the protection you need.

Can a store require a credit card ID before it cashes a check?
"Yes."

Dear Mr. Alderman:
A store told me it wouldn't take my personal check unless I showed the clerk a driver's license and a major credit card. I refused, and the clerk made me pay cash. What purpose is served by showing a credit card? My driver's license proves who I am. Is it legal to require a credit card to cash a check?

I agree with you that a credit card doesn't really do anything to help establish identity. But basically, a store isn't required to take a personal check unless it wants to. Therefore, it can place whatever requirements it wants on the customer. If the store wants to require you to show a credit card, I see no reason why it can't.

I cashed a check for a friend. How am I liable?
"When you sign a check, you become responsible."

Dear Mr. Alderman:
A friend asked me to cash a $1,000 check he had been given by someone else. I gave him the cash and then deposited the check in my account. My bank gave me credit for the check, and I thought that was the end of it. It was not. My bank now has taken $1,000 out of my account because the check bounced. Why am I responsible for this? It wasn't even my check. What are my rights?

Unfortunately for you, the bank had the right to do just what it did. You now will have to try to recover the $1,000 from either your friend or the person who wrote the check to your friend.

When someone makes out a check, the check is merely his or her promise to pay the money. The bank on which the check is drawn has no liability on the check. It simply takes money out of the person's account to pay what that person promised. If there is no money in the account, the check will be returned, and the person who wrote it will be responsible, not the bank.

But the person who wrote the check is not the only one responsible. Anyone who endorses the check also promises to pay. Therefore, when your friend endorsed the check to you, he became liable to you. When you endorsed the check to your bank to deposit it, you became responsible to the bank.

When the check bounced, three people were responsible to your bank: the person who wrote the check, your friend, and you. The bank chose to collect from the easiest person, you. Now you have the right to try to collect from your friend or the person who wrote the check.

Cashing a check for someone is like making him or her a loan. You are giving that person money that you hope will be reimbursed by the check you deposit. Unfortunately, as you found out, signing your name to the check also makes you responsible and can be very expensive.

What are my rights on an unsigned check?
"Your rights are on the 'underlying obligation.'"

Dear Mr. Alderman:
I did some work for someone. He paid me with a check. I deposited the check and it was returned. It turns out the person never signed the check, and I didn't notice. Now he says I can't sue him. What are my rights?

Whenever someone owes you money and pays you with a check, there are two separate obligations. First, there is what the law calls the "underlying obligation" based on the contract for your services. Second, there is the obligation "on the instrument" that arises from the check. In your case, the person who gave you the check is correct with respect to the obligation on the instrument. If a check is not signed, you generally may not sue the person who issued the check.

On the other hand, the fact that the check is not signed does not affect your right to sue on the underlying obligation. When you agreed to perform work in exchange for money, you entered into a contract. You may enforce this contract even if the check was not signed.

The bottom line is simple: You did the work, and you are entitled to be paid.

How can my bank pay a postdated check?
"The law allows it."

Dear Mr. Alderman:

I gave someone a postdated check. At that time I didn't have enough money in my account to cover it. I assumed it would not be paid until after the date on the check. Instead, the person I gave the check to deposited it, and my bank paid it. This caused many of my other checks to bounce. The bank charged me $25 for each of these checks. How can this happen?

A postdated check is a check that you date sometime in the future. Many people believe, as you did, that this means the check may not be paid until the date that appears on the check. Unfortunately, this is not the law.

A bank is allowed to pay a postdated check whenever it is presented to the bank. It may pay the check in good faith even if it is presented many days before the date on the check. In most cases, checks are processed electronically, and the date on a check is not even viewed when it is paid.

If you want to make sure a postdated check is not paid before the date on the check, you must notify the bank that you have written a postdated check. If you do this, the bank has no legal right to pay the check early.

I should point out that even though you have no claim against the bank, you do have rights against the person to whom you gave the check. If the check was given with the understanding that it would not be deposited until the date on the check, the person you gave the check to should be responsible for the fees you incurred when your other checks bounced. I suggest you let him know you expect him to reimburse you.

Who is responsible for a counterfeit cashier's check?
"The person who dealt with the thief."

Dear Mr. Alderman:

I sold something and sent it to someone out of state. As payment, I received a cashier's check. The check turned out to be counterfeit. The bank says I owe it the money I withdrew. Is this right?

This is becoming a very common and very serious problem. Basically, whenever you deposit or cash a check, your endorsement when you deposit or cash it is a promise to reimburse the bank in the event the check is not paid. After you repay the bank—or, more likely, the bank simply withdraws the money from your account—you still have a claim against the person who gave you the check. In most cases, the loss will fall on the person who dealt with the person who issued the counterfeit check.

The best way to avoid this problem in the future is to withhold delivery of the goods until the check has cleared and been finally paid by the bank. Because of the law, banks often must give you a "provisional" credit for a deposited check before it is actually paid. I suggest you do not withdraw any of these funds until the bank assures you the check has been finally paid by the bank on which the check was drawn.

Does "paid in full" mean I don't owe any additional money? "Usually not."

Dear Mr. Alderman:
I owe my credit card company $1,500. I cannot afford to pay the full amount, so I sent a check for $750 clearly marked "accepted as payment in full." The credit card company cashed the check, and is now trying to collect the remaining $750. Do I owe any more money? I thought "paid in full" meant the debt is settled.

You are correct that giving someone a check as payment in full *may* constitute a complete satisfaction of the debt. In your case, however, this law does not apply. If getting out of debt were as simple as giving someone a "paid in full" check, none of us would owe anything.

Under the law, when you attempt, in good faith, to settle a disputed debt by offering payment in full, acceptance of the payment by the other party will constitute full satisfaction, and you will no longer owe any additional money. For this law to apply, however, there must be a dispute about the debt, the debtor must offer the check as payment in good faith, and the creditor must obtain payment. For example, suppose someone repaired your car and you did not think the job was done correctly. The mechanic says you owe $700, but you believe that the repairs are worth only $300. In an effort to resolve the dispute, you send the mechanic a check for $350, marked "accepted as payment in full." Under the law, if the mechanic cashes the check, the debt would be discharged and you would not owe any additional money. On the other hand, if the job was done properly, and you just didn't want, or couldn't afford, to pay the full amount, sending a $350 check marked "accepted as payment in full" would have no legal effect, and the mechanic would be entitled to pursue his claim for the remaining $350.

In your case, there is no dispute regarding the existence and amount of your obligation to the credit card company. Therefore, it has the right to cash the check and collect the remaining amount.

Does giving someone a check mean you cannot get out of the deal? "It depends."

Dear Mr. Alderman:
What is the law in the state of Texas if someone writes you a check to hold a boat that is for sale, and then backs out of the deal the next day.

As far as the law is concerned, once two parties agree to a price to buy and sell an item, they have an enforceable contract. If he agreed to buy the boat and gave you money to hold it until he came to pay the rest, his refusal to do so would be a breach of contract.

The issue in your case, however, is whether he gave you the check as a down payment on a contract, or to have you hold the boat so he had more time to decide whether he wanted to buy it. The legal question is: Did the buyer say something that meant, "I agree to buy the boat. Here is a check to hold it for me. I'll come back and pick it up and pay the rest," or "I think I want the boat. Here is a check to hold it for me and I'll come back in a few days and let you know if I want it."

If the facts of your case are the first example, he has breached the contract. On the other hand, if the facts are the second example, you never had a contract. If you had a contract, the amount of your damage would be the difference between what the buyer agreed to pay and what you ultimately sell the boat for. If the boat is sold for the same price, there would not be any damages, even though there was a breach of contract.

CHAPTER 4

Contracts

In a certain sense, there is no such thing as a "contract." You can't buy one, you can't hold one, and you can't pick one up and tote it around. A contract is simply a legal term for a promise that the law will enforce. Sometimes this promise is evidenced by a piece of paper, but that paper is not a contract; the legally enforceable agreement is.

Any agreement you enter into may be legally enforceable and may become a contract, no matter what words you may use, and regardless of whether it is oral or written. For example, suppose the neighborhood boy comes by your house and yells, "Hey, lady. Want your lawn cut?" A nod of your head will result in a contract, and after he finishes the task, you will have to pay.

So you see, your life consists of one contract followed by another. When you buy gas for your car or groceries at the store or have your laundry cleaned, you enter into a contract. Some basic knowledge of contract law should help you with your everyday problems.

As you will find in the next few letters, you don't need very specific language, and you usually don't need anything written to enter into a binding contract.

Must a contract be formal?
"Just an agreement."

Dear Mr. Alderman:
I own a house at the lake that's about twenty years old. The fence needed repairs, and my neighbor told me he would split the cost if I had the fence repaired. We talked about it a while, and ultimately I agreed to have it fixed, and he agreed to pay half. The bill amounted to $350, and now my neighbor refuses to pay. The price, I feel, is very reasonable, but my neighbor says we didn't have any kind of a formal arrangement, and there is nothing I can do. Is he right?

The law of contracts is not as complicated as many people think. If you agree to do something in exchange for someone's promise to do something else, there probably is a legally enforceable agreement. To put it simply, if you intended to be legally bound, you probably are.

In your case, each party made a promise to the other. You promised to fix the fence, and he promised to pay you one-half the cost. Based on your letter, it seems that at the time of the agreement you both thought you had entered into a contract. Your agreement is probably legally enforceable.

Contract law long ago dispensed with the need for any formalities before an agreement could be enforceable in a court of law. The modern trend is to enforce every agreement that the parties intended to be binding. You can't get out of a contract by simply saying, "I know what I said before, but it wasn't really a formal contract." If your neighbor doesn't pay you the money he owes, I suggest you take him to justice court. Maybe the judge can convince him he has entered into a legally enforceable agreement.

Can an Internet company be sued in Texas?
"Probably."

Dear Mr. Alderman:
About two months ago I purchased something over the Internet from an out-of-state company. My credit card was immediately charged. I still have not received what I bought. What can I do to get my money back?

Generally, when a company does business in Texas, it may be sued in Texas. This means that you probably have the right to file a claim against the company in your local justice court. Unfortunately, once you win, it probably will be necessary to go to the state where the company is located to collect. You should consider the likelihood of collecting before you spend the money to file a lawsuit. But a lawsuit probably is not necessary.

As you have discovered, dealing with an unknown company involves the risk that the company will not perform as promised. Fortunately, however, you used a credit card. Under federal law, if you are billed for goods you never received, you may dispute the bill and refuse to pay the credit card company. Using a credit card protects you against problems like the one you now face. You should immediately contact the credit card company in writing and let it know your bill contained a billing error—a charge for goods never received. To learn more about your rights when you use a credit card, review the questions in Chapter 5.

What if she doesn't give me the gift?
"There's not much you can do about it."

Dear Mr. Alderman:

For the past five years my grandmother has been ill. Weekly, I would go to her home, help with her chores, and buy her groceries. Last month she told me she really appreciated everything I had done for her and she wanted me to have her diamond pin. Yesterday, I went to her house and asked about the pin. She said she had changed her mind and given it to my sister. My dear sibling has never done anything for my grandmother. Is there any way I can make my grandmother keep her promise?

P.S.: I even have a written promise that reads, "In exchange for the love and affection shown to me by my granddaughter, Betsy, I promise to give her my diamond pin before the end of the year."

The fact that you have a signed written promise does not mean you can force a person to do what she promised to do. *As a general rule, promises to make gifts are not enforceable.* This is because of the legal doctrine known as "consideration."

Under the law, a promise is enforceable only if given in exchange for something. In legalese there must be a "quid pro quo"—something for something. For example, suppose I promise to pay you to paint my house. What we have actually done is exchange promises. I have promised to pay you in return for your promise to paint. We have each given something in exchange for something else. The promises are enforceable, and we have a contract. The exchange, however, must be for something in the future. If you promise to pay someone for something that has already happened, the promise is not enforceable—it is a promise to make a gift. For example, if you paint my house without my asking, and after you finish I say, "You did a good job. I promise to pay you next week," the promise would not be enforceable because it was not made in exchange for performance. For every enforceable promise there is a quid pro quo, something exchanged for something else.

So what does all this mean to you? Your grandmother promised to make you a gift for what you had done in the past—and such promises cannot be enforced in a court of law. Even though your grandmother may be morally bound to give you the pin, there is no legally enforceable obligation. Things would be different, though, if your grandmother had said, "If you help me with the groceries, I will give you my pin." In that case there would be a legally enforceable promise because she would have made her promise in exchange for yours.

The bottom line is, not all promises, even those in writing, are enforceable. If someone promises to give you a gift and doesn't, you usually can't force him to.

There is, however, one exception to this that you should know. If you rely on the promise and suffer a loss, you may be able to force the person to compensate you for your loss. For example, suppose your grandmother told you she was going to give you $500 to buy a coat, and relying on this you put down a $50 nonrefundable deposit. If your grandmother changed her mind, you couldn't force her to pay the $500, but you could collect the $50 you spent in reliance on her promise.

Is a contract valid if I don't sign?
"It probably doesn't matter."

Dear Mr. Alderman:

My driveway needed repair, so I called a contractor to fix it. We discussed what he would do, and he sent me an estimate of $1,500. I phoned him back and told him to go ahead and begin work. The next day, when he arrived with his crew, I informed him I had changed my mind and was going to fix it myself. He was very mad and told me he was going to lose $100 because he had to pay his crew for showing up. I told him I was sorry, that it wasn't my fault, and besides, we never had a real contract because I never signed anything. I have now received a letter informing me he is planning to sue me in justice court for the $100. Because I didn't sign anything, do I have to pay?

Most people are surprised to find out they usually don't have to sign anything to have an enforceable contract. In your case, your contract was for the performance of a service, and such contracts do not require a signature *unless they can't be performed within a year.* Your contract clearly was to be performed in less than a year, and you are responsible for any loss the contractor incurred.

Under the law, most contracts do not have to be in writing or be signed to be enforceable. But some contracts are considered more important than others, and there is a law called the **Statute of Frauds** that requires certain kinds of contracts be "evidenced" by a signed writing. The most common types of contracts that need a signed writing are contracts for the sale of land, contracts that cannot be performed within one year, contracts for the sale of goods that cost more than $500, and contracts to pay the debts of another. To enforce these types of contracts, there must be sufficient writing to show a contract has been made, signed by the person against whom the contract is being enforced. A brief example will show you how this law works.

Suppose I agree to sell you my house. Because contracts for the sale of land are covered by the Statute of Frauds, the agreement is not enforceable unless we have a writing. We orally agree to the sale, and I then go home and write you a letter telling you how excited I am about the deal and discussing all the details. I sign the letter and mail it to you. At this point there is an enforceable contract against me because I signed a writing, indicating we made a contract and giving the important terms. But the contract probably would not be enforceable against you because you did not sign anything. *If you are worried about the enforceability of an agreement, protect yourself: Put it in a signed writing.*

The Statute of Frauds is designed to prevent one person from forcing another into a contract by falsely stating they had an agreement. Without the writing, the agreement is not enforceable. But the law does not like people to use the Statute of Frauds to get out of contracts that they made and other people relied on. For example, suppose you agreed to buy a custom-made boat from me for $2,500. After I build the boat, you change your mind and say you won't pay. The contract is for the sale of goods that cost more than $500, so I need a signed writing to sue you. Am I out of luck? Not in this case. As noted above, there are some exceptions to the law that require a writing, and this is one of them. Because the goods were specially manufactured, I can sue you even without the writing. All I have to do is prove you orally agreed. The same rule applies whenever one party has performed its part of the deal and then the other party tries to get out of the contract after performance.

Remember, most contracts do not require a writing. Even when a writing is required, the requirement may be waived if it is unfair to one of the parties. Best advice: If you make an oral contract, be prepared to keep your promise.

Does an agreement to split lottery winnings have to be in writing? "Probably not."

Dear Mr. Alderman:
Several of my friends and I buy lottery tickets each week. Each of us puts in $2, and we buy 10 tickets. We have agreed that if we win we will split the winnings. I know it is unlikely, but if we did win, could I force everyone to split the money? Do we have to have a written agreement?

You have the right to force everyone to divide the money, provided you can convince a court that you really did make the agreement. Basically, you and your friends have entered into a contract. The terms of the contract are that each of you will provide part of the proceeds to buy the tickets and, if you win, you will divide the proceeds equally.

This agreement is enforceable without any form of a writing. As I stated in the prior letter, most contracts do not have to be in writing to be enforceable. This contract, because it could be performed in less than one year, is an example of one type of contract that does not have to be in writing. You would need a writing, however, if your agreement to buy tickets was for more than one year and did not end even if you won the lottery earlier.

This does not mean, however, that it would not be a good idea to put your agreement in a written form. Even though your agreement is enforceable, there still may be problems proving it if you were to win. The best way to avoid any future problems is to write an agreement and have everyone sign it. "Friendly" agreements such as this always seem to become harder to enforce when there is a large amount of money involved.

Can I share lottery winnings with my children?
"Yes, but prepare a contract."

Dear Mr. Alderman:
I know I may be dreaming, but I have a question about what happens if I win the lottery. Is it legal for me to share the winnings with my children? Can I give them a share of what I won without paying any extra taxes?

There is nothing illegal about giving some or all of your lottery winnings to your children. However, how you structure the transaction will determine the tax ramifications. Obviously you will be taxed on any winnings you receive. You cannot avoid being taxed on those winnings by transferring part or all of the money to your children. Your children, however, pay no taxes on the money you give them. This could be where you got the idea about paying an extra tax.

Alternatively, you could enter into a contract with your children to share the winnings. An agreement between you and your children to split the winnings of a lottery ticket that any of you purchase is an enforceable contract. This agreement should be in writing. This way, if you do win, checks will be issued to you and your children. With this arrangement, ordinary income tax would be owed individually by each person receiving a check. In other words, you would pay taxes at your income tax rate, and your children would pay at their tax rates.

Finally, if you do win a large amount of money, you may want to speak to an attorney who specializes in estate planning before accepting payment. He or she will let you know the best way to structure any lottery winnings.

What if he doesn't do what he promised?
"There's no punishment."

Dear Mr. Alderman:

I signed a contract to purchase a television from a local store. When I went back the next day to pick it up, the manager told me he had just sold it to another customer and that he couldn't get another one for several weeks. I was really mad . . . because I knew the manager didn't like me and had sold it just for spite. I went to another store, right around the corner, and I bought the same TV for a much better price. Now I want to know if I can do anything about the fact that the store manager didn't sell me the original TV. I have a written contract.

The law of contracts is designed to do one thing: ensure that you get the benefit of your bargain. If someone breaches a contract, you are entitled to money damages to put you in the same place you would have been in if the contract had been performed. *It is very rare that punitive damages are awarded for breach of contract. All the law requires is that the breaching party put the other party in as good a position as he would be in if the contract had been performed.*

In your case, you were better off after the store breached the contract than you would have been had the store performed, so you are not entitled to any damages. If you had to pay more for the TV at the other store, you could recover the difference in price. But in your case, you saved money. Even though you have a written contract, you cannot get any kind of penalty from the merchant for not living up to his part of the bargain.

The damages for breach of contract can be demonstrated in this way:

market price	(what it will cost you to get the same thing somewhere else)
− contract price	(what you would have paid)
= damages	
+ consequential loss	(whatever else you lost because of the breach)
= total recovery	

For example, suppose the television cost $100 more at every other store and you had to drive an extra 50 miles to find one. You would then be entitled to $100 (the difference between the market price and the contract price) plus a reasonable amount for your mileage (a consequential loss). In your case, though, the formula results in a negative number, and even though you don't owe the store, it doesn't have to pay you any damages.

The law requires that you perform any contract you enter into, but damages are designed to compensate, not punish. If the other party's breach didn't hurt you economically, you are probably not entitled to any damages.

If you agree to hold an item for a buyer, can he just back out?
"It depends on your agreement."

Dear Mr. Alderman:
What is the law in the state of Texas if someone writes you a check to hold a boat that is for sale, and then backs out of the deal the next day?

As far as the law is concerned, once two parties agree to a price to buy and sell an item they have an enforceable contract. If someone agreed to buy the boat and gave you money to hold it until he came to pay the rest, his refusal to do so would be a breach of contract.

The issue in your case, however, is whether he gave you the check as a down payment on a contract or to have you hold the boat so he had more time to decide whether he wanted to buy it. The legal question is: Did the buyer say something that meant "I agree to buy the boat. Here is a check to hold it for me. I'll come back and pick it up and pay the rest," or "I think I want the boat. Here is a check to hold it for me and I'll come back in a few days and let you know if I want it."

If the facts of your case match the first example, he has breached the contract. On the other hand, if they match the second example, you never had a contract. If you had a contract, the amount of your damage would be the difference between what the buyer agreed to pay and what you ultimately sell the boat for. If the boat is sold for the same price, there would not be any damages, even though there was a breach of contract.

I couldn't afford to pay for my layaway.
Don't I get my money back?
"It depends."

Dear Mr. Alderman:
A few months ago I saw a great dress at a little store near my house. I asked if the store did layaways, and the clerk said yes. She gave me something to sign and told me I had to pay $10 a week and that in ten weeks the dress would be mine. The dress was marked $100, so this seemed fair. I paid for five weeks and then lost my job. When I went back and told the clerk I couldn't make the payments anymore, she said, "Fine. We'll keep your money and the dress." Then she showed me the paper I signed, which said the store could do this. I

know I should have read it before I signed, but I just assumed that if I stopped paying I would get my money back. Can I do anything?

You asked a good question, and I was surprised I couldn't find a Texas law dealing directly with the area of layaways. It is a matter of private contract between you and the store. Whatever you agree to is enforceable, as any other contract would be. *It is very important that you carefully read the agreement before you sign it.* You should always get the seller's layaway policy in writing, and review and understand the plan's terms. Look to see how much time you have to pay for the merchandise or service, when the payments are due, and the minimum payment required. You also should see if any interest is charged, whether there are any cancellation fees, and whether there are any other possible charges.

Nevertheless, this does not mean the store has the right to do whatever it wants. It is still subject to the Texas Deceptive Trade Practices Act. Under this law, the store would be liable if it misrepresented the terms of the agreement. For example, if the clerk told you that you would get your money back, the store could not hold you to a written agreement that said otherwise. In that case, by keeping your money the store would violate the Deceptive Trade Practices Act, and you could get up to three times your damages (read Chapter 10).

This law also prohibits the store from doing anything "unconscionable." This is defined as an act that takes grossly unfair advantage of a customer's knowledge, ability, experience, or capacity. In your case, the conduct of the store—charging $50 and giving you nothing in return—could be considered unconscionable if you lacked the ability to protect yourself from such a bad deal and the store took advantage of you. A court would make this determination. However, in my opinion, the store seems to have taken advantage of you, and this act could be considered unconscionable.

If you think you were deceived or that the store acted unconscionably under the Deceptive Trade Practices Act, you should consider letting the store know and going to justice court if necessary. Remember, though, that before you use this law you must do certain things, so read Chapter 10 carefully.

Who owns my dental records?
"Your dentist."

Dear Mr. Alderman:
I recently changed dentists. To avoid taking additional X-rays, I asked my former dentist for the X-rays he had. He refused to give them to me. Can he do this? I paid for the X-rays; aren't they mine?

Under the law, what you paid for were the services of the dentist. The records of the dentist, including X-rays, belong to the dentist. If he or she does not want to give them to you, you have no right to them.

The law does, however, require that the dentist retain your records for at least five years and provide you with a copy of your records, including radiographs. A dentist who provides you with copies is entitled to charge a reasonable fee for the copying services.

Should I cosign a note for my friend?
"Being a cosigner can be dangerous."

Dear Mr. Alderman:

A good friend of mine is having a problem getting credit because of financial problems she had more than four years ago. She is now back on her feet but still has a bad credit report. She has asked me to cosign a note to buy a car. I fully trust this person and know she will pay. Recently, however, someone told me that if my friend doesn't pay, it could hurt my credit. Is this true? Can her default show up on my credit report?

Being a cosigner may seem like the nice thing to do, but unfortunately the old saying "No good deed goes unpunished" often applies to cosigners. When you cosign or guarantee someone else's signature, you are in effect agreeing to the same obligation as that person. If that person does not pay, you must. And if you do not, your credit report will reflect it. In other words, don't cosign unless you are willing to bear full responsibility for the obligation.

I should point out, however, that you are not without recourse if you must pay. If you, as a cosigner, pay, you are entitled to seek recovery against the person primarily responsible on the note. For example, if your friend didn't pay and you had to, you would be entitled to reimbursement from your friend.

How long do I have to change my mind after I sign a contract?
"Usually no time!"

Dear Mr. Alderman:

Last week I went to buy a new car. It was late at night, and after a very hard sell, I signed a contract. The next morning I thought about the terms and decided they were more than I really could afford. When I called the car dealer to cancel, he said I couldn't. I thought you had three days to get out of a contract after you signed it. Isn't that the law in Texas?

In fact, as far as I know, it isn't the law anywhere. In most cases, once you sign a contract you are obligated by its terms. Unless you were tricked, deceived, or defrauded into signing the agreement, you are usually bound. (Read Chapter 10 if this is the case.)

The existence of a three-day cooling-off period is one of the most widely held misconceptions about the law. There are only very limited instances in which you have three days to change your mind. For example, you have this right if you sign a contract that puts a lien on your home, a contract for time-share property, a health spa contract, or most contracts negotiated door-to-door. In other cases, though, once you sign you are bound.

The bottom line is simple. Don't sign anything until you have had time to read it and think about it. And as far as that high-pressure salesperson is concerned, go home and really think about the deal. If it really is a good deal, it will still be there the next day.

How can I get out of a long-term health club contract? "There is a law."

Dear Mr. Alderman:
Like everyone else, my New Year's resolution was to get back in shape. The first thing I did was rush off to the local health club to sign up. The salesperson told me the club had a special that day and it would only cost $19.99 a month. He told me that to save time I should just sign the forms and he would have them ready when I came back that afternoon. I signed and then picked them up a few hours later. When I got home, I was shocked to see the membership cost $19.99 a month plus an initiation fee of $300. I don't have that kind of money. When I called and told him I wanted to cancel, his manager told me a contract is a contract and I should have read it before I signed. What can I do? Is this just an expensive lesson not to sign anything before you read it?

Although learning not to sign blank forms is a good lesson to learn, it is not all you can do in this case. Texas has a **Health Spa Act** that protects you. Basically, this law protects against false and deceptive acts or misrepresentations, such as what you describe. More important, this law has a cooling-off period and requires that health clubs post bonds with the secretary of state.

Under the law, any health spa contract must give you three days to cancel. The law requires that notice of this policy appear in bold print in the contract. The law also requires a bold notice telling consumers not to sign a contract with any blanks.

I suggest you contact the manager again and let her know you know about this law. If she doesn't agree to cancel it, you should file a complaint with the secretary of state. That is the office that enforces this law and keeps the bonds health clubs must file.

What happens if the photographer dies?
"You should get your money back."

Dear Mr. Alderman:
We hired a photographer to take pictures at an event. We gave him a large deposit. Before the event occurred, the photographer died. His office called and said it was going to hire a replacement. We did not want just any photographer and refused the offer. The office now refuses to return our deposit, saying it was nonrefundable. What are our rights?

The first thing you should do is read your agreement with the photographer. If the contract has a provision dealing with this situation, that provision controls your rights. If the contract doesn't say anything about the death of the photographer, you should have the right to have the deposit returned. In most contracts, the person who delivers the goods or performs the service is not important, and you would have to allow substitute performance. In personal service contracts of this kind, however, the person providing the service does not have the right simply to provide another person. As far as I am concerned, you do not have to accept a substitute photographer, and you are entitled to the return of your deposit.

Can a fifteen-year-old be liable on a contract?
"Minors generally cannot be forced to pay."

Dear Mr. Alderman:
My fifteen-year-old son joined an online video club. After buying a few DVDs, he stopped paying. The company now wants my husband and me to pay. Do we have to? What is our son's liability?

Basically, you have no liability for contracts entered into by your son. If you did not agree to pay, you do not have any liability to the music club.

Your son also may not have any liability. Under the law, a minor generally cannot enter into enforceable contracts. Some exceptions exist for necessities, such as food, basic furniture, and housing. These exceptions do not apply in this case.

From an ethical or moral standpoint, you should take care of liabilities incurred by your family members. As far as the law is concerned, however, there may not be a legal obligation on your part or your son's to the music company.

My insurance company refuses to pay for "diminished value." "Your insurance company has no liability for 'diminished value.'"

Dear Mr. Alderman:
I was in an accident that was my fault. Is there a special approach I should take in justice court to sue for "diminished value"? My insurance company refuses to pay. After all the repairs, the vehicle is worth $2,500 less than before because of the accident.

You are correct that in some cases, even a repaired car may suffer a "diminished value" due to the repairs. In other words, a repaired car may not be worth as much as a new car, even if all the repairs are properly performed. Your insurance company refuses to pay, however, because the Texas Supreme Court has held that insurance companies have no liability to their insured for diminished value. In other words, if the accident was your fault, you cannot collect damages for diminished value from your own insurance company.

Your right to recover against your insurance company for damages resulting from an accident you caused is based on your insurance contract. The Texas Supreme Court reviewed the standard auto policy and concluded that it does not obligate the insurance company to compensate you for the diminished value of a fully repaired vehicle. Bottom line: Don't waste your time suing for something you are not entitled to.

Is a parking lot responsible for damage to my car? "Usually not."

Dear Mr. Alderman:
I parked my car in a local parking lot. When I returned to leave I noticed the car had a big dent on the side. I spoke with the manager of the parking lot, who showed me signs that stated they were "not responsible for damage or theft." He also pointed out that the same language was on the ticket I received when the car was parked. Are these disclaimers valid? Do I have any rights against the parking lot?

The disclaimers on signs and parking receipts are usually valid, assuming that the damage was not caused as a result of the negligence of the parking lot owner or employee. For example, if you paid to park in the lot, parked the car yourself, and the damage was caused by another person using the lot, the parking lot has no liability. It was not negligent, and the disclaimers make it clear that it is not guaranteeing the safety of your car. In other words, the damage was not the fault of the parking lot or its employees.

On the other hand, if the attendant parked your car, and while speeding around a turn he damaged your car, my opinion is the parking lot is responsible, regardless of the signs. No matter what it says on your parking ticket, the parking lot owes you a duty to act reasonably in handling your car and not damage your property.

The bottom line is that a parking lot does not guarantee the safety of your car, or the possessions inside it. It does, however, owe you a duty to act reasonably in parking and protecting your car. If the parking lot has acted negligently—for example, by not providing reasonable security or lighting, or properly training and supervising its employees—the parking lot should be responsible for all the damages resulting from its negligence.

Does "all sales final" mean I am out of luck?
"You are not stuck with defective goods."

Dear Mr. Alderman:
I received a gift for the holidays. When I opened it, I discovered it was broken. I went to exchange it and the clerk pointed to a sign that said "All Sales Final," and told me I was out of luck. Is that right? This does not seem fair.

It doesn't seem fair and, in my opinion, that is not what the sign means. The store is correct that your rights are subject to the store policy of "all sales final." This does not mean, however, that you must accept a defective product.

Whenever you buy something, you enter into a contract with the store. The terms of that contract are generally not discussed. For example, little is usually said about warranties or about your right to return an item if you do not like it. This means that your rights are what a reasonable person would expect them to be. Generally, when nothing is said the product you buy comes with standard warranties (as discussed in Chapter 18), and if you are not satisfied with it, you may return it for a refund or exchange. These rights, however, may be changed by agreement.

For example, a store may sell an item subject to a "final sale." This means that the customer does not have the right to return it if he does not like it or changes his mind. Similarly, a store may limit a buyer's right to a refund by stating, "No refund: store credit or exchange only." If the person who buys the gift is informed of these conditions prior to the sale—for example, by a sign near the register—the conditions become part of the contract.

Clauses such as "all sales final," or "exchange or store credit only," however, do not change the customer's warranty rights. Whenever you buy something from a store, you get an "implied" warranty that it will work the way it is supposed to work. If an item is defective, a customer has the right to return it to the store and have it replaced or repaired, or to receive a refund. A store may sell an item without a warranty, but simply saying "all sales final" does not do this. If the store had said all sales are "as is," there would be no warranty and you would be stuck. "As is" really means buyer beware.

The bottom line: Whenever you receive a gift you are bound by whatever agreement the person who purchased the gift entered into with the store. But "all sales are final" does not mean you must accept defective goods.

Does a store have to honor the price in its advertisement? "It must meet reasonable demand."

Dear Mr. Alderman:
I went shopping for an item I saw advertised in the morning paper.
When I arrived, I was told they had sold out. I was there just a few
hours after they opened. Can I force them to give me a rain check?

Under the law, an advertisement must either disclose that only a limited number of the item are available, or the store must have enough to meet "reasonable demand." If the store does either of these things, there is no requirement that any business give you a "rain check." I suggest you read the ad carefully to see if the quantity was limited. If the quantity was not limited, speak with a manager if you feel the store did not have a reasonable supply of the item.

CHAPTER 5

Credit Cards

In Chapter 1, you saw how important credit is and that there are laws to help you obtain credit at a fair price. But once you have credit, all sorts of complications can arise while using it.

Have you ever wondered if you could stop payment on a credit card the same way you can on a check? Or who is responsible when your credit card is lost or stolen and the tacky thief enjoys an around-the-world trip—via your charge cards?

As you will see, credit cards offer more protection than any other payment plan. And credit card laws are changing rapidly. To stay current, visit my website, www.peopleslawyer.net.

What can I do when I have dispute with a merchant? "Luckily, you used a credit card."

Dear Mr. Alderman:

Approximately three weeks ago, I bought a new houseplant. It was quite expensive, and the local florist told me it was in excellent shape and, with good care, would be a real showpiece. As soon as I got it home, I noticed it had a horrible case of spider mites. The plant was so infested I couldn't even bring it into the house. I immediately returned it to the florist, who told me the mites must have come from my house, as his plants were "all spotless." I told him I just bought it a few hours ago and the plant was never in my house. It was obvious the mites had been there a long period of time. He said he was sorry, but he wasn't going to do anything, and according to him, I could have the plant back or leave it with him. He then laughed and said, "Remember the old maxim 'caveat emptor': Let the buyer beware." At any rate, last week I received my credit card bill with the $80 charge for the plant on it. Can I do anything?

If you had paid for the plant with cash, your only remedies would be to try to get the merchant to refund your money or to go to justice court. But luckily you used a credit card and, as you will see, this gives you substantial rights. Under federal law, a charge card company is not allowed to recover any amount from you that the merchant would not be allowed to recover. In legal jargon, the card company takes the account subject to all "claims and defenses" the buyer has against the merchant.

What this means is you have a chance to explain to the charge card company why you don't want to pay. For example: If the florist tried to collect the $80 from you, you would be able to refuse, saying the goods were defective and did not live up to the promise of being show quality.

Under the law, the charge card company is treated like the merchant. You can say to the charge card company, "I don't have to pay my bill because the goods I purchased and tried to return are defective." You have this right against the charge card company *until you pay the charge* and if the following three conditions have been met:

1. You have made a good faith effort to settle the matter with the merchant.

2. The goods cost more than $50.

3. The sale took place within your home state or within 100 miles of your home address.

This law protects you whenever you pay for goods or services with a charge card. If you receive your bill and there is a charge for goods or services that you did not receive or that were defective, you should immediately contact the charge card company in writing and tell the company of the dispute.

Do not pay the charge you are disputing!

You must write the credit card company and explain you are disputing the charge. Check the back of your billing statement or the company's website for the proper address. Sometimes the credit card company will listen to your version of the dispute over the phone. But to fully retain all your rights under the law, follow up any phone call with a letter sent via certified mail, return receipt requested, confirming the call. You also should check the website to see if there is a process to dispute the charge online. Most credit card issuers now have a dispute process online.

The law we are discussing is called the **Fair Credit Billing Act.** To find out more about how to use this law, read the next letter.

What can I do when a company goes bankrupt?
"Next time, use a credit card."

Dear Mr. Alderman:
It seems like every day another business goes bankrupt or just disap-
pears. I am worried I will buy something from a business and before
it is delivered the company will go bankrupt. Some of my friends are
stuck with tickets on bankrupt airlines. How can I protect myself?

As a consumer, you can't prevent a company from going bankrupt, but by
using a credit card, you can usually protect yourself from having to bear
any loss. Under the Fair Credit Billing Act, a credit card company may not
collect for goods or services you purchased but never received. This rule
would probably apply if you charged a plane ticket and never had an opportunity to use it because the airline has gone bankrupt, canceling your flight.

The law is easy to use, but you must follow a few simple rules:

1. You must send a separate, written billing error notice to the card
   company (your billing insert will give you the address), or file a
   dispute online.

2. Your notice must reach the card company within 60 days after the
   first bill containing the error was mailed to you.

These steps must be explained in your bill. Usually there will be a statement like the following:

BILLING RIGHTS SUMMARY
(In Case of Errors or Questions About Your Bill)

If you think your bill is wrong or if you need more information about
a transaction on your bill, write us (on a separate sheet) at (the address
shown on your bill) as soon as possible. We must hear from you no
later than 60 days after we sent you the first bill on which the error or
problem appeared. You can telephone us, but doing so will not preserve your rights. In your letter, give us the following information:

• Your name and account number.
• The dollar amount of the suspected error.
• A description of the error, and explain, if you can, why you believe
  there is an error. If you need more information, describe the item you
  are unsure about.

You do not have to pay any amount in question while we are inves-
tigating, but you are still obligated to pay the parts of your bill not in

question. While we investigate your question, we cannot report you as delinquent or take any action to collect the amount you question.

Special Rule for Credit Card Purchases

If you have a problem with the quality of goods or services that you purchased with a credit card, and you have tried in good faith to correct the problem with the merchant, you may not have to pay the remaining amount due on the goods or services. You have this protection only when the purchase price was more than $50 and the purchase was made in your home state or within 100 miles of your mailing address. (If we [The credit card company] own or operate the merchant, or if we mailed you the advertisement for the property or services, all purchases are covered regardless of amount or location of purchase.)

You may use the following form for your letter. Send this letter to your credit card company at the address listed on your monthly statement. Send it via certified mail, return receipt requested:

Date   Your name
                                                          Address

Credit Card Company
Address
RE: Account # _____

I am disputing the charge in my (<u>month</u>) statement in the amount of $(<u>give amount</u>), for the purchase of (<u>item</u>).

State reasons for refusal to pay. For example, the writer of the prior letter would say:

This charge was for the purchase of a plant that the store told me was in great condition, a showpiece. The plant was infected with mites. I have returned the plant and refuse to pay because it is defective. The store now has the plant.

Please remove this charge from my bill. Thank you for your expected cooperation.

_____
Signed

Next time you buy goods or services, think about the advantages of using your credit card. If the goods or services never arrive or the company goes out of business, you will not have to bear a loss because the law allows you to dispute your bill and assert your legal rights against the credit card company.

THE FAIR CREDIT BILLING ACT

The Fair Credit Billing Act (FCBA) protects you in the case of "billing errors." Billing errors are defined by the law and include:

1. Charges not made by you or anyone authorized to use your account.

2. Charges that are incorrectly identified or for which the wrong amount or date is shown.

3. Charges for goods or services that you did not accept or that were not delivered as agreed.

4. Computational or similar errors.

5. Failure to properly reflect payments or other credits, such as returns.

6. Not mailing or delivering bills to your current address (provided you give a change of address at least twenty days before the billing period ends).

7. Charges for which you request an explanation or written proof of purchase.

This law applies to any business you have an account with, including stores, credit card companies, and even bank overdraft checking accounts. If you feel a billing error has occurred, you must send the creditor a billing error notice or file a written complaint online. This notice must reach the creditor within 60 days after you receive the first bill containing the error. Send the notice to the address provided on your bill, or file online. In your letter or online dispute you should include the following information:

1. Name and account number.

2. A statement that you believe your bill contains an error and that includes the dollar amount involved.

3. A statement describing why you think there is an error.

The law requires only that you send this notice, but to protect yourself, send it certified mail, return receipt requested. You should also receive confirmation for any online dispute.

What must the creditor do?

The creditor must acknowledge your dispute claiming a billing error within 30 days after he receives it, unless the problem is resolved within that time period. In any event, within two billing cycles (but not more than 90 days) the creditor must conduct a reasonable investigation and either correct the mistake or explain why he believes the bill to be correct.

What happens while a bill is being disputed?

You may withhold payment of the amount in dispute, including the affected portions of minimum payments and finance charges, until the dispute is resolved. You are still required to pay any part of the bill that is not disputed, including finance and other charges.

While the FCBA dispute settlement procedure is going on, the creditor cannot take any legal or other action to collect the disputed amount. Your account cannot be closed or restricted in any way, except the disputed amount may be applied against your credit limit.

What about your credit rating?

While a bill is being disputed, the creditor cannot threaten to damage your credit rating or report you as delinquent to anyone. The creditor is, however, permitted to report you are disputing your bill.

Another federal law, the **Equal Credit Opportunity Act,** prohibits creditors from discriminating against credit applicants who in good faith exercise their rights under the FCBA. You cannot be denied credit merely because you have disputed a bill.

What if the creditor makes a mistake?

If your bill is found to contain a billing error, the creditor must write to you explaining the corrections to be made on your account. In addition to crediting your account with the amount not owed, the creditor must remove all finance charges, late fees, and other charges relating to the amount. If the creditor concludes you owe part of the disputed amount, this too must be explained in writing. You also have the right to request copies of documents proving you owe the money.

What if the bill is correct?

If the creditor investigates and still believes the bill to be correct, you must be told promptly in writing how much you owe and why. You may also request copies of relevant documents. At this point, you will owe the disputed amount plus any finance charges accumulated while the amount was being disputed.

What if the creditor doesn't follow the procedures?

Any creditor who fails to strictly follow the Fair Credit Billing Act dispute settlement procedure is penalized by not being allowed to collect the first $50 of the amount in dispute, even if the bill turns out to be correct. For example: This penalty would apply if a creditor acknowledges your complaint in 45 days (15 days too late) or takes more than two billing cycles to resolve a dispute. It also applies if a creditor threatens to report or improperly reports your billing situation. Thus, if you owed $200, the creditor's delay would mean he can only recover $150.

The bottom line: Use a credit card whenever you have any doubts about a company or whenever you are buying something to arrive or to be used in the future.

Don't I have to give my consent for someone to get my credit report?
"No."

Dear Mr. Alderman:

I just learned a mortgage company got a copy of my credit report. I was never told the company requested this. I thought anyone who requested a credit check needed my permission. Am I wrong?

Under the Fair Credit Reporting Act, a company can get a copy of your report if it is using the report to furnish you credit or review your account. Credit reports may also be provided in connection with employment and insurance. Based on what you say in your letter, the mortgage company had a legitimate basis for requesting the report and therefore was entitled to it. There is no need for your permission.

The best way to find out who has requested copies of your report is to contact one of the three major credit bureaus. They keep records of who has made inquiries. If you feel a report was requested for unlawful reasons, you should let the credit bureau and the Federal Trade Commission know.

What happens when my card is stolen?
"Good news for you."

Dear Mr. Alderman:

The other day I went into a restaurant and paid for my meal with a credit card. The waiter had me sign the receipt but forgot to return my card. I didn't discover this until several days later, when I went to charge another meal and found the card missing. Of course, I immediately called the restaurant and was told the waiter had been fired. I informed the credit card company my card was stolen and was told to write the credit card company a letter confirming this. Now I am worried about what will happen if my card is used by the waiter.

Don't worry, federal law protects you when your credit card is lost or stolen. Under the law, your maximum liability for the unauthorized use of your credit card is $50. But that liability may be even less if you quickly notify the credit card company. You have no liability for charges incurred after you have given the company notice that your card was stolen or lost. Notice may be given in any reasonable way, including over the telephone. In your case, you will not have to pay for any charges after the date you phoned the card company, and the most you will have to pay for unauthorized charges made before you gave notice is $50.

If you want to make certain you never have to pay anything if your credit card is lost or stolen, keep the telephone number for the credit card company handy and call as soon as you find your card is missing. A quick phone call could save you $50.

Good advice: Make a copy of the contents of your wallet with contact phone numbers so you can quickly report any lost or stolen credit card.

Someone is charging things to my account. What are my rights?
"You may not have to pay anything."

Dear Mr. Alderman:
I received my credit card bill, and there were three charges for things I didn't buy. I disputed the charges as you suggested and was told they were for mail-order items charged to my account and sent to someone else. The store said it was a phone order and it got my account number that way. I didn't make these calls, and I don't feel I should have to pay anything, even the $50.

I agree; I don't believe you have any liability. Under the law you don't have to pay for any unauthorized charge. A store that simply accepts a credit card number over the phone and mails the merchandise to a different address runs the risk that the cardholder won't pay. I suggest you make it clear to the credit card company that you did not order the items and you do not intend to pay.

As far as the $50 is concerned, I don't think you should have to pay even that much. As I stated earlier, if you lose your card or it is stolen, you may be required to pay up to the first $50. In my opinion, this rule doesn't apply when someone fraudulently uses your number but not the card. In other words, the law imposes some obligations on you if you are careless and lose the card, or if it is stolen. But as long as you have the card, you have no liability for the unauthorized use of your card number.

Can a credit card company issue a card to an unemployed nineteen-year-old?
"It may issue a card to whomever it wants."

Dear Mr. Alderman:
Our nineteen-year-old son recently received a credit card in his name. He is unemployed and has no money. Is it legal for a credit card company to issue a credit card to someone in his position?

Basically, a credit card company may issue a credit card to whomever it wants. Of course, as a practical matter, most companies will not issue a card if they suspect the person will not be able to pay his or her bills or that they will be unable to collect.

For example, as a general rule, a minor—that is, a person under eighteen years of age—may not enter into binding contracts. This means that a credit card company cannot sue a minor, even if the minor signs an application agreeing to pay. It does not mean the company may not issue a card to a minor.

Similarly, if a person is unemployed he or she may not have the ability to pay bills. A credit card company, however, still has the right to issue that person a credit card with the expectation that he or she will pay.

The bottom line is that the credit card company has the right to issue a card to your son. Your son must now exercise good judgment when using it.

I lost my debit card. What now?
"All plastic is not equal."

Dear Mr. Alderman:
I recently used a walk-up teller machine to get some cash. I withdrew $50 and left. Apparently I dropped my card, because I can't find it. I have looked everywhere, but it is just missing. I remember reading something about the fact that I am only liable for $50 if I lose my credit card. Am I protected if someone finds my bank card and uses it?

The law protecting you in the case of lost credit cards does not apply to cards that electronically transfer money directly out of your account. Unlike a credit card, which extends credit during the period between the time of making the charge and the time you pay the bill, a debit card immediately debits your account.

The law regarding debit cards such as MPACT, Pulse, or any so-called bank card, is very different from the law regarding credit cards. If your debit card is lost or stolen, *your liability depends on how quickly you report the loss.* Your liability is limited to $50 only if you notify the institution within two business days of learning of the loss. If you wait, your liability may be as high as $500. And should you fail to report the loss within 60 days after your statement is mailed to you, you are responsible for all transfers made after 60 days (even if they total more than $500). This means you could lose all the money in your account, plus any overdraft protection you may have with the bank.

For example, suppose your automated teller machine card is stolen by some nefarious thief who has also discovered your code number. (*Remember: A good way to protect yourself is to keep your code number a secret.*) The first stop the villain makes is the ATM, where he promptly withdraws $75 from your account. The next day, he returns and withdraws a hefty $200 (he's getting greedy!). A week later you attempt to use your card only to discover it's missing.

If you call the bank within two business days after you discover the card missing, all you lose is $50. But should you wait a week, you will be responsible for the entire $275; if you wait longer you may lose all the money in your account. For instance, many people put their bank statements aside or don't check them online, planning to find a "free moment" later to look them over. Meanwhile, two and a half months go by. The thief decides to hit the ATM again and, with your card and code in hand, wipes out your entire account, which amounts to $1,000. Because you did not report the discrepancy in your statement within 60 days after the bank mailed the statement, the entire loss will fall on your shoulders.

Remember: A delay of two days in reporting the loss of a debit card could cost you $500. Promptly review all bank statements and report any unauthorized transfer of funds.

The law regulating misuse of debit cards is called the **Electronic Fund Transfer Act.** It covers not only your debit cards, but also any preauthorized payments you allow the bank to make. For example, many of us use electronic fund transfers to pay some of our monthly bills automatically, such as utility and mortgage payments. As the answer to this letter indicates, using a debit card does not provide the same legal protections as a credit card. Many people prefer debit cards because they help them manage their budgets and not overspend. The trade-off is the loss of the protections of a credit card.

When are my payments really due?
"On the stated date."

Dear Mr. Alderman:
I have been paying on an installment loan on my truck for the past year. Payments are due on the 1st and I have a fifteen-day grace period. I always mail my payment by the 15th. For the past two months the company I'm paying has called me on the 16th and demanded payment, asking why I am late. It has even threatened to repossess my car. What can I do to stop this harassment?

You seem to believe that because you mailed your payment on the 15th you are paying your note on time. In fact, in most cases the due date is when the payment must arrive, not when it must be sent.

In your case the payment is due on the 1st of the month. The creditor has given you a fifteen-day grace period to help you make sure the payment arrives. I suggest you mail the payment on a date that ensures it arrives before the 15th. If you do not, you run the risk of having your truck repossessed.

By the way, since 2010, a credit card company must give you a twenty-one-day grace period.

Is there a new credit card law?
"Yes, and it offers consumers substantial protections."

Dear Mr. Alderman:
I just received a notice from my credit card company increasing my interest rate. I have never been late with a payment, and almost always pay more than the minimum. Is this legal? I heard there is a new law that protects consumers.

You are correct. Congress passed a credit card law that stops practices like the one you describe. In early 2009, Congress enacted the Credit Card Accountability Responsibility and Disclosure Act, commonly referred to as the Credit CARD Act. The most significant of the Act's provisions prevent credit card companies from raising interest rates whenever they want. The new law became effective in February 2010, but many people still are not familiar with its provisions. Under the Credit CARD Act, card issuers:

- Cannot increase interest rates on your existing balances unless you are at least sixty days late on the account. Rates cannot be increased on new accounts in their first year unless you are sixty days late in payment.

- Must provide clear disclosure of terms before you open an account.
- Must honor promotional interest rates for at least six months.
- Cannot charge over-limit fees unless they obtain the account holder's prior consent to accept and process over-limit transactions.
- Cannot charge fees or penalties for accepting payments by mail, phone, electronic transfer, or any other means, unless the payment is processed through an expedited service processor.
- Are prohibited from double-cycle billing, in which a customer's interest and finance charges are based on two months of the account's balance. This practice hurts people who may have paid off the balance in one month but not the other.
- Are banned from universal default practices, in which cardholders' interest rates are raised because of late payments made to others, such as mortgage or insurance companies.

You can learn much more about this law on the Consumer Financial Protection Bureau's website, www.consumerfinance.gov.

Can my credit card company change the terms of our agreement? "Maybe, but they must give you forty-five days' notice."

Dear Mr. Alderman:
I just got a letter from my credit card company telling me that it is raising my interest rate. I cannot afford to pay the higher rate. Will the new rate take effect immediately? Can I pay the balance off under the original terms?

First, under the Credit CARD Act, a credit card company may no longer just raise your interest rate whenever it wants to. Interest rates may not be raised unless it is a promotional rate that has expired, a floating rate tied to an index, or you are at least sixty days late on the account. Additionally, assuming that the company has the right to change your interest rate, the law requires that you be given at least forty-five days' notice before the rate is changed. During those forty five days, you may close or cancel the card and continue to pay off the balance under the original terms.

Is it legal for a store to print my credit card number on a receipt?
"Neither a credit card number nor a driver's license number may be printed on a receipt."

Dear Mr. Alderman:
I bought something and paid for it with a credit card. The store printed out the receipt, and then added my driver's license number to it. In light of all the credit card fraud and identity theft you read about, this seems very dangerous. Is it legal?

You are correct to be worried about credit card fraud and identity theft, and so is the government. Under federal law, only the last five digits of a credit or debit card transaction may be printed on electronically printed receipts. A new addition to Texas law also prohibits a person from printing a driver's license number on a receipt.

Can a business issue a gift card that expires in two months?
"Not anymore."

Dear Mr. Alderman:
I was given a gift card for the holidays. I went to the store to spend it and found out that it expired after one year. Is this legal? Seems like a rip-off to me.

I agree, gift cards with short expiration dates are a rip-off, but it used to be legal to limit gift cards to a short period of time or charge substantial fees. Short expiration dates and most inactivity fees mean that billions of dollars spent on gift cards are forfeited directly to the business. But this has changed.

Since July 2010, the Credit CARD Act prohibits gift cards from expiring within five years. The law also eliminates most monthly inactivity fees. Inactivity fees will only be permitted if there is no activity on the card for the previous year.

The Credit CARD Act goes a long way toward ensuring that consumers get what they pay for when they purchase a gift card.

Can I be charged more if I use a credit card?
"Not under Texas law."

Dear Mr. Alderman:
The other day I went shopping for a new microwave oven for my wife. I found one I like, but when I went to pay, the store told me I would

*have to pay a 5 percent surcharge if I paid by credit card. The man-
ager told me the credit card company charges him a surcharge and
he was simply passing it on to me. As he explained it, he only gets 95
cents on a dollar from the credit card company, and therefore he has
to charge me more to make the same profit. I paid the extra 5 percent,
but now I don't think it was right. The store advertises it takes credit
cards, and it doesn't seem fair that I have to pay more. Is this legal?*

In simple terms: No, it is not legal! Texas law currently says a merchant,
with the exception of a governmental body, may not charge a customer
more if he uses a credit card instead of cash. Of course, the law doesn't
require that merchants take credit cards, but once they do, they may not
charge you more. I suggest you let the store manager know he didn't have
the right to charge you the extra 5 percent, and that if he doesn't refund it,
you will file a complaint with the attorney general. In my opinion, charging
this illegal extra amount may also violate the Deceptive Trade Practices
Act. To file a complaint under this law, contact the Texas Attorney General's office, texasattorneygeneral.gov.

Finally, I must note that a recent decision of the United States Supreme
Court may affect the continued validity of this law. If you find many stores
starting to charge a surcharge for a credit card, it may be this law has been
invalidated or repealed.

Can I be charged a surcharge for using a debit card?
"Texas law prohibits debit card surcharges."

*Dear Mr. Alderman:
I know that a surcharge for a credit card is unlawful, but a discount
may be give for cash. What about a debit card? Can I be charged a
surcharge if I use a debt card?*

Texas law prohibits debit card surcharges. Unlike the credit card surcharge
law, however, this law is enforced by the Texas Attorney General. To file a
complaint, contact the Consumer Protection Division, (800) 621-0508 or
www.texasattorneygeneral.gov/cpd/consumer-protection.

If credit surcharges are illegal, how can a store give a discount for cash?
"They are not the same."

*Dear Mr. Alderman:
I don't understand. I heard you on TV, and you said it was illegal in
Texas to charge more if someone uses a credit card. The next day I*

went to a gas station, and it had two prices, one for cash and one for credit. The credit price was higher. Isn't this illegal? What should I do about it?

I know this is confusing, but charging more for credit is illegal, while giving a discount for cash is not. Let me give you an example. Suppose a store sells a TV with a list price of $100. If it charged you $104 when you used a credit card, that would be illegal. But if you paid cash and only had to pay $96, this discount would be legal and logical. Here is why:

When you pay with a credit card, the credit card company does not give the merchant 100 cents for every dollar you charge. It discounts the amount it pays the merchant. For example, the credit card company may only give the merchant 96 or 97 cents for every dollar you charge. *In other words, a merchant pays for the credit when you use a credit card.* By giving you a discount for cash the merchant is simply recognizing that it saves money when you pay cash, and it passes that savings on to you. That is what the company is doing.

Because the merchant doesn't know who is going to pay cash and who isn't, the price of any item includes the cost of the credit (the amount the credit card company will deduct). If a merchant doesn't give you a discount for cash, the merchant is in effect charging you for credit you didn't use. As far as I am concerned, every merchant should have two prices: one cash, one credit. If he doesn't, the cash customers are paying more to subsidize those who use credit. (Of course, the bottom line, whether you pay cash or credit, is to always shop for the best price.)

Can a merchant require I provide a photo when I pay with a credit card? "Maybe."

Dear Mr. Alderman:
I have not had this arise, but I am still curious. Can a store demand to see a photo ID when I pay with a credit card? Some places ask, and many do not.

Until recently, the only law that controlled whether a store could ask for a photo ID from a customer was the contract between the credit card issuer and the merchant. For most credit cards, this contract prohibits asking for an ID if the card is signed. If the card is unsigned, the merchant has the right to demand to see a photo ID. Here is what each credit company contract says:

- **Visa:** Merchants cannot require ID if the credit card is signed. However, if the credit card is not signed, the merchant can ask you to show a government-issued ID and sign your credit card on the spot.
- **Mastercard:** Merchants cannot require ID if the credit card is signed. However, if the credit card is not signed, the merchant can ask you to show a government-issued ID and sign your credit card on the spot.
- **American Express:** Merchants should verify that the customer is the actual cardholder, but there are no specific requirements for (or against) requesting to see an ID.
- **Discover:** Merchants can request an ID if they believe the credit card isn't valid. For unsigned credit cards, the merchant can request two forms of identification, one of which must be a government-issued photo ID.

Recently, however, Texas enacted a law that allows Texas merchants to ask for photo identification for credit and debit card purchases—and turn down transactions if a buyer won't show it. The legal issue is whether this law or the contract between the store and the credit card issuer controls. In my opinion, because the law says a merchant "may" decline a transaction without a photo ID, the contract between the merchant and the credit card company controls. We will all have to wait for the lawsuit that I know will be filed after the law takes effect in 2018 to see if I am right.

CHAPTER 6

Debt Collection

Everyone will surely agree we all should pay our bills and they should be paid on time. But once in a while things happen, and somehow we just can't. If you are unable to pay all your bills all the time, you should know federal and state laws exist to protect you from unscrupulous debt collectors.

Most consumers pay their debts. Even though only a small percent of all consumer credit obligations ever become delinquent, late or unpaid accounts total billions of dollars. As one might expect, with this vast sum of money at stake, debt collectors often devote considerable energy to collection of delinquent debts, and some of their efforts are illegal.

Debt collection usually begins with a polite letter from the company informing the late party that the bill is overdue and requesting payment, or at least requesting a payment plan. If nothing can be resolved, additional letters will be sent telling the debtor of more drastic actions to follow.

But if the letters fail to get the needed funds, the account is usually forwarded or sold to a collection agency. The correspondence at this point becomes more urgent, and the tone more harsh. The debtor also may receive telephone calls, both at home and at work, pleading for payment. If payment does not result, the next step is to turn the matter over to an attorney, who may file suit. But suing is expensive and only used as a last resort. If possible, the debt collector wants to be paid without going to court, and sometimes this means resorting to more forceful, and often illegal, means. The ingenuity of debt collectors is unlimited, and unfortunately, their approaches are oftentimes questionable. Tales of the misconduct of debt collectors could fill the pages of many books.

The aggressive tactics of some debt collectors became so abusive that Congress found it necessary to pass a law to protect debtors. This law is called the **Fair Debt Collection Practices Act,** and it provides protection to consumers who experience harassing and threatening conditions at the hands of pesky debt collectors. This law, along with the **Texas Debt Collection Act,** should ensure that honest debtors, who are trying to do their best but just get in a little over their heads, are treated fairly and humanely by debt collectors.

Before talking about these laws, however, you should know what legal rights your creditors have if they do sue you. To stay current with all the laws that regulate debt collection in Texas, check out the "LAWS" section at www.peopleslawyer.net, and consider subscribing to my free Consumer News Alert while you are there.

What can the debt collector get?
"Not much."

Dear Mr. Alderman:

I owe a local department store about $1,000. I have been unable to pay in full, and even though I send as much as I can each month, the store has said it will sue me. I have a steady job and a small house with a large mortgage. Every penny I earn goes to pay my bills. If the store sues, what can it get from me?

Every state has a law that "exempts" some of a debtor's property from his creditors, even after a lawsuit. Exempt property is property your creditors can never take. No matter how much money you owe, there is some property the state feels is so important to you that you should be able to keep it. *Texas has about the most favorable exemption statutes in the country.* Under Texas law, after a lawsuit your creditors cannot take your homestead or a specified amount of personal property, in most cases up to $100,000. Here is what the law says:

TEXAS PROPERTY CODE

PERSONAL PROPERTY EXEMPTION

Sec. 42.001. PERSONAL PROPERTY EXEMPTION.
(a) Personal property, as described in Section 42.002, is exempt from garnishment, attachment, execution, or other seizure if:
   (1) the property is provided for a family and has an aggregate fair market value of not more than $100,000, exclusive of the amount of any liens, security interests, or other charges encumbering the property; or
   (2) the property is owned by a single adult, who is not a member of a family, and has an aggregate fair market value of not more than $50,000, exclusive of the amount of any liens, security interests, or other charges encumbering the property.

(b) The following personal property is exempt from seizure and is not included in the aggregate limitations prescribed by Subsection (a):

 (1) current wages for personal services, except for the enforcement of court-ordered child support payments;

 (2) professionally prescribed health aids of a debtor or a dependent of a debtor;

 (3) alimony, support, or separate maintenance received or to be received by the debtor for the support of the debtor or a dependent of the debtor; and

 (4) a religious bible or other book containing sacred writings of a religion that is seized by a creditor other than a lessor of real property who is exercising the lessor's contractual or statutory right to seize personal property after a tenant breaches a lease agreement for or abandons the real property.

(c) Except as provided by Subsection (b)(4), this section does not prevent seizure by a secured creditor with a contractual landlord's lien or other security in the property to be seized.

(d) Unpaid commissions for personal services not to exceed 25 percent of the aggregate limitations prescribed by Subsection (a) are exempt from seizure and are included in the aggregate.

(e) A religious bible or other book described by Subsection (b)(4) that is seized by a lessor of real property in the exercise of the lessor's contractual or statutory right to seize personal property after a tenant breaches a lease agreement for the real property or abandons the real property may not be included in the aggregate limitations prescribed by Subsection (a).

Sec. 42.002. PERSONAL PROPERTY.

(a) The following personal property is exempt under Section 42.001(a):

 (1) home furnishings, including family heirlooms;

 (2) provisions for consumption;

 (3) farming or ranching vehicles and implements;

 (4) tools, equipment, books, and apparatus, including boats and motor vehicles used in a trade or profession;

 (5) wearing apparel;

 (6) jewelry not to exceed 25 percent of the aggregate limitations prescribed by Section 42.001(a);

 (7) two firearms;

 (8) athletic and sporting equipment, including bicycles;

(9) a two-wheeled, three-wheeled, or four-wheeled motor vehicle for each member of a family or single adult who holds a driver's license or who does not hold a driver's license but who relies on another person to operate the vehicle for the benefit of the nonlicensed person;

(10) the following animals and forage on hand for their consumption:

    (A) two horses, mules, or donkeys and a saddle, blanket, and bridle for each;

    (B) 12 head of cattle;

    (C) 60 head of other types of livestock; and

    (D) 120 fowl; and

(11) household pets.

(b) Personal property, unless precluded from being encumbered by other law, may be encumbered by a security interest under Subchapter B, Chapter 9, Business & Commerce Code, or Subchapter F, Chapter 501, Transportation Code, or by a lien fixed by other law, and the security interest or lien may not be avoided on the ground that the property is exempt under this Chapter.

Sec. 42.0021. ADDITIONAL EXEMPTION FOR CERTAIN SAVINGS PLANS.

(a) In addition to the exemption prescribed by Section 42.001, a person's right to the assets held in or to receive payments, whether vested or not, under any stock bonus, pension, annuity, deferred compensation, profit-sharing, or similar plan, including a retirement plan for self-employed individuals, or a simplified employee pension plan, an individual retirement account or individual retirement annuity, including an inherited individual retirement account, individual retirement annuity, Roth IRA, or inherited Roth IRA, or a health savings account, and under any annuity or similar contract purchased with assets distributed from that type of plan or account, is exempt from attachment, execution, and seizure for the satisfaction of debts to the extent the plan, contract, annuity, or account is exempt from federal income tax, or to the extent federal income tax on the person's interest is deferred until actual payment of benefits to the person under Section 223, 401(a), 403(a), 403(b), 408(a), 408A, 457(b), or 501(a), Internal Revenue Code of 1986, including a government plan or church plan described by Section 414(d) or (e), Internal Revenue Code of 1986. For purposes of this subsection, the interest of a person in a plan, annuity, account, or contract acquired by reason of the death of another person, whether as an owner, participant, beneficiary, survivor, coannuitant, heir, or legatee, is exempt to the same extent that the interest of the person from whom the plan, annuity, account, or contract was acquired was exempt on the date of the person's death. If this subsection is held invalid or preempted by federal law in whole or in part or in certain circumstances, the subsection remains in effect in all other respects to the maximum extent permitted by law.

(b) Contributions to an individual retirement account that exceed the amounts permitted under the applicable provisions of the Internal Revenue Code of 1986 and any accrued earnings on such contributions are not exempt under this section unless otherwise exempt by law. Amounts qualifying as nontaxable rollover contributions under Section 402(a)(5), 403(a)(4), 403(b)(8), or 408(d)(3) of the Internal Revenue Code of 1986 before January 1, 1993, are treated as exempt amounts under Subsection (a). Amounts treated as qualified rollover contributions under Section 408A, Internal Revenue Code of 1986, are treated as exempt amounts under Subsection (a). In addition, amounts qualifying as nontaxable rollover contributions under Section 402(c), 402(e)(6), 402(f), 403(a)(4), 403(a)(5), 403(b)(8), 403(b)(10), 408(d)(3), or 408A of the Internal Revenue Code of 1986 on or after January 1, 1993, are treated as exempt amounts under Subsection (a). Amounts qualifying as nontaxable rollover contributions under Section 223(f)(5) of the Internal Revenue Code of 1986 on or after January 1, 2004, are treated as exempt amounts under Subsection (a).

(c) Amounts distributed from a plan, annuity, account, or contract entitled to an exemption under Subsection (a) are not subject to seizure for a creditor's claim for 60 days after the date of distribution if the amounts qualify as a nontaxable rollover contribution under Subsection (b).

(d) A participant or beneficiary of a plan, annuity, account, or contract entitled to an exemption under Subsection (a), other than an individual retirement account or individual retirement annuity, is not prohibited from granting a valid and enforceable security interest in the participant's or beneficiary's right to the assets held in or to receive payments under the exempt plan, annuity, account, or contract to secure a loan to the participant or beneficiary from the exempt plan, annuity, account, or contract, and the right to the assets held in or to receive payments from the plan, annuity, account, or contract is subject to attachment, execution, and seizure for the satisfaction of the security interest or lien granted by the participant or beneficiary to secure the loan.

(e) If Subsection (a) is declared invalid or preempted by federal law, in whole or in part or in certain circumstances, as applied to a person who has not brought a proceeding under Title 11, United States Code, the subsection remains in effect, to the maximum extent permitted by law, as to any person who has filed that type of proceeding.

(f) A reference in this section to a specific provision of the Internal Revenue Code of 1986 includes a subsequent amendment of the substance of that provision.

Sec. 42.0022. EXEMPTION FOR COLLEGE SAVINGS PLANS.

(a) In addition to the exemption prescribed by Section 42.001, a person's right to the assets held in or to receive payments or benefits under any of the following is exempt from attachment, execution, and seizure for the satisfaction of debts:

(1) any fund or plan established under Subchapter F, Chapter 54, Education Code, including the person's interest in a prepaid tuition contract;

(2) any fund or plan established under Subchapter G, Chapter 54, Education Code, including the person's interest in a savings trust account; or

(3) any qualified tuition program of any state that meets the requirements of Section 529, Internal Revenue Code of 1986, as amended.

(b) If any portion of this section is held to be invalid or preempted by federal law in whole or in part or in certain circumstances, this section remains in effect in all other respects to the maximum extent permitted by law.

Sec. 41.001. INTERESTS IN LAND EXEMPT FROM SEIZURE

(a) A homestead and one or more lots used for a place of burial of the dead are exempt from seizure for the claims of creditors except for encumbrances properly fixed on homestead property.

(b) Encumbrances may be properly fixed on homestead property for:

(1) purchase money;

(2) taxes on the property;

(3) work and material used in constructing improvements on the property if contracted for in writing as provided by Sections 53.254(a), (b), and (c);

(4) an owelty of partition imposed against the entirety of the property by a court order or by a written agreement of the parties to the partition, including a debt of one spouse in favor of the other spouse resulting from a division or an award of a family homestead in a divorce proceeding;

(5) the refinance of a lien against a homestead, including a federal tax lien resulting from the tax debt of both spouses, if the homestead is a family homestead, or from the tax debt of the owner;

(6) an extension of credit that meets the requirements of Section 50(a)(6), Article XVI, Texas Constitution; or

(7) a reverse mortgage that meets the requirements of Sections 50(k)–(p), Article XVI, Texas Constitution.

(c) The homestead claimant's proceeds of a sale of a homestead are not subject to seizure for a creditor's claim for six months after the date of sale.

Sec. 41.002. DEFINITION OF HOMESTEAD

(a) If used for the purposes of an urban home or as both an urban home and a place to exercise a calling or business, the homestead of a family or a single, adult person, not otherwise entitled to a homestead, shall consist of not more than 10 acres of land which may be in one or more contiguous lots, together with any improvements thereon.

(b) If used for the purposes of a rural home, the homestead shall consist of:

(1) for a family, not more than 200 acres, which may be in one or more parcels, with the improvements thereon; or

(2) for a single, adult person, not otherwise entitled to a homestead, not more than 100 acres, which may be in one or more parcels, with the improvements thereon.

(c) A homestead is considered to be urban if, at the time the designation is made, the property is:

(1) located within the limits of a municipality or its extraterritorial jurisdiction or a platted subdivision; and

(2) served by police protection, paid or volunteer fire protection, and at least three of the following services provided by a municipality or under contract to a municipality:

(A) electric;

(B) natural gas;

(C) sewer;

(D) storm sewer; and

(E) water.

(d) The definition of a homestead as provided in this section applies to all homesteads in this state whenever created.

So what does all this mean to you? In summary, it means you can keep your home, free from all your creditors except for a few exceptions, such as a home equity loan or someone who loaned you the money to buy the house or improve it. If you don't pay these debts, or if you don't pay your taxes, your house may be sold to pay your debts. You also can keep all life insurance and personal property, up to $100,000 for a family, so long as the property is included in the list and you didn't voluntarily give your creditor a lien. For example, if you own a car, your general creditors cannot take it to satisfy your debt. But the dealer who sold you the car can repossess it if he took a lien when he sold it to you. On the other hand, if you own a boat, an item not included on the list, your creditors could sue you and have the sheriff or constable take the boat and sell it to pay off the debt.

As you can see, most of what the average person owns is exempt. This means even if you are sued, you do not have to worry about losing your property. Of course, the person who extended credit to you to buy an expensive item may have a lien allowing him to take the goods back if you don't pay.

And remember: your creditors also know the law. They know they can't force you to pay and therefore would probably like to talk with you about finding a way to work things out.

Can they take my wages?
"Probably not . . ."

Dear Mr. Alderman:

I owe lots of people money, but my family comes first. I buy groceries and clothing, and everything else I earn goes to pay my bills. I am worried that if I don't pay my bills soon, the creditors will take part of my wages. I couldn't even afford the basics if this happened. Can they do this?

The Texas Constitution guarantees that a person's wages are protected from his or her creditors. Under the law there are three groups of debts you must be concerned with: student loans, child support, and taxes. If you owe money for either of these, your wages may be attached to pay the debt. *In all other cases, your creditors may not take any of your wages.*

Remember, this is a Texas law. In nearly every other state a portion of your wages may be taken by any creditor to satisfy the debt. For example, if you work part-time in Texas and part-time in Oklahoma, your Oklahoma wages may be subject to your creditors.

Best advice: As you can tell from this letter and the one right before it, creditors in Texas have few legal remedies when it comes to enforcing debts. Because of this they are usually more than willing to work with you to arrange a fair payment plan. *If you are having trouble with your creditors and just need some time to rearrange your debts, contact your creditors and see what you can work out. It is in everyone's best interest to reach a compromise.*

Is there a law that protects me from abusive debt collectors? "Actually, there are two laws."

Dear Mr. Alderman:
I am being harassed by a bill collector. He calls me day and night, yells profanities, and threatens my family. How do I stop this? Is there a law that protects me?

There actually are two laws that protect you against abusive debt collection practices. Texas has a law called the **Texas Debt Collection Act.** There also is a federal law called the **Fair Debt Collection Practices Act.** Both of these laws prohibit certain abusive conduct; however, they define the term "debt collector" very differently.

Under the state law, anyone collecting a debt is a debt collector subject to the law. Under the federal law, however, only someone collecting a debt for another—a third-party debt collector—is covered. For example, if the local department store calls you about a past-due bill, it would be a debt collector for purposes of the Texas Debt Collection Act, but not the federal Fair Debt Collection Practices Act. On the other hand, if Jones Debt Collection services calls about the same debt, it will be subject to both laws. This is an important distinction because the federal law has restrictions not included in the state law.

Here are the major provisions of both these laws that protect you against abusive practices. For specific application of these laws, look at the questions in the remainder of this chapter.

FAIR DEBT COLLECTION PRACTICES ACT
[UNITED STATES CODE]

Sec. 805. COMMUNICATION IN CONNECTION WITH DEBT COLLECTION [15 U.S.C. Sec. 1692C]

(a) COMMUNICATION WITH THE CONSUMER GENERALLY. Without the prior consent of the consumer given directly to the debt collector or the express permission of a court of competent jurisdiction, a debt collector may not communicate with a consumer in connection with the collection of any debt—

(1) at any unusual time or place or a time or place known or which should be known to be inconvenient to the consumer. In the absence of knowledge of circumstances to the contrary, a debt collector shall assume that the convenient time for communicating with a consumer is after 8 o'clock antemeridian and before 9 o'clock postmeridian, local time at the consumer's location;

(2) if the debt collector knows the consumer is represented by an attorney with respect to such debt and has knowledge of, or can readily ascertain, such attorney's name and address, unless the attorney fails to respond within a reasonable period of time to a communication from the debt collector or unless the attorney consents to direct communication with the consumer; or

(3) at the consumer's place of employment if the debt collector knows or has reason to know that the consumer's employer prohibits the consumer from receiving such communication.

(b) COMMUNICATION WITH THIRD PARTIES. Except as provided in section 804, without the prior consent of the consumer given directly to the debt collector, or the express permission of a court of competent jurisdiction, or as reasonably necessary to effectuate a post-judgment judicial remedy, a debt collector may not communicate, in connection with the collection of any debt, with any person other than a consumer, his attorney, a consumer reporting agency if otherwise permitted by law, the creditor, the attorney of the creditor, or the attorney of the debt collector.

(c) CEASING COMMUNICATION. If a consumer notifies a debt collector in writing that the consumer refuses to pay a debt or that the consumer wishes the debt collector to cease further communication with the consumer, the debt collector shall not communicate further with the consumer with respect to such debt, except—

(1) to advise the consumer that the debt collector's further efforts are being terminated;

(2) to notify the consumer that the debt collector or creditor may invoke specified remedies which are ordinarily invoked by such debt collector or creditor; or

(3) where applicable, to notify the consumer that the debt collector or creditor intends to invoke a specified remedy.

If such notice from the consumer is made by mail, notification shall be complete upon receipt.

(d) For the purpose of this section, the term "consumer" includes the consumer's spouse, parent (if the consumer is a minor), guardian, executor, or administrator.

Sec. 806. HARASSMENT OR ABUSE [15 U.S.C. Sec. 1692D]

A debt collector may not engage in any conduct the natural consequence of which is to harass, oppress, or abuse any person in connection with the collection of a debt. Without limiting the general application of the foregoing, the following conduct is a violation of this section:

(1) The use or threat of use of violence or other criminal means to harm the physical person, reputation, or property of any person.

(2) The use of obscene or profane language or language the natural consequence of which is to abuse the hearer or reader.

(3) The publication of a list of consumers who allegedly refuse to pay debts, except to a consumer reporting agency or to persons meeting the requirements of section 603(f) or 604(3)1 of this Act.

(4) The advertisement for sale of any debt to coerce payment of the debt.

(5) Causing a telephone to ring or engaging any person in telephone conversation repeatedly or continuously with intent to annoy, abuse, or harass any person at the called number.

(6) Except as provided in section 804, the placement of telephone calls without meaningful disclosure of the caller's identity.

Sec. 807. FALSE OR MISLEADING REPRESENTATIONS [15 U.S.C. Sec. 1692E]

A debt collector may not use any false, deceptive, or misleading representation or means in connection with the collection of any debt. Without limiting the general application of the foregoing, the following conduct is a violation of this section:

(1) The false representation or implication that the debt collector is vouched for, bonded by, or affiliated with the United States or any State, including the use of any badge, uniform, or facsimile thereof.

(2) The false representation of—
   (A) the character, amount, or legal status of any debt; or
   (B) any services rendered or compensation which may be lawfully received by any debt collector for the collection of a debt.

(3) The false representation or implication that any individual is an attorney or that any communication is from an attorney.

(4) The representation or implication that nonpayment of any debt will result in the arrest or imprisonment of any person or the seizure, garnishment, attachment, or sale of any property or wages of any person unless such action is lawful and the debt collector or creditor intends to take such action.

(5) The threat to take any action that cannot legally be taken or that is not intended to be taken.

(6) The false representation or implication that a sale, referral, or other transfer of any interest in a debt shall cause the consumer to—
   (A) lose any claim or defense to payment of the debt; or
   (B) become subject to any practice prohibited by this title.

(7) The false representation or implication that the consumer committed any crime or other conduct in order to disgrace the consumer.

(8) Communicating or threatening to communicate to any person credit information which is known or which should be known to be false, including the failure to communicate that a disputed debt is disputed.

(9) The use or distribution of any written communication which simulates or is falsely represented to be a document authorized, issued, or approved by any court, official, or agency of the United States or any State, or which creates a false impression as to its source, authorization, or approval.

(10) The use of any false representation or deceptive means to collect or attempt to collect any debt or to obtain information concerning a consumer.

(11) The failure to disclose in the initial written communication with the consumer and, in addition, if the initial communication with the consumer is oral, in that initial oral communication, that the debt collector is attempting to collect a debt and that any information

obtained will be used for that purpose, and the failure to disclose in subsequent communications that the communication is from a debt collector, except that this paragraph shall not apply to a formal pleading made in connection with a legal action.

(12) The false representation or implication that accounts have been turned over to innocent purchasers for value.

(13) The false representation or implication that documents are legal process.

(14) The use of any business, company, or organization name other than the true name of the debt collector's business, company, or organization.

(15) The false representation or implication that documents are not legal process forms or do not require action by the consumer.

(16) The false representation or implication that a debt collector operates or is employed by a consumer reporting agency as defined by section 603(f) of this Act.

Sec. 808. UNFAIR PRACTICES [15 U.S.C. Sec. 1692F]

A debt collector may not use unfair or unconscionable means to collect or attempt to collect any debt. Without limiting the general application of the foregoing, the following conduct is a violation of this section:

(1) The collection of any amount (including any interest, fee, charge, or expense incidental to the principal obligation) unless such amount is expressly authorized by the agreement creating the debt or permitted by law.

(2) The acceptance by a debt collector from any person of a check or other payment instrument postdated by more than five days unless such person is notified in writing of the debt collector's intent to deposit such check or instrument not more than ten nor less than three business days prior to such deposit.

(3) The solicitation by a debt collector of any postdated check or other postdated payment instrument for the purpose of threatening or instituting criminal prosecution.

(4) Depositing or threatening to deposit any postdated check or other postdated payment instrument prior to the date on such check or instrument.

(5) Causing charges to be made to any person for communications by concealment of the true propose of the communication. Such charges include, but are not limited to, collect telephone calls and telegram fees.

(6) Taking or threatening to take any nonjudicial action to effect dispossession or disablement of property if—
   (A) there is no present right to possession of the property claimed as collateral through an enforceable security interest;
   (B) there is no present intention to take possession of the property; or
   (C) the property is exempt by law from such dispossession or disablement.
(7) Communicating with a consumer regarding a debt by post card.
(8) Using any language or symbol, other than the debt collector's address, on any envelope when communicating with a consumer by use of the mails or by telegram, except that a debt collector may use his business name if such name does not indicate that he is in the debt collection business.

TEXAS DEBT COLLECTION ACT [TEXAS FINANCE CODE]

Sec. 392.301. THREATS OR COERCION.
(a) In debt collection, a debt collector may not use threats, coercion, or attempts to coerce that employ any of the following practices:
   (1) using or threatening to use violence or other criminal means to cause harm to a person or property of a person;
   (2) accusing falsely or threatening to accuse falsely a person of fraud or any other crime;
   (3) representing or threatening to represent to any person other than the consumer that a consumer is willfully refusing to pay a nondisputed consumer debt when the debt is in dispute and the consumer has notified in writing the debt collector of the dispute;
   (4) threatening to sell or assign to another the obligation of the consumer and falsely representing that the result of the sale or assignment would be that the consumer would lose a defense to the consumer debt or would be subject to illegal collection attempts;
   (5) threatening that the debtor will be arrested for nonpayment of a consumer debt without proper court proceedings;
   (6) threatening to file a charge, complaint, or criminal action against a debtor when the debtor has not violated a criminal law;
   (7) threatening that nonpayment of a consumer debt will result in the seizure, repossession, or sale of the person's property without proper court proceedings; or

(8) threatening to take an action prohibited by law.
(b) Subsection (a) does not prevent a debt collector from:
    (1) informing a debtor that the debtor may be arrested after proper court proceedings if the debtor has violated a criminal law of this state;
    (2) threatening to institute civil lawsuits or other judicial proceedings to collect a consumer debt; or
    (3) exercising or threatening to exercise a statutory or contractual right of seizure, repossession, or sale that does not require court proceedings.

Sec. 392.302. HARASSMENT; ABUSE.

In debt collection, a debt collector may not oppress, harass, or abuse a person by:
(1) using profane or obscene language or language intended to abuse unreasonably the hearer or reader;
(2) placing telephone calls without disclosing the name of the individual making the call and with the intent to annoy, harass, or threaten a person at the called number;
(3) causing a person to incur a long distance telephone toll, telegram fee, or other charge by a medium of communication without first disclosing the name of the person making the communication; or
(4) causing a telephone to ring repeatedly or continuously, or making repeated or continuous telephone calls, with the intent to harass a person at the called number.

Sec. 392.303. UNFAIR OR UNCONSCIONABLE MEANS.

(a) In debt collection, a debt collector may not use unfair or unconscionable means that employ the following practices:
    (1) seeking or obtaining a written statement or acknowledgment in any form that specifies that a consumer's obligation is one incurred for necessaries of life if the obligation was not incurred for those necessaries; or
    (2) collecting or attempting to collect interest or a charge, fee, or expense incidental to the obligation unless the interest or incidental charge, fee, or expense is expressly authorized by the agreement creating the obligation or legally chargeable to the consumer;
    (3) collecting or attempting to collect an obligation under a check, draft, debit payment, or credit card payment, if:
    (A) the check or draft was dishonored or the debit payment

or credit card payment was refused because the check or draft was not drawn or the payment was not made by a person authorized to use the applicable account;

(B) the debt collector has received written notice from a person authorized to use the account that the check, draft, or payment was unauthorized; and

(C) the person authorized to use the account has filed a report concerning the unauthorized check, draft, or payment with a law enforcement agency, as defined by Article 59.01, Code of Criminal Procedure, and has provided the debt collector with a copy of the report.

(b) Notwithstanding Subsection (a)(2), a creditor may charge a reasonable reinstatement fee as consideration for renewal of a real property loan or contract of sale, after default, if the additional fee is included in a written contract executed at the time of renewal.

(c) Subsection (a)(3) does not prohibit a debt collector from collecting or attempting to collect an obligation under a check, draft, debit payment, or credit card payment if the debt collector has credible evidence, including a document, video recording, or witness statement, that the report filed with a law enforcement agency, as required by Subsection (a)(3)(C), is fraudulent and that the check, draft, or payment was authorized.

Sec. 392.304. FRAUDULENT, DECEPTIVE, OR MISLEADING REPRESENTATIONS.

(a) Except as otherwise provided by this section, in debt collection or obtaining information concerning a consumer, a debt collector may not use a fraudulent, deceptive, or misleading representation that employs the following practices:

(1) using a name other than the:
  (A) true business or professional name or the true personal or legal name of the debt collector while engaged in debt collection; or
  (B) name appearing on the face of the credit card while engaged in the collection of a credit card debt;

(2) failing to maintain a list of all business or professional names known to be used or formerly used by persons collecting consumer debts or attempting to collect consumer debts for the debt collector;

(3) representing falsely that the debt collector has information or something of value for the consumer in order to solicit or discover information about the consumer;

(4) failing to disclose clearly in any communication with the debtor the name of the person to whom the debt has been assigned or is owed when making a demand for money;

(5) in the case of a third-party debt collector, failing to disclose, except in a formal pleading made in connection with a legal action:

    (A) that the communication is an attempt to collect a debt and that any information obtained will be used for that purpose, if the communication is the initial written or oral communication between the third-party debt collector and the debtor; or

    (B) that the communication is from a debt collector, if the communication is a subsequent written or oral communication between the third-party debt collector and the debtor;

(6) using a written communication that fails to indicate clearly the name of the debt collector and the debt collector's street address or post office box and telephone number if the written notice refers to a delinquent consumer debt;

(7) using a written communication that demands a response to a place other than the debt collector's or creditor's street address or post office box;

(8) misrepresenting the character, extent, or amount of a consumer debt, or misrepresenting the consumer debt's status in a judicial or governmental proceeding;

(9) representing falsely that a debt collector is vouched for, bonded by, or affiliated with, or is an instrumentality, agent, or official of, this state or an agency of federal, state, or local government;

(10) using, distributing, or selling a written communication that simulates or is represented falsely to be a document authorized, issued, or approved by a court, an official, a governmental agency, or any other governmental authority or that creates a false impression about the communication's source, authorization, or approval;

(11) using a seal, insignia, or design that simulates that of a governmental agency;

(12) representing that a consumer debt may be increased by the addition of attorney's fees, investigation fees, service fees, or other charges if a written contract or statute does not authorize the additional fees or charges;

(13) representing that a consumer debt will definitely be increased by the addition of attorney's fees, investigation fees, service fees, or other charges if the award of the fees or charges is subject to judicial discretion;

(14) representing falsely the status or nature of the services rendered by the debt collector or the debt collector's business;

(15) using a written communication that violates the United States postal laws and regulations;

(16) using a communication that purports to be from an attorney or law firm if it is not;

(17) representing that a consumer debt is being collected by an attorney if it is not;

(18) representing that a consumer debt is being collected by an independent, bona fide organization engaged in the business of collecting past due accounts when the debt is being collected by a subterfuge organization under the control and direction of the person who is owed the debt; or

(19) using any other false representation or deceptive means to collect a debt or obtain information concerning a consumer.

(b) Subsection (a)(4) does not apply to a person servicing or collecting real property first lien mortgage loans or credit card debts.

(c) Subsection (a)(6) does not require a debt collector to disclose the names and addresses of employees of the debt collector.

(d) Subsection (a)(7) does not require a response to the address of an employee of a debt collector.

(e) Subsection (a)(18) does not prohibit a creditor from owning or operating a bona fide debt collection agency.

Can I lose my car if I don't pay my credit card bills?
"No, and a threat to take it may be unlawful."

Dear Mr. Alderman:
A debt collector for a credit card company has threatened to sue me. He told me if I didn't pay he would sue me and take my car. This will leave me without a way to get to work. Then I will not be able to pay any of my bills. Is there anything I can do to protect my car?

You do not have to do anything. The debt collector for the credit card company has no legal right to take your car. As I pointed out earlier, under Texas law, certain property is "exempt." Even if a creditor sues and gets a judgment against you, he may not take exempt property. Included in the list of exempt property is your car. This means that the debt collector cannot take your car, even if he sues and wins.

You also may want to read the rest of the material in this chapter. The debt collector's threats to take your car probably violate state and federal debt collection laws. Under both statutes, it is unlawful for a debt collector to threaten to take action that the law prohibits. As far as I am concerned, threatening to take exempt property violates our debt collection laws.

Can my creditors take my IRA?
"Not anymore!"

Dear Mr. Alderman:
I lost my job and have fallen behind in paying my bills. I am trying to keep up, but some of my creditors want to be paid in full and have threatened to sue me. I heard you say they can't take my wages, but I am concerned we will lose our savings if they take our IRA. Is there any way I can protect my retirement money?

Before September 1, 1987, a creditor that sued you and won in court could probably take your IRA funds to satisfy the judgment. This was an unfortunate situation because, as the previous letters show, most other property is exempt from your creditors. The legislature has changed this, however, by passing a law that exempts most retirement plans and IRAs from your creditors.

Under this law a qualified IRA, including a Roth IRA, may not be taken by your creditors, even if they go to court, sue, and win. This money is considered so important for your retirement that the state has decided to allow you to keep it. In other words, the answer to your question about protecting your money is . . . keep it in the IRA. Of course, as I pointed out before, other savings, such as a simple savings account, may be taken by your creditors once they sue and win.

Is money from my IRA exempt?
"Not after you remove it from the account."

Dear Mr. Alderman:
I am going to cash out an IRA to pay some bills and repair my home. There will be about $4,000 left after I pay my bills. If I put the money left in the bank, can my creditors seize it?

As you apparently know, in Texas an IRA is "exempt" property. This means that even if you are sued, your creditors may not seize your IRA.

Once you cash the IRA in, however, the funds generally lose their exempt status and may be subject to your creditors. This means that if you put the $4,000 in a bank account, it could be subject to a writ of garnishment.

The best way to avoid this problem is to not withdraw more money from your IRA than you are going to spend. That way, the balance remaining in your IRA account will continue to be exempt.

Is an IRA in another state exempt?
"It probably depends on the law of the other state."

Dear Mr. Alderman:
I read that in Texas an IRA is exempt from creditors. I live in Texas, but I have an IRA with a California bank. Can my creditors take it, or is it still exempt?

Good question. If the account was in a Texas bank, and a creditor attempted to enforce a judgment in Texas, Texas law would govern. Under Texas law, the creditor could not take the money in the account.

If, however, a creditor tried to collect the judgment in California, California law may apply. There has been some litigation in this area, and the courts are not uniform in their decisions. The best thing to do may be to transfer the money into a local bank account to ensure the protection of Texas law.

Can my creditors take my wife's property?
"Maybe not."

Dear Mr. Alderman:
I have a judgment rendered against me in Harris County by a California credit card company. I have not heard from the company about trying to enforce the judgment. I have no assets or funds that would be available to the company if it tried to enforce the judgment. I am now concerned because my wife may inherit a large sum of money. She is not named in the judgment. Can the company try to collect against her if she inherits the money?

As I discuss in Chapter 7, Texas is a "community property state." This means most of the property owned by a husband and wife is "community." Community property may be viewed as being jointly owned. Community property, therefore, is generally subject to the debts of either of the spouses.

On the other hand, "separate property" is property that belongs to just one spouse and is not subject to the debts of the other. Separate property includes property owned before the marriage, *as well as property inherited.* In your case, your wife's inheritance probably would be considered separate property and would not be subject to your debt. She should be careful not to commingle the property or do anything to ratify your debt. If she does, the inheritance could become subject to the debt.

Can I stop harassing phone calls?
"They must stop."

Dear Mr. Alderman:
My creditors won't leave me alone. I know I should pay my bills, and I will as soon as I can, but I am going to lose my job if I don't get some sleep. The most annoying thing they do is call me in the middle of the night and say things like, "I don't know how a deadbeat like you can sleep. Don't you feel guilty about not paying your bills?" I have started pulling my phone cord out at night, but as soon as I plug it in, the calls begin. How can I stop this? Do I report it to the telephone company? I have even tried changing my phone number.

As the introduction to this chapter points out, two laws protect you from harassment by debt collectors, the **Texas Debt Collection Act,** and the federal **Fair Debt Collection Practices Act.** Both laws prohibit debt collectors from harassing you over the phone.

The federal law makes it illegal for "debt collectors" to engage in any conduct designed to harass, oppress, or abuse you in connection with the collection of a debt. It is specifically made illegal to cause a phone to ring repeatedly with intent to annoy, abuse, or harass; to call without giving the caller's identity; or to call after 9 p.m. or before 8 a.m. The federal law also states that once you notify the debt collector in writing that you want him to stop communication with you, *the debt collector must stop all communication except advising you of his next step.*

Under the Fair Debt Collection Practices Act, you can stop the debt collector from calling you, and he may have already violated the law by his conduct so far. *But the Fair Debt Collection Practices Act applies only to a "debt collector," that is, someone in the business of collecting debts for another.* It doesn't apply to a creditor collecting his own debts. If the calls have been from a collection agency, the federal law applies. If the calls are directly from the creditor—for example, a store—the federal law does not apply, but the Texas law does.

Unlike the federal law, the Texas Debt Collection Act applies to anyone trying to collect a debt. This includes the store that sold you the goods and any agency it hires to collect the debt. Although the Texas law is not as broad as the federal law, you still can use it to prevent any further harassment. Under the Texas law, it is illegal to oppress, harass, or abuse any person in connection with the collection of a debt. The law specifically provides that a debt collector may not place phone calls without disclosing the name of the person calling, may not call with the intent to annoy or harass, and may not cause the phone to ring repeatedly or continuously with the intent to harass.

If you feel you are being harassed, immediately contact the creditor and the debt collector (if they are not the same person), and tell them you expect them to cease all further harassment. Do it in writing and mail it certified, return receipt requested. You also should contact the appropriate state and federal agencies. The federal law is enforced by the Consumer Financial Protection Bureau, www.consumerfinance.gov, and the state law is enforced by the attorney general's office, texasattorneygeneral.gov. Additionally, both these laws can be enforced in a private lawsuit, and you can collect substantial civil damages if you have been injured as a result of unlawful collection. If you have suffered injury, see a private attorney about filing a lawsuit. I should remind you that, if you are successful, you are entitled to recover your attorney's fees as well.

Can they tell my boss?
"You may be protected."

Dear Mr. Alderman:
I owe several stores money. I just got a new job, and I am paying them back as fast as I can. Most of the creditors have been nice and have allowed me to pay as best I can, but one debt collector told me that if I don't pay everything I owe, he will call my boss and tell him he has a deadbeat working for him. I know I will be fired if he does that. The only way I can pay this particular store is to not pay anyone else. Is there any way to protect myself? Can the debt collector tell people that I owe money?

If it really is a "debt collector" calling you, as opposed to the store itself, then it is illegal for him to call your boss. The federal law governing debt collection, which applies only to someone trying to collect a debt owed to someone else, says debt collectors may only communicate with other people to try to locate you. *The law expressly makes it illegal for them to call your employer and try to force him to make you pay.*

I suggest you contact the debt collector in writing and demand he stop all communication with third parties. The federal law also provides that if you write debt collectors to stop collection efforts, they must cease all communication except to tell you they are stopping and what they intend to do next. If they continue, contact the Consumer Financial Protection Bureau, www.consumerfinance.gov. If their action has harmed you, you may also consider seeing an attorney to bring a private lawsuit. Under the law you may be entitled to punitive damages, as well as to your actual loss and attorney's fees.

Be aware that this law does not apply to people collecting their own debts. They are governed by the Texas law, which probably lets them contact your employer, unless it is done in a harassing or abusive manner.

My check bounced. What can they do?
"It may be a crime."

Dear Mr. Alderman:
The new dress at the department store was irresistible. The only problem was that the check I used didn't have any money to back it up. After the check bounced I told the store manager that as soon as I got paid I would pay off the check, but the manager insisted I pay right away. The manager said it is criminal to pay for something with a check that bounces and unless I paid soon, the store would turn it over to the district attorney. Can the store do this? I didn't steal the dress—I plan to pay for it.

What you have done is probably criminal under Texas law, and the store has the right to turn the matter over to the district attorney, who could prosecute. *I strongly recommend you immediately pay the store the money you owe it.*

Under Texas law the issuance of a "bad check" is a Class C misdemeanor, and you could receive a fine or even be put in jail. This law states it is illegal to give someone a check knowing you do not have enough money in the bank to cover it. As a practical matter, if you quickly pay the check, you probably will not be prosecuted; but based on what you say in your letter, you have violated the law.

You should be aware, however, of the difference between passing a bad check and stopping payment for a reason. It is not illegal to stop payment on a check when you have enough money in your account to pay it. For example, suppose when you got the dress home, you discovered it was damaged, so you took it back to the store. The store refused to give you back your money, even though it had a sign saying it would give a refund if the goods were returned within twenty-four hours. If you stopped payment on the check, the store could not have you prosecuted under this law. If the store wanted to try to collect the money, it would have to pursue its civil remedies.

But be careful if you are thinking about stopping payment on a check to a mechanic. Read the next letter before you do.

My check bounced. Can they repossess my car?
"They can if the check was for repairs."

Dear Mr. Alderman:
The other day I had the brakes fixed on my car. I paid the bill of $79.95 with a check. I thought I had more than enough money in the bank, but apparently I didn't. The check bounced, and a few days later I found my car missing. When I called the police to report it stolen, they said it had been repossessed. I called the repo man and was told I had to pay the $79.95 plus $550 in repossession costs to get it back. I paid, and now I am mad. What are my rights?

You have probably heard me say that in most cases if someone isn't paid for what he sells you, he can't just come and take it back. He has to go to court and sue you. Well, unfortunately for you there is one big exception to this.

A mechanic has a lien on your car whenever he repairs it. Until you pay he does not have to give it back. And if you pay with a check that is dishonored or if you stop payment, the mechanic has the right to repossess your car. The mechanic cannot forcefully take your car, but he can have a repo man come out in the middle of the night and remove it. So it looks like the mechanic does have the right to take your car back.

The harder question is, what are your rights with respect to the repo man who charged you $550 for taking the car and held it until you paid. Under the law, the repo man has the right to keep the car until you pay. The law limits how much you owe, however, to a reasonable fee. If $550 is an unreasonable amount, you should be entitled to the return of the excessive portion. Do a little research on repo fees and consider justice court.

Can my mechanic keep my car if I don't pay?
"He can if he has a mechanic's lien."

Dear Mr. Alderman:
A mechanic told me he could repair my car for $700. I agreed to this after he assured me that $700 would be the total cost. I told him I couldn't afford to pay any more. After he started the work he discovered the damage was much more serious than he expected. He now wants me to pay $1,200 for the repairs. What are my legal rights? I have offered him $700. He will not give me my car until I pay $1,200.

First, the mechanic is probably asserting his mechanic's lien, and this will make it difficult to get your car without paying or suing. The mechanic has the right to retain your car if you do not pay money that you owe. In my opinion, however, you do not owe more than the $700 you agreed to pay. The mechanic assured you that this would be the total, and he should assume the risk that he underestimated what was required.

The problem, however, is that as long as the mechanic asserts that you owe the money, he may retain the car. Only after it is determined that you do not owe the additional $500—for example, through a court proceeding—will his assertion of the lien for that amount be considered wrongful. At that point you would be entitled to the return of your car and damages. Your damages could include the cost of a rental car for the period during which you were disputing the charge.

Challenging the lien, however, could be costly and time-consuming. The first thing you should do is speak with the mechanic and try to resolve the dispute. Let him know you do not believe you should have to pay for repairs you did not authorize and that are in excess of the amount originally stated. You may want to remind him that if a court determines he is wrong, he could owe you a substantial amount of money. Perhaps you could pay a small percentage of the additional costs as a means of settling the dispute.

If you cannot work things out, another alternative, if you can afford it, is to pay the disputed $500 "under protest," and then file a claim in justice court to get your money back. In my opinion, however, the bottom line is that you do not owe the additional amount. The mechanic's representations are the basis of your contract with him. His attempt to collect additional money breaches that agreement and may also violate the Texas Deceptive Trade Practices Act. Hopefully, once the mechanic knows you know your legal rights, you will be able to work things out.

How long is a judgment good for?
"A judgment can be good forever."

Dear Mr. Alderman:
In 1986 my house was foreclosed on, and I was sued. The bank got a judgment against me. How long will this appear on my credit report? How long is the judgment good for? I was told the judgment is only good for ten years. Is there some period of time after which I will no longer be obligated to pay?

As a general rule, negative information stays on your credit report for only seven years. A judgment, however, remains enforceable "until the governing statute of limitations period has expired." In Texas, a judgment is enforceable and attaches to your property for ten years. In my opinion, that would be the "governing statute of limitations period." Therefore, the information could be reported for ten years.

If nothing is done during the ten-year period, the judgment will expire and no longer be legally enforceable. The creditor, however, may take steps before the end of the ten years to renew the judgment for another ten years. As long as the creditor takes steps to preserve the judgment, it may be enforced.

The buyer of my house didn't make his payments.
How can I owe the money?
"That is how an assumption works."

Dear Mr. Alderman:
I sold my house to a buyer who assumed my existing mortgage. I have now discovered the buyer has not paid the mortgage and has moved out of the house. The mortgage company has asked me to pay the full amount owed and to continue making payments. I don't mind picking up the future installments, but it doesn't seem fair that I have to pay the past-due amounts.

It may not seem fair, but legally you are obligated for these payments. When a house is sold and a buyer assumes the mortgage, the buyer is simply agreeing to pay the money the seller owes on the mortgage. The seller, however, is still obligated on the note and is responsible if the buyer doesn't make the payments. If the buyer defaults, the seller is responsible for all payments the buyer may have missed, as well as any future payments.

So what will happen if you do not make these payments? The mortgage company will probably foreclose on the house and sell it to pay off the note. As the next letter indicates, that may not be the end of your problems. When a buyer assumes a seller's mortgage, the seller remains legally obligated on the note. To eliminate this problem, the seller can require that the buyer arrange his own financing and pay off the seller's note.

My house was foreclosed. How can I still owe money?
"Foreclosure does not extinguish a debt."

Dear Mr. Alderman:
Several years ago we had financial problems, and our house was foreclosed. Since that time, we have been able to get back on our feet

and are paying all our bills on time. Now we have received a letter saying we owe $23,000 on our house note. How is this possible? Do we have to pay this? What are our alternatives?

Unfortunately, your letter is not the only one I have received about this problem. Many other people find themselves in the same situation. And from a legal standpoint, you owe the money.

When property is foreclosed upon, the property is sold, and the proceeds are applied to the debt. If the sale price is more than what you owe, you will get money back. If the sale price is less, as was the case with your house, you still owe the difference between the sale price and the debt. You also will owe the costs of the foreclosure proceeding. In other words, you are legally responsible for the money. As a practical matter, however, you should first see if the creditor will work with you. Perhaps you can come up with a payment plan you can live with.

Because of the large amount involved, you also should consider bankruptcy. I realize many people think of bankruptcy as a radical alternative, but it may be the best way to really get a fresh start on your finances. As discussed in Chapter 2, many attorneys handle consumer bankruptcy, and you should look for a board-certified bankruptcy specialist.

My car was repossessed. How do I still owe money? "Repossession doesn't extinguish a debt."

Dear Mr. Alderman:
I bought a new car and could not keep up the payments. After receiving several letters I returned the car to the lender. I have now received a letter saying I owe $6,000. How is this possible? I don't even have the car anymore.

Many people do not understand how a repossession works. When you buy a car, you sign two documents. The first is a note promising to pay back a certain sum of money. The second is an agreement giving the lender the right to take the car back if you do not pay and to apply the proceeds to your note. The repossession, however, doesn't extinguish the note. If the money obtained from the sale of the car is not sufficient to pay off the note, you owe the difference.

For example, suppose you buy a new car and finance $13,000. After paying $1,000, you default, and the car is repossessed. The car will then be sold. Assume the costs of the repossession are $500. The balance remaining on your debt is $12,500. If the car is sold for $10,000, the proceeds are applied to what you owe. You still owe a balance of $2,500.

In your case the car was apparently sold for substantially less than what you owed on the note. I suggest you ask the lender for a full explanation of your situation, and then try to work out a settlement. Under the law, you are entitled to be notified how and why your car will be sold and to be given an accounting of how much was obtained. If the lender did not act reasonably, you may not owe anything.

How do I collect from a defunct corporation?
"You cannot."

Dear Mr. Alderman:
I successfully sued a business in justice court. When I tried to collect, I discovered the company had gone out of business. What can I do? Can I collect from the man who ran the company?

Unfortunately, based on what you say in your letter, you may be out of luck. This is because the business you sued was a corporation. Under the law, a corporation is a separate legal entity. When it ceases to do business, the officers or shareholders of the corporation generally have no personal liability, and you cannot collect from them. Unless the business still has some assets to pay you, such as cash in the bank or inventory, there is little you can do.

Can a business refuse to deal with me based on an old debt?
"They may do business with whomever they want."

Dear Mr. Alderman:
I just placed an order with a company I used to do business with. They told me I had a ten-year-old debt with them and that unless I paid they would not do business with me. I probably owe the money, but isn't there a time limit on collecting debts?

Actually there is no time limit on how long you owe a debt. Until it is paid, it exists. On the other hand, there are time limits on what legal steps may be taken to collect it. For example, a lawsuit generally must be filed within four years of the time you default. If the person waits longer, they will be barred from filing a suit. Also, negative information on your credit report becomes obsolete after seven years and generally may not be reported.

There is no legal limitation, however, on an individual refusing to deal with someone else who still owes him or her money. If the business says "pay up or go elsewhere," the choice is yours.

Do I have to pay my sister's debts?
"Probably not."

Dear Mr. Alderman:
My sister was in a nursing home before she died. The nursing home is now sending me the bills for the last two months she was in there. Am I responsible?

Generally, a person is not responsible for the debts of another unless she agreed in advance to pay them. When a person dies, her estate is responsible for her bills, and if there is no money in the estate, the bills do not get paid. If you did not agree to pay your sister's nursing home bills, I do not know any reason why you would be responsible.

On the other hand, you should check with the home and see whether you did, in fact, agree to be responsible for your sister's bills. You may have signed such a statement when she was admitted and not remembered. I suggest you contact the home and ask why it feels you are responsible for your sister's debt.

Can my sister go to jail if she doesn't pay her debts?
"No."

Dear Mr. Alderman:
My sister has gotten over her head in debt. Now one of the credit card companies is threatening her. In the past, our family has always helped her out. Now we cannot, and we are afraid of what may happen. Can she go to jail if she doesn't pay?

There is no longer debtors' prison in this country. Although a creditor has the right to try to collect its debt, the law prohibits it from threatening a person. I suggest your sister write the creditor and insist it stop threatening her. If it does not, it will be violating the law.

If a creditor is not paid, it always has the right to try to collect by suing. In most cases, however, once a creditor knows you really are making a good faith effort to pay, it will work with you to come up with a payment plan you can live with. Hopefully this will happen for your sister.

I forgot to return the video to the store.
"This could be a criminal matter."

Dear Mr. Alderman:
I rented a video and forgot to return it. I received a letter from the
store telling me that if I don't return the tape and pay the fees, I will
be charged with a crime. I have taken care of the account, but I am
still curious. Is this really a criminal matter?

It may be. The Texas Penal Code includes a crime titled "Theft of Ser-vice." This law applies when you rent something, including a video, and do not return it. If the store sends you a notice demanding the return of the property and you do not return it within ten days, the law presumes criminal intent.

As you discovered, if you return the property and pay the fees within ten days after receiving the written notice, the matter is resolved. If you do not, however, the store may have criminal charges filed against you.

How long can I be billed for an old debt?
"You may owe the debt forever."

Dear Mr. Alderman:
I just got an invoice for a five-year-old doctor's bill. How long do
they have to collect a bill? Can I still be sued?

As a legal matter, the doctor has four years to file suit to collect the bill. After four years, you have a defense to any lawsuit based on what is known as the "statute of limitations." This does not mean, however, that you do not owe the bill after that time, or that steps cannot be taken to try to collect.

Although legal action to collect may be foreclosed, you "owe" the bill until it is paid or discharged in bankruptcy. The debt will also remain on your credit report for seven years.

The doctor has the right to request payment, and may continue to do so even ten or twenty years from now. Unless the debt is discharged in bankruptcy, you owe the money and have a moral obligation to pay. In my opinion, if you have the ability to pay, you should, but there will not be any legal consequences if you politely refuse.

How much notice do I get before a foreclosure?
"At least twenty days."

Dear Mr. Alderman:
I am behind in my mortgage payments. I know the bank can fore-
close, but I was wondering what type of notice I will get. How long
before the house is sold do they have to notify me?

In Texas, most foreclosures are "nonjudicial." Before a mortgage company can foreclose, they have to send you a notice stating you are delinquent, and that they are accelerating your note. They then must give you
twenty days to cure the default. Then, they have to send a second notice to
you by certified mail at least twenty-one days before any foreclosure sale.
This notice will tell you the exact date that the mortgage company intends
to foreclose.

In Texas, foreclosure sales are held only on the first Tuesday of each
month. At this point, you should make sure you pick up any certified mail
sent to you. That way you will know if your mortgage company intends to
foreclose. As a general rule, mortgage companies begin foreclosure proceedings when you become four to six months delinquent on your mortgage payment.

Can I redeem my property after a foreclosure?
"Not unless it was for back taxes or an HOA lien."

Dear Mr. Alderman:
We have been unable to keep up with our mortgage payments. Our
house has been listed for foreclosure by the bank. We were wonder-
ing, can we redeem the house after the sale by buying it back from the
purchaser, or do we just lose it once it is sold?

Basically, once a house is sold at a foreclosure sale, the new buyer takes
title and cuts off the prior owner's rights. Unless the foreclosure was for
delinquent property taxes or an HOA lien, there is no Texas law providing
for a homeowner to redeem the property after a foreclosure. If the foreclosure was done for delinquent taxes, there is a right to redeem the home for
two years if it was your resident homestead, or six months if it was not.
If the foreclosure was for an HOA assessment, the owner may redeem for
180 days.

Can I just hold property of someone who doesn't pay a debt?
"Not without an agreement."

Dear Mr. Alderman:
I recently asked my daughter to move out of my home. She owes me
over $3,000 for money I loaned her while she lived with me. Now
she is refusing to pay it back or make payments toward the debt.
Her washer and dryer are still in my home. Can I just hold on to the
appliances until she pays me at least part of what she owes me? Can
I sell them if she still refuses to pay?

As a general rule, if someone owes you money you cannot just take, or
hold, their property if they don't pay you. To be able to use someone's
property as collateral for a loan, you need a special agreement, called a
security agreement. In most cases, a security agreement is in writing. For
example, when you purchase a car, you sign such an agreement that allows
the lender to take your car in the event you do not pay. Because you have
the property, the agreement may be oral; however, your daughter must
have agreed *at the time of the loan* that you could keep or sell her appliances if she did not pay. In my opinion, based on what you say, you do not
have the right to refuse to give her the appliances or sell them if she does
not pay.

How can I sell my house with a lien?
"The lien does not attach to a homestead."

Dear Mr. Alderman:
A credit card company successfully sued me. I have not been able to
pay the judgment and have not heard from them for over a year. I am
now trying to sell the house I live in and have been told that if I don't
pay the judgment, I will not be able to get a title policy to sell the
house. Is this right? If I have to pay the judgment I will not be able to
afford a new house. I thought a homestead was exempt?

Until recently, selling your homestead after a judgment was entered against
you was difficult. Even though your house is exempt and cannot be taken
to enforce the lien, title companies would not issue a policy when there
was an outstanding judgment. Under current law, however, it is clear that
a judgment lien does not "attach" to your homestead. You now may file a
Homestead Affidavit that operates to release any lien on your homestead.
Unless the creditor contests what you say, you should not have trouble
getting a title policy after filing the affidavit. Here is a sample affidavit:

Before me, the undersigned authority, on this day personally appeared _____ ("Affiant[s]") (insert name of one or more affiants) who, being first duly sworn, upon oath states:

HOMESTEAD AFFIDAVIT AS RELEASE OF JUDGMENT LIEN

(1) My/our name is/are _____ (insert name of Affiant[s]). I/we own the following described land ("Land"):

  (describe the property claimed as homestead)
(2) This affidavit is made for the purpose of effecting a release of that judgment lien recorded in (refer to recording information of judgment lien) ("Judgment Lien") as to the Land.
(3) The Land includes as its purpose use for a home for Affiant(s) and is the homestead of Affiant(s), as homestead is defined in Section 41.002, Property Code. The Land does not exceed:
  (A) 10 acres of land, if used for the purposes of an urban home or as both an urban home and a place to exercise a calling or business; or
  (B) 200 acres for a family or 100 acres for a single, adult person not otherwise entitled to a homestead, if used for the purposes of a rural home.
(4) Attached to this affidavit is evidence that:
  (A) Affiant(s) sent a letter and a copy of this affidavit, without attachments and before execution of the affidavit, notifying the judgment creditor in the Judgment Lien of this affidavit and the Affiant(s)' intent to file for record this affidavit; and
  (B) the letter and this affidavit were sent by registered or certified mail, return receipt requested, 30 or more days before this affidavit was filed to:
    (i) the judgment creditor's last known address;
    (ii) the address appearing in the judgment creditor's pleadings in the action in which the judgment was rendered or another court record, if that address is different from the judgment creditor's last known address;
    (iii) the address of the judgment creditor's last known attorney as shown in those pleadings or another court record; and

(iv) the address of the judgment creditor's last known attorney as shown in the records of the State Bar of Texas, if that address is different from the address of the attorney as shown in those pleadings or another court record.

(5) This affidavit serves as a release of the Judgment Lien as to the Land in accordance with Section 52.0012, Property Code.

Signed on this ___ day of _____,

_____
(Signature of Affiant[s])

State of _____

County of _____

SWORN TO AND SUBSCRIBED before me on the ___ day of _____, 20___ .

My commission expires: _____

_____
Notary Public, State of Texas

Notary's printed name: _____

Divorce, Marriage & Child Custody

Few things in a person's life are as traumatic as family law problems—for example, divorce. No matter who wants the divorce or how agreeable the parties are, divorce is always difficult to deal with. And when children are involved, divorce becomes even more complicated—both psychologically and legally.

In most cases, the parties to a divorce will be represented by attorneys, and legal questions will be answered by that person. But knowing a little bit of law before you see an attorney can help you understand the process that is about to so seriously affect you—for example, how long it should take, what will happen, and what factors can simplify or complicate the process.

As with any other legal service that usually requires the assistance of an attorney, I strongly urge you to shop around before you hire one. Shop around and compare prices. You may be surprised how much money you can save. And to keep current with the changes in this area of law, visit my website, www.peopleslawyer.net.

How long do we have to live together to have a common-law marriage?
"One second."

Dear Mr. Alderman:

My "friend" and I have been living together for nearly six years. We are very much in love but just don't want to be married. Last week, one of my friends told me that if we lived together for seven years we would have a common-law marriage, whether we wanted it or not. This has us concerned. Should we live apart for a while? Does it matter if we put it in writing that we are not married? What can we do?

You may not have to do anything. Just living together, for any length of time, is not enough to form a common-law marriage. To have a common-law marriage in Texas you must do three things: You must agree to be married, hold yourself out as married, and live together. Simply living together is not enough. Once you agree you want to be married and hold yourselves out as married (for example, by using the titles Mr. and Mrs.), the moment you live together you are husband and wife under Texas law. On the other hand, if you keep your separate names and let people know you are not married, you can live together forever and probably not have a common-law marriage. If you do not want to be considered married, make sure you take all possible steps to maintain your separate identities, and let people know you are not husband and wife. If you decide to marry, I recommend you have a civil or church ceremony just to end any doubts about your relationship.

Is there such a thing as common-law divorce?
"Not really."

Dear Mr. Alderman:
I lived with a man for five years. During that time, we probably were a common-law husband and wife. We split up about six years ago, and I assumed I was single and free to marry again. Now I am concerned. I thought I heard you say there is no such thing as a common-law divorce. Do I have to go to court and get divorced before I remarry?

As I said above, a common-law marriage is no different from any other form of marriage. You are married. This means you will have to get a divorce to end the marriage.

There is, however, one provision in the law that may help some people end their common-law marriages. Under the law, if a marriage is not asserted within two years of the date when the parties stopped living together, there is a presumption that there was no marriage. This means the party who wants to assert the marriage after that time has the burden to prove it existed. This change in the law does not appear to help in your case.

If you wish to legally remarry, I suggest you file for divorce.

Can a seventeen-year-old have a common-law marriage?
"No."

Dear Mr. Alderman:
I am seventeen and live with my boyfriend as his wife. I want to know what I need to do to legally establish a common-law marriage.

There is nothing you can do. A person under the age of eighteen cannot have a common-law marriage.

I married without getting divorced.
Which person is now my husband?
"You can have only one spouse."

Dear Mr. Alderman:
I was married about ten years ago. Shortly after we married my
spouse left me. I have not seen or heard from him in almost seven
years. Two years ago I fell in love with a wonderful man who asked
me to marry him. I said yes and we had a simple ceremony. Am I now
married to both men? Does my second wedding invalidate my first?
I never told my husband that I was married before.

Under the law, you can have only one marriage. A marriage entered into
when either party has an existing marriage is void. In other words, you are
still married to your first spouse and your second marriage has no legal
effect.

The only way to remedy this situation is get a divorce from your first
spouse and dissolve that marriage. Once you legally terminate your first
marriage, your second marriage will automatically become valid if you
continue to live together and hold yourselves out as married. I know it
will be uncomfortable but you should tell the man you love your situation
and promptly speak with a family law attorney about dissolving your first
marriage.

Can I receive alimony?
"Texas has limited alimony."

Dear Mr. Alderman:
I have been married more than fifteen years. I have just discovered my
husband has been seeing another woman. I am pretty sure he is going
to ask me for a divorce. I have no interest in continuing this relation-
ship; however, I am afraid of living on my own. I have not worked
since we got married, and it will take me some time to find a job. I
heard Texas now allows alimony. Is this true? Will I be entitled to it?

Until 1995, Texas law did not permit any form of alimony. At the time of
a divorce, community property was divided, and child support could be
awarded; however, the court could not order continuing support for an
ex-spouse. The legislature changed this by enacting a law allowing for a
form of alimony called post-divorce "maintenance payments."

The law designates who is eligible for maintenance payments. Rather
than try to paraphrase this law, here is what the Texas Family Code says:

Sec. 8.051. ELIGIBILITY FOR MAINTENANCE. In a suit for dissolution of a marriage or in a proceeding for maintenance in a court with personal jurisdiction over both former spouses following the dissolution of their marriage by a court that lacked personal jurisdiction over an absent spouse, the court may order maintenance for either spouse only if the spouse seeking maintenance will lack sufficient property, including the spouse's separate property, on dissolution of the marriage to provide for the spouse's minimum reasonable needs and:

(1) the spouse from whom maintenance is requested was convicted of or received deferred adjudication for a criminal offense that also constitutes an act of family violence, as defined by Section 71.004, committed during the marriage against the other spouse or the other spouse's child and the offense occurred:

  (A) within two years before the date on which a suit for dissolution of the marriage is filed; or

  (B) while the suit is pending; or

(2) the spouse seeking maintenance:

  (A) is unable to earn sufficient income to provide for the spouse's minimum reasonable needs because of an incapacitating physical or mental disability;

  (B) has been married to the other spouse for 10 years or longer and lacks the ability to earn sufficient income to provide for the spouse's minimum reasonable needs; or

  (C) is the custodian of a child of the marriage of any age who requires substantial care and personal supervision because of a physical or mental disability that prevents the spouse from earning sufficient income to provide for the spouse's minimum reasonable needs.

Once a court determines a person is eligible for maintenance, it must determine the amount and duration of the payments. Section 8.052 of the Family Code directs the court to consider all relevant factors, including:

(1) each spouse's ability to provide for that spouse's minimum reasonable needs independently, considering that spouse's financial resources on dissolution of the marriage;

(2) the education and employment skills of the spouses, the time necessary to acquire sufficient education or training to enable the spouse seeking maintenance to earn sufficient income, and the availability and feasibility of that education or training;

(3) the duration of the marriage;

(4) the age, employment history, earning ability, and physical and emotional condition of the spouse seeking maintenance;

(5) the effect on each spouse's ability to provide for that spouse's minimum reasonable needs while providing periodic child support payments or maintenance, if applicable;

(6) acts by either spouse resulting in excessive or abnormal expenditures or destruction, concealment, or fraudulent disposition of community property, joint tenancy, or other property held in common;

(7) the contribution by one spouse to the education, training, or increased earning power of the other spouse;

(8) the property brought to the marriage by either spouse;

(9) the contribution of a spouse as homemaker;

(10) marital misconduct, including adultery and cruel treatment, by either spouse during the marriage; and

(11) any history or pattern of family violence, as defined by Section 71.004.

Maintenance probably will not be awarded if the person asking for it has not exercised due diligence in seeking employment or developing the skills necessary to become self-sufficient. An exception to this requirement is made for an individual who is physically or mentally incapacitated.

Once maintenance is awarded, it generally may not continue for more than five to ten years, depending on the length of the marriage. The law directs the court to limit payments to the shortest period of time reasonably necessary for the person seeking maintenance to obtain the necessary employment or training skills. Payments may, however, continue longer if the spouse receiving payment is incapacitated because of physical or mental disability.

Finally, a court may not issue a maintenance order for more than the lesser of $5,000 a month or 20% of the person's average monthly gross income.

Based on what you say in your letter, you should be eligible to receive an award of maintenance. The attorney you hire to assist you with your divorce, however, will be better able to analyze your situation.

My ex-husband was supposed to pay the debts.
Now creditors are coming after me. Can they do this?
"A divorce decree is just between you and your spouse."

Dear Mr. Alderman:
My husband and I were divorced about a year ago. In our settlement he agreed to pay all the debts, including a mortgage on the house. He

paid some of them but has not paid the mortgage. I should also point out that he was given the house and lives there. Now the mortgage company has contacted me and wants me to pay. I sent the company a copy of the divorce decree, but the creditor said it didn't matter. How can this be? I thought my husband was legally obligated to pay. Can the mortgage company really sue me if I don't pay?

Unfortunately, the answer is probably yes. Even though your divorce decree says your husband agreed to pay the mortgage, if he does not, you are still obligated. This would be true of any debt you incurred while you were married.

The reason is that when you incurred the debt, you and your husband entered into a contract with the creditor in which you promised to pay. When you were divorced, you entered into an agreement between you and your husband determining who would pay what. That agreement is not between you and the creditor. In effect, your husband has agreed to pay what you owe the creditor. If he does not, the creditor comes after you, and then you have to go after your ex.

The bottom line is, a divorce decree only affects the relationship between the parties to the marriage. It does not release either party from existing obligations. To protect yourself against this, make sure debts are paid in full before the divorce becomes final or get the creditor to agree in writing. If you trust your ex-spouse to pay and he or she does not, you may end up footing the bill.

Is a house owned before marriage community property?
"Probably not."

Dear Mr. Alderman:
Four years before we married, my wife bought a home. A few years after we married, I used $50,000 of my money to pay off the mortgage. We are now divorcing. Is the home community property? Do I have any rights?

The home is not community property. You may have a right of reimbursement, however, for the money you paid. In other words, you should be entitled to additional money as part of the divorce settlement. For more information about community and separate property, see Chapter 19.

Does separate property become community?
"No."

Dear Mr. Alderman:
My husband inherited a one-half interest in a house. I know that his interest is separate property. However, we just purchased the other half from his brother. Is the house now community property?

As you seem to recognize, the half your husband inherited is his separate property, and remains so. Assuming you purchased the other half with community funds, however, the half you purchased is community property. In other words, you basically have an interest in one-fourth of the house.

How much child support should I get?
"There are statutory guidelines."

Dear Mr. Alderman:
I have been married seven years. Last month my husband left me. I have decided to file for divorce, and I was wondering how much money I could get my husband to pay for the children. He has a good job and left me with little. I asked him how much he would pay, and he told me, "As little as I can. I will have a new family soon, and I need my money." This doesn't seem fair. I think my children should get paid before his new family. What does the law say?

Until the 1980s, no set guidelines for how much money a spouse should pay in child support existed. The judge looked at all the facts of the case and did what he or she thought was fair. In 1989, however, the legislature enacted a law providing guidelines for awarding child support. Although the guidelines are not binding on the court, they are generally followed and should give you a good idea of how much you are entitled to.

What follows is the relevant part of this law. Section numbers refer to the Texas Family Code. Although the guidelines can get complicated, support payments are generally 20 percent of net resources for one child, and increase by 5 percent for each additional child.

COURT-ORDERED CHILD SUPPORT

Sec. 154.001. SUPPORT OF CHILD. The court may order either or both parents to support a child in the manner specified by the order:

(1) until the child is 18 years of age or until graduation from high school, whichever occurs later;

(2) until the child is emancipated through marriage, through removal of the disabilities of minority by court order, or by other operation of law;

(3) until the death of the child; or

(4) if the child is disabled as defined in this chapter, for an indefinite period.

Sec. 154.002. CHILD SUPPORT THROUGH HIGH SCHOOL GRADUATION.

(a) The court may render an original support order, or modify an existing order, providing child support past the 18th birthday of the child to be paid only if the child is:

  (1) enrolled:

    (A) under Chapter 25, Education Code, in an accredited secondary school in a program leading toward a high school diploma;

    (B) under Section 130.008, Education Code, in courses for joint high school and junior college credit; or

    (C) on a full-time basis in a private secondary school in a program leading toward a high school diploma; and

  (2) complying with:

    (A) the minimum attendance requirements of Subchapter C, Chapter 25, Education Code; or

    (B) the minimum attendance requirements imposed by the school in which the child is enrolled, if the child is enrolled in a private secondary school.

(b) The request for a support order through high school graduation may be filed before or after the child's 18th birthday.

(c) The order for periodic support may provide that payments continue through the end of the month in which the child graduates.

Sec. 154.010. NO DISCRIMINATION BASED ON MARITAL STATUS OF PARENTS OR SEX.

The amount of support ordered for the benefit of a child shall be determined without regard to:

(1) the sex of the obligor, obligee, or child; or

(2) the marital status of the parents of the child.

SUBCHAPTER B. COMPUTING NET RESOURCES AVAILABLE FOR PAYMENT OF CHILD SUPPORT

Sec. 154.061. COMPUTING NET MONTHLY INCOME.

(a) Whenever feasible, gross income should first be computed on an annual basis and then should be recalculated to determine average monthly gross income.

(b) The Title IV-D agency shall annually promulgate tax charts to compute net monthly income, subtracting from gross income social security taxes and federal income tax withholding for a single person claiming one personal exemption and the standard deduction.

Sec. 154.062. NET RESOURCES.

(a) The court shall calculate net resources for the purpose of determining child support liability as provided by this section.

(b) Resources include:

(1) 100 percent of all wage and salary income and other compensation for personal services (including commissions, overtime pay, tips, and bonuses);

(2) interest, dividends, and royalty income;

(3) self-employment income;

(4) net rental income (defined as rent after deducting operating expenses and mortgage payments, but not including noncash items such as depreciation); and

(5) all other income actually being received, including severance pay, retirement benefits, pensions, trust income, annuities, capital gains, social security benefits other than supplemental security income, United States Department of Veterans Affairs disability benefits other than nonservice-connected disability pension benefits, as defined by 38 U.S.C. Section 101(17), unemployment benefits, disability and workers' compensation benefits, interest income from notes regardless of the source, gifts and prizes, spousal maintenance, and alimony.

(c) Resources do not include:

(1) return of principal or capital;

(2) accounts receivable;

(3) benefits paid in accordance with the Temporary Assistance for Needy Families program or another federal public assistance program; or

(4) payments for foster care of a child.

Text of subsection (d) effective until September 01, 2018

(d) The court shall deduct the following items from resources to determine the net resources available for child support:

(1) social security taxes;

(2) federal income tax based on the tax rate for a single person claiming one personal exemption and the standard deduction;

(3) state income tax;

(4) union dues;

(5) expenses for the cost of health insurance or cash medical support for the obligor's child ordered by the court under Section 154.182; and

(6) if the obligor does not pay social security taxes, nondiscretionary retirement plan contributions.

Text of subsection effective on September 01, 2018

(d) The court shall deduct the following items from resources to determine the net resources available for child support:

(1) social security taxes;

(2) federal income tax based on the tax rate for a single person claiming one personal exemption and the standard deduction;

(3) state income tax;

(4) union dues;

(5) expenses for the cost of health insurance, dental insurance, or cash medical support for the obligor's child ordered by the court under Sections 154.182 and 154.1825; and

(6) if the obligor does not pay social security taxes, nondiscretionary retirement plan contributions.

Text of subsection (e) effective until September 01, 2018

(e) In calculating the amount of the deduction for health care coverage for a child under Subsection (d)(5), if the obligor has other minor dependents covered under the same health insurance plan, the court shall divide the total cost to the obligor for the insurance by the total number of minor dependents, including the child, covered under the plan.

Text of subsection effective on September 01, 2018

(e) In calculating the amount of the deduction for health care or dental coverage for a child under subsection (d)(5), if the obligor has other minor dependents covered under the same health or dental insurance plan, the court shall divide the total cost to the obligor for the insurance by the total number of minor dependents, including the child, covered under the plan.

(f) For purposes of subsection (d)(6), a nondiscretionary retirement plan is a plan to which an employee is required to contribute as a condition of employment.

Sec. 154.063. PARTY TO FURNISH INFORMATION.

The court shall require a party to:

(1) furnish information sufficient to accurately identify that party's net resources and ability to pay child support; and

(2) produce copies of income tax returns for the past two years, a financial statement, and current pay stubs.

Sec. 154.064. HEALTH INSURANCE FOR CHILD PRESUMPTIVELY PROVIDED BY OBLIGOR.

The guidelines for support of a child are based on the assumption that the court will order the obligor to provide health insurance coverage for the child in addition to the amount of child support calculated in accordance with those guidelines.

Text of section 154.064 effective September 1, 2018

MEDICAL SUPPORT AND DENTAL SUPPORT FOR CHILD PRESUMPTIVELY PROVIDED BY OBLIGOR.

The guidelines for support of a child are based on the assumption that the court will order the obligor to provide medical support and dental support for the child in addition to the amount of child support calculated in accordance with those guidelines.

Sec. 154.065. SELF-EMPLOYMENT INCOME.

(a) Income from self-employment, whether positive or negative, includes benefits allocated to an individual from a business or undertaking in the form of a proprietorship, partnership, joint venture, close corporation, agency, or independent contractor, less ordinary and necessary expenses required to produce that income.

(b) In its discretion, the court may exclude from self-employment income amounts allowable under federal income tax law as depreciation, tax credits, or any other business expenses shown by the evidence to be inappropriate in making the determination of income available for the purpose of calculating child support.

Sec. 154.066. INTENTIONAL UNEMPLOYMENT OR UNDER-EMPLOYMENT.

(a) If the actual income of the obligor is significantly less than what the obligor could earn because of intentional unemployment or underemployment, the court may apply the support guidelines to the earning potential of the obligor.

(b) In determining whether an obligor is intentionally unemployed or underemployed, the court may consider evidence that the obligor is a veteran, as defined by 38 U.S.C. Section 101(2), who is seeking or has been awarded:

(1) United States Department of Veterans Affairs disability benefits, as defined by 38 U.S.C. Section 101(16); or

(2) nonservice-connected disability pension benefits, as defined by 38 U.S.C. Section 101(17).

Sec. 154.067. DEEMED INCOME.

(a) When appropriate, in order to determine the net resources available for child support, the court may assign a reasonable amount of deemed income attributable to assets that do not currently produce income. The court shall also consider whether certain property that is not producing income can be liquidated without an unreasonable financial sacrifice because of cyclical or other market conditions. If there is no effective market for the property, the carrying costs of such an investment, including property taxes and note payments, shall be offset against the income attributed to the property.

(b) The court may assign a reasonable amount of deemed income to income-producing assets that a party has voluntarily transferred or on which earnings have intentionally been reduced.

Sec. 154.068. WAGE AND SALARY PRESUMPTION.

(a) In the absence of evidence of a party's resources, as defined by Section 154.062(b), the court shall presume that the party has income equal to the federal minimum wage for a 40-hour week to which the support guidelines may be applied.

(b) The presumption required by subsection (a) does not apply if the court finds that the party is subject to an order of confinement that exceeds 90 days and is incarcerated in a local, state, or federal jail or prison at the time the court makes the determination regarding the party's income.

Sec. 154.069. NET RESOURCES OF SPOUSE.

(a) The court may not add any portion of the net resources of a spouse to the net resources of an obligor or obligee in order to calculate the amount of child support to be ordered.

(b) The court may not subtract the needs of a spouse, or of a dependent of a spouse, from the net resources of the obligor or obligee.

SUBCHAPTER C. CHILD SUPPORT GUIDELINES

Sec. 154.121. GUIDELINES FOR THE SUPPORT OF A CHILD.
The child support guidelines in this subchapter are intended to guide the court in determining an equitable amount of child support.

Sec. 154.122. APPLICATION OF GUIDELINES REBUTTABLY PRESUMED IN BEST INTEREST OF CHILD.

(a) The amount of a periodic child support payment established by the child support guidelines in effect in this state at the time of the hearing is presumed to be reasonable, and an order of support conforming to the guidelines is presumed to be in the best interest of the child.

(b) A court may determine that the application of the guidelines would be unjust or inappropriate under the circumstances.

Sec. 154.123. ADDITIONAL FACTORS FOR COURT TO CONSIDER.

(a) The court may order periodic child support payments in an amount other than that established by the guidelines if the evidence rebuts the presumption that application of the guidelines is in the best interest of the child and justifies a variance from the guidelines.

(b) In determining whether application of the guidelines would be unjust or inappropriate under the circumstances, the court shall consider evidence of all relevant factors, including:

(1) the age and needs of the child;

(2) the ability of the parents to contribute to the support of the child;

(3) any financial resources available for the support of the child;

(4) the amount of time of possession of and access to a child;

(5) the amount of the obligee's net resources, including the earning potential of the obligee if the actual income of the obligee is significantly less than what the obligee could earn because the obligee is intentionally unemployed or underemployed

and including an increase or decrease in the income of the obligee or income that may be attributed to the property and assets of the obligee;

(6) child care expenses incurred by either party in order to maintain gainful employment;

(7) whether either party has the managing conservatorship or actual physical custody of another child;

(8) the amount of alimony or spousal maintenance actually and currently being paid or received by a party;

(9) the expenses for a son or daughter for education beyond secondary school;

(10) whether the obligor or obligee has an automobile, housing, or other benefits furnished by his or her employer, another person, or a business entity;

(11) the amount of other deductions from the wage or salary income and from other compensation for personal services of the parties;

(12) provision for health care insurance and payment of uninsured medical expenses;

(13) special or extraordinary educational, health care, or other expenses of the parties or of the child;

(14) the cost of travel in order to exercise possession of and access to a child;

(15) positive or negative cash flow from any real and personal property and assets, including a business and investments;

(16) debts or debt service assumed by either party; and

(17) any other reason consistent with the best interest of the child, taking into consideration the circumstances of the parents.

Sec. 154.125. APPLICATION OF GUIDELINES TO NET RESOURCES.

(a) The guidelines for the support of a child in this section are specifically designed to apply to situations in which the obligor's monthly net resources are not greater than $7,500 or the adjusted amount determined under subsection (a)(1), whichever is greater.

(1) The dollar amount prescribed by subsection (a) is adjusted every six years as necessary to reflect inflation. The Title IV-D agency shall compute the adjusted amount, to take effect beginning September 1 of the year of the adjustment, based on the percentage change in the consumer price index during the 72-month period preceding March 1 of the year

of the adjustment, as rounded to the nearest $50 increment. The Title IV-D agency shall publish the adjusted amount in the Texas Register before September 1 of the year in which the adjustment takes effect. For purposes of this subsection, "consumer price index" has the meaning assigned by Section 341.201, Finance Code.

(b) If the obligor's monthly net resources are not greater than the amount provided by subsection (a), the court shall presumptively apply the following schedule in rendering the child support order:

CHILD SUPPORT GUIDELINES
BASED ON THE MONTHLY NET RESOURCES OF THE OBLIGOR

1 child	20% of obligor's net resources
2 children	25% of obligor's net resources
3 children	30% of obligor's net resources
4 children	35% of obligor's net resources
5 children	40% of obligor's net resources
6+ children	Not less than the amount for 5 children

Sec. 154.126. APPLICATION OF GUIDELINES TO ADDITIONAL NET RESOURCES.

(a) If the obligor's net resources exceed the amount provided by Section 154.125(a), the court shall presumptively apply the percentage guidelines to the portion of the obligor's net resources that does not exceed that amount. Without further reference to the percentage recommended by these guidelines, the court may order additional amounts of child support as appropriate, depending on the income of the parties and the proven needs of the child.

(b) The proper calculation of a child support order that exceeds the presumptive amount established for the portion of the obligor's net resources provided by Section 154.125 (a) requires that the entire amount of the presumptive award be subtracted from the proven total needs of the child. After the presumptive award is subtracted, the court shall allocate between the parties the responsibility to meet the additional needs of the child according to the circumstances of the parties. However, in no event may the obligor be required to pay more child support than the greater of the presumptive amount or the amount equal to 100 percent of the proven needs of the child.

Sec. 154.127. PARTIAL TERMINATION OF SUPPORT OBLIGATION.

(a) A child support order for more than one child shall provide that, on the termination of support for a child, the level of support for the remaining child or children is in accordance with the child support guidelines.

(b) A child support order is in compliance with the requirement imposed by subsection (a) if the order contains a provision that specifies:

(1) the events, including a child reaching the age of 18 years or otherwise having the disabilities of minority removed, that have the effect of terminating the obligor's obligation to pay child support for that child; and

(2) the reduced total amount that the obligor is required to pay each month after the occurrence of an event described by subdivision (1).

Sec. 154.183. MEDICAL SUPPORT ADDITIONAL SUPPORT DUTY OF OBLIGOR.

(a) An amount that an obligor is ordered to pay as medical support for the child under this chapter, including the costs of health insurance coverage or cash medical support under Section 154.182;

(1) is in addition to the amount that the obligor is required to pay for child support under the guidelines for child support;

(2) is a child support obligation; and

(3) may be enforced by any means available for the enforcement of child support, including withholding from earnings under Chapter 158.

(b) If the court finds and states in the child support order that the obligee will maintain health insurance coverage for the child at the obligee's expense, the court shall increase the amount of child support to be paid by the obligor in an amount not exceeding the actual cost to the obligee for maintaining health insurance coverage, as provided under Section 154.182 (b-1).

(c) As additional child support, the court shall allocate between the parties, according to their circumstances:

(1) the reasonable and necessary health care expenses, including vision and dental expenses, of the child that are not reimbursed by health insurance or are not otherwise covered by the amount of cash medical support ordered under Section 154.182 (B)(3); and

(2) amounts paid by either party as deductibles or copayments in obtaining health care services for the child covered under a health insurance policy.

EFFECTIVE Sep. 1, 2018
MEDICAL AND DENTAL SUPPORT ADDITIONAL SUPPORT DUTY OF OBLIGOR.

(a) An amount that an obligor is ordered to pay as medical support or dental support for the child under this chapter, including the costs of health insurance coverage or cash medical support under Section 154.182 and the costs of dental insurance under Section 154.1825:

    (1) is in addition to the amount that the obligor is required to pay for child support under the guidelines for child support;

    (2) is a child support obligation; and

    (3) may be enforced by any means available for the enforcement of child support, including withholding from earnings under Chapter 158.

(b) If the court finds and states in the child support order that the obligee will maintain health insurance coverage, dental insurance coverage, or both, for the child at the obligee's expense, the court shall increase the amount of child support to be paid by the obligor in an amount not exceeding the actual cost to the obligee for maintaining the coverage, as provided under Sections 154.182 (b-1) and 154.1825 (d).

(c) As additional child support, the court shall allocate between the parties, according to their circumstances:

    (1) the reasonable and necessary health care expenses, including vision and dental expenses, of the child that are not reimbursed by health or dental insurance or are not otherwise covered by the amount of cash medical support ordered under Section 154.182; and

    (2) amounts paid by either party as deductibles or copayments in obtaining health care or dental care services for the child covered under a health insurance or dental insurance policy.

**Do I get less child support when there are children
from another marriage?**
"There are different rules for children from more than one family."

Dear Mr. Alderman:
I am receiving child support. The person paying is about to get
divorced again and has a child by that second marriage. What hap-
pens to the amount of my support?

As discussed in the previous letter, the amount of child support paid is
generally based on guidelines in the Texas Family Code. For example: For
one child the amount is 20 percent of net resources; for two children 25
percent.

In the event that the person paying support has children from different
households, however, there are different rules. In your case, the person
will be paying support for two children but the amount is not 25 percent.
Instead, the guidelines suggest an amount of 17 percent for each child.
This is a compromise that recognizes that although an additional child
places increased financial burdens on the payer, the first child should not
be forced to receive a substantially reduced payment.

Here is what the relevant statutes say:

Sec. 154.128. COMPUTING SUPPORT FOR CHILDREN IN
MORE THAN ONE HOUSEHOLD.
(a) In applying the child support guidelines for an obligor who has
    children in more than one household, the court shall apply the
    percentage guidelines in this subchapter by making the following
    computation:
    (1) determine the amount of child support that would be ordered
        if all children whom the obligor has the legal duty to sup-
        port lived in one household by applying the schedule in this
        subchapter;
    (2) compute a child support credit for the obligor's children
        who are not before the court by dividing the amount deter-
        mined under subdivision (1) by the total number of children
        whom the obligor is obligated to support and multiplying that
        number by the number of the obligor's children who are not
        before the court;
    (3) determine the adjusted net resources of the obligor by sub-
        tracting the child support credit computed under subdivision
        (2) from the net resources of the obligor; and
    (4) determine the child support amount for the children before the
        court by applying the percentage guidelines for one house-
        hold for the number of children of the obligor before the court
        to the obligor's adjusted net resources.

(b) For the purpose of determining a child support credit, the total number of an obligor's children includes the children before the court for the establishment or modification of a support order and any other children, including children residing with the obligor, whom the obligor has the legal duty of support.

(c) The child support credit with respect to children for whom the obligor is obligated by an order to pay support is computed, regardless of whether the obligor is delinquent in child support payments, without regard to the amount of the order.

Sec. 154.129. ALTERNATIVE METHOD OF COMPUTING SUPPORT FOR CHILDREN IN MORE THAN ONE HOUSEHOLD.

In lieu of performing the computation under the preceding section, the court may determine the child support amount for the children before the court by applying the percentages in the table below to the obligor's net resources:

Multiple Family Adjusted Guidelines (% of Net Resources)

		Number of Children before the Court						
		1	*2*	*3*	*4*	*5*	*6*	*7*
Number of	0	20.00	25.00	30.00	35.00	40.00	40.00	40.00
Other Children for Whom	1	17.50	22.50	27.38	32.20	37.33	37.71	38.00
the Obligor	2	16.00	20.63	25.20	30.33	35.43	36.00	36.44
Has a Duty of Support	3	14.75	19.00	24.00	29.00	34.00	34.67	35.20
	4	13.60	18.33	23.14	28.00	32.89	33.60	34.18
	5	13.33	17.86	22.50	27.22	32.00	32.73	33.33
	6	13.14	17.50	22.00	26.60	31.27	32.00	32.62
	7	13.00	17.22	21.60	26.09	30.67	31.38	32.00

How long do I have to pay child support?
"It depends on what the decree says."

Dear Mr. Alderman:
At what age does court-ordered child support end? My daughter is nineteen, and I am still paying support. Do I have to continue to pay?

In most cases, the divorce decree will specify at what point in time the obligation to pay child support ends. If the decree says nothing, however, support generally stops when the child reaches the age of eighteen. The length of time may be extended by the court if the child is enrolled in an accredited high school program. In some cases, however, the obligation may end sooner.

For example, the obligation to pay child support ends if the person who is required to pay for the child dies. It also stops if the child gets married. In either case, the age of the child does not matter.

As I said, the obligation to pay child support and the length of time that obligation continues for are usually spelled out in the divorce decree. Read your decree carefully to see what it says.

How often can support be modified?
"As often as there is a substantial change in circumstances."

Dear Mr. Alderman:

Four months ago, my ex-spouse took me back to court to increase the amount of child support I must pay. Now she is threatening to do it again unless I voluntarily give her additional money. Going to court is very expensive. Can she just keep taking me back to court whenever she wants?

The Texas Family Code provides that support orders may be modified only when there has been a material and substantial change in circumstances. She cannot take you back to court whenever she wants, but she can petition to have the amount modified whenever there has been a material and substantial change in circumstances regarding you or the child.

Do I need an attorney to file for divorce?
"No, but it sure can make life simpler."

Dear Mr. Alderman:

My wife and I have decided that our brief attempt at marriage isn't going to work. We know Texas is a "no-fault" divorce state, so there wouldn't be any trouble getting a divorce, but we don't have a lot of extra money and can't afford to spend a fortune on attorney's fees. We have no children and agree on how everything should be split. Is it legal to do your own divorce, and do you think we could handle it ourselves?

Anyone can represent themselves in court. Whether you should do it is another question. Even though a simple divorce is not complicated, any attempt at practicing law by a layperson can be difficult, and there are many traps for the amateur to fall into. There are, however, several books on the market and online websites that will take you step-by-step through the divorce. You may want to look at them and see if you think you could do it.

As far as I am concerned, a better approach is to shop around and find an attorney who will handle your divorce inexpensively. Many competent attorneys will do a simple divorce for a few hundred dollars in attorney's fees. I realize this is still more than it will cost to just buy the book and do it yourself, but with an attorney you are assured it will be done properly, and you may save enough time to make it worth your while. Again, the important thing is to shop around and get prices from several lawyers before you make a selection.

Do I have to live in Texas to get divorced there?
"Usually."

Dear Mr. Alderman:

I am in the process of relocating to Texas. I am coming without my wife. We have decided to get a divorce, but neither of us has seen a lawyer or filed any papers. I will not live in Texas until two months from now, but I would like to get things going on the divorce. Can I file in Texas now?

To file for divorce, the court you file with has to have what is called "jurisdiction." This is a legal term meaning the court has the power to hear the case and make a decision. In the case of a divorce, a court only has jurisdiction if you have been a domiciliary of this state for the preceding six months and a resident of the county where you file for the preceding ninety days. In other words, if you want to get a divorce in Texas you will have to wait until you have made Texas your permanent home for six months. Then you can file where you have lived for the past ninety days. If you want a divorce sooner than that, you will probably have to file in the state where you presently live.

I should point out that the rule would be different if your spouse lived in Texas. If one spouse has lived in Texas for the last six months, a spouse living in another state may file for divorce in the county where the Texas spouse lives.

How can I get my husband to pay child support?
"He may be thrown in jail."

Dear Mr. Alderman:

I have been divorced for five years. I have two children, ages seven and nine. My ex-husband is supposed to pay child support each month, but for the last three months he has not paid. He says he has too many other bills and can't afford it. I know he has other obligations, but I need the money to support the kids. What can I do?

Unlike most debts, child support obligations are very enforceable in Texas. If a person doesn't pay as ordered, his wages can be garnished (taken by the court), or, in some cases, he can even be thrown in jail until he pays. All this will have to be done through the courts—usually with the assistance of an attorney.

You may want to talk with the attorney who handled your divorce and ask him or her for assistance. Another alternative is to contact the Child Support Enforcement Division of the Texas Attorney General's Office, (512) 460-6000, or www.texasattorneygeneral.gov/cs/welcome-to-the-child-support-division. This division exists to assist in the enforcement of child support obligations. Usually, once an ex-husband understands the consequences of not paying, he will begin to do so.

How can I collect child support?
"You can take a driver's license away."

Dear Mr. Alderman:
Is it true I can have my ex-husband's driver's license taken away if he does not pay child support?

Under a new law, a person who doesn't pay child support may lose a professional license, such as a license to practice law or medicine, or a driver's license. I should point out that wage garnishment also may be used to enforce a child support obligation.

My ex-husband is not making his child support payment.
May I prevent him from seeing the children?
"No."

Dear Mr. Alderman:
Seven years ago I was divorced. Until recently, my husband made all his child support payments. He is now two months behind. I told him that until he makes his payments he couldn't see the children on his weekends. He told me I couldn't do this. Who is right?

Your husband is correct. As discussed in the letters above, there are many ways to enforce child support obligations. Denying visitation rights, however, is not one of them. Child support and visitation are two separate issues. Even if your husband does not pay his support payments, you cannot deny him his visitation rights.

What must I show to get a divorce?
"Just that you don't get along."

Dear Mr. Alderman:
My husband and I have had problems for several years. We seem
to do nothing but fight. Finally, we decided we just are not right for
each other and that we should get a divorce. No one in my family has
ever been divorced, and we don't know much about it. Our first ques-
tion is, what do we have to prove to end our marriage? Do I have to
say he committed adultery or beat me?

It used to be that to get a divorce it was necessary to show "fault," (for
example, cruelty, adultery, abandonment) or that you had lived apart for
three years. This is no longer necessary. The law now allows the court to
grant a divorce if you show:

> *that the marriage has become insupportable because of discord or conflict*
> *of personalities that destroys the legitimate ends of the marriage relation-*
> *ship and prevents any reasonable expectations of reconciliation.*

What this legalese means is that Texas now is a "no-fault" divorce state.
You can get a divorce simply by showing that you no longer get along. It is
not necessary to prove either party did anything wrong or to explain why
you can't remain married. In fact, if one party doesn't want to be married
and the other does, this difference alone would be enough for the court to
grant the divorce.

What do I have to show to get an annulment?
"Much more than necessary to get divorced."

Dear Mr. Alderman:
A friend of mine is trying to get a divorce from her husband of four
months. She rushed into the marriage and is now finding out various
things about him. The marriage was based on a big lie. Can she get
an annulment?

Getting an annulment may be much harder than getting a divorce. As I
said in the letter above, obtaining a divorce in Texas is simple and does not
require proof of any fault on the part of either party.

To obtain an annulment, it is necessary to prove one of several things.
An annulment may be granted if it is shown that:

- at the time of the marriage you were under the influence of alcoholic beverages or narcotics and as a result did not have the capacity to consent to the marriage
- either party was permanently impotent at the time of the marriage and the other party did not know about it
- the other party used fraud, duress, or force to induce you to enter into the marriage
- at the time of the marriage the petitioner did not have the mental capacity to consent to marriage or to understand the nature of the marriage ceremony because of a mental disease or defect
- the other party got divorced from a third party within a thirty-day period preceding the date of the marriage ceremony and you did not know of the divorce
- the marriage ceremony took place during the seventy-two-hour period immediately following the issuance of a marriage license.

To obtain an annulment on any of the above grounds, it is also necessary to show that the person requesting the annulment has not voluntarily cohabited with the other party after discovery of the grounds for the annulment.

As you can tell, obtaining an annulment requires much more proof and is usually much more time-consuming and expensive than obtaining a divorce.

I just got divorced. When can I remarry?
"In thirty days."

Dear Mr. Alderman:
My divorce was finalized last year. My ex-husband and I have been living apart for more than two years, and I have been seeing another man for almost a year. He wants to marry me but says we have to wait a year after the divorce. I want to get married right now. Do I have to wait a year?

Under Texas law you may remarry thirty days after the day your divorce is decreed. In fact, in some cases you can marry even sooner. For example, if you wanted to remarry your ex-husband there is no waiting period. Also, in special circumstances a court may waive the thirty days prohibition if requested. In other words, if he really wants to marry you, the most you should have to wait is thirty days.

How do I find my adopted child?
"There may be help available if he wants to be found."

Dear Mr. Alderman:
Many years ago I placed my son for adoption. I have no regrets and
still believe it was the right thing to do. Now, however, I am curious
to know how things turned out and what kind of person he is. Is there
any way for me to find out who adopted my son?

Although it is generally difficult to find out who adopted your child, it
may be possible if the child also wants to contact you. The Texas Department of State Health Services maintains a Voluntary Adoption Registry.
This is a system that allows adopted children, birth parents, and biological
siblings to locate each other if they wish. To get more information about
the registry, contact the Central Adoption Registry, Texas Department of
State Health Services, Austin, Texas; www.dshs.state.tx.us/vs/REQPROC/
adoptionregistry.shtm.

What name can I use after the divorce?
"This must be determined at the time of the divorce."

Dear Mr. Alderman:
I was divorced more than a year ago, and now I have decided I want
to start using my maiden name again. Can I just do it?

Nike's instructions notwithstanding, you cannot "just do it." Under the law
in Texas, a woman must legally change her name if she wishes to use her
maiden name after a divorce. This is usually done as part of the divorce
proceedings. In your case, however, it will be necessary to file a separate
pleading to legally change your name.

I suggest you either contact different attorneys to see what they will
charge for a name change, or file the petition yourself. If you want to do
it yourself, check with your local bookstore, law library, or online legal
service to see if you can find the proper forms. If you use an attorney, shop
around for the best price. This routine legal service should not be expensive. A few phone calls may save you a lot of money.

Does a grandparent have the right to visit with the grandchildren?
"Only in very limited circumstances."

Dear Mr. Alderman:

My daughter had a child two years ago. She and her husband decided that it was in the best interest of the child to keep her away from me. I was heartbroken. Don't I have the legal right to see my own grandchild?

Not necessarily. In Texas, a grandparent has very limited rights when it comes to visiting with the grandchild. First, to petition for access, the grandparent must allege that denial of access will "significantly impair the child's physical health or mental well-being." Also, if both parents do not want the grandparent to see the child, the grandparent generally does not have the legal right to do so. Here is the text of the law:

RIGHTS OF GRANDPARENT, AUNT, OR UNCLE

Sec. 153.431. APPOINTMENT OF GRANDPARENT, AUNT, OR UNCLE AS MANAGING CONSERVATOR.
If both of the parents of a child are deceased, the court may consider appointment of a parent, sister, or brother of a deceased parent as a managing conservator of the child, but that consideration does not alter or diminish the discretionary power of the court.

Sec. 153.432. SUIT FOR POSSESSION OR ACCESS BY GRANDPARENT.
(a) A biological or adoptive grandparent may request possession of or access to a grandchild by filing:
(1) an original suit; or
(2) a suit for modification as provided by Chapter 156.
(b) A grandparent may request possession of or access to a grandchild in a suit filed for the sole purpose of requesting the relief, without regard to whether the appointment of a managing conservator is an issue in the suit.
(c) In a suit described by subsection (a), the person filing the suit must execute and attach an affidavit on knowledge or belief that contains, along with supporting facts, the allegation that denial of possession of or access to the child by the petitioner would significantly impair the child's physical health or emotional well-being. The court shall deny the relief sought and dismiss the suit unless the court determines that the facts stated in the affidavit, if true, would be sufficient to support the relief authorized under Section 153.433.

Sect. 153.433. POSSESSION OF OR ACCESS TO GRANDCHILD.

(a) The court may order reasonable possession of or access to a grandchild by a grandparent if:

    (1) at the time the relief is requested, at least one biological or adoptive parent of the child has not had that parent's parental rights terminated;

    (2) the grandparent requesting possession of or access to the child overcomes the presumption that a parent acts in the best interest of the parent's child by proving by a preponderance of the evidence that denial of possession of or access to the child would significantly impair the child's physical health or emotional well-being; and

    (3) the grandparent requesting possession of or access to the child is a parent of a parent of the child and that parent of the child:

        (A) has been incarcerated in jail or prison during the three-month period preceding the filing of the petition;

        (B) has been found by a court to be incompetent;

        (C) is dead; or

        (D) does not have actual or court-ordered possession of or access to the child.

(b) An order granting possession of or access to a child by a grandparent that is rendered over a parent's objections must state, with specificity that:

    (1) at the time the relief was requested, at least one biological or adoptive parent of the child had not had that parent's parental rights terminated;

    (2) the grandparent requesting possession of or access to the child has overcome the presumption that a parent acts in the best interest of the parent's child by proving by a preponderance of the evidence that the denial of possession of or access to the child would significantly impair the child's physical health or emotional well-being; and

    (3) the grandparent requesting possession of or access to the child is a parent of a parent of the child and that parent of the child:

        (A) has been incarcerated in jail or prison during the three-month period preceding the filing of the petition;

        (B) has been found by a court to be incompetent;

        (C) is dead; or

        (D) does not have actual or court-ordered possession of or access to the child.

How old do I have to be to get married?
"Eighteen; sixteen or seventeen with court approval."

Dear Mr. Alderman:
I am a fifteen-year-old high school junior and very much in love. My parents do not want me to see my boyfriend. I was told that if we got married, my parents could not stop me from moving out and living with him. Would this be legal?

If you were to get married, you would have the right to move out and live with your husband. The problem is that under Texas law you cannot marry at age fifteen. Generally you must be eighteen to marry. You may marry at age sixteen or seventeen but only with court approval.

Can a person marry a cousin?
"Not anymore."

Dear Mr. Alderman:
I have a friend who says he is going to marry his cousin. Is this legal?

In the past, the law did not prohibit marriage between cousins. This law was changed, however, in 2005 and now it appears you may not marry a first cousin.

Does living together nullify our divorce?
"No, but you may have remarried."

Dear Mr. Alderman:
My husband and I were recently divorced. We realized we made a mistake and have moved back in together. Does living together nullify the divorce?

Once a divorce is final, living together does not nullify it. You are divorced. Living together, however, may give rise to a common-law marriage. If you and your ex-husband agree to be married again, hold yourselves out as married, and live together as married, you probably have established a common law marriage. In other words, you were married, got divorced, and now have remarried.

CHAPTER 8

Door-to-Door Sales

Historically, few salespeople were as persuasive as those who traveled door-to-door. We have all heard stories of the person who bought the high-priced vacuum cleaner, a new roof or siding for their home, or the set of encyclopedias from a smooth-talking, fast-moving traveling salesperson only to discover later that the price was too high, or the goods never arrived or were unnecessary.

Although the number of people selling door-to-door has been substantially reduced due to the proliferation of many other shopping options, door-to-door selling still provides a alternative for people who are unable to go out and shop or who, because of their obligations at home, must remain at home during the day. While the Internet has almost replaced door-to-door sales, door-to-door selling remains a convenient and practical way for some to shop at home.

So how do we balance the problems of high-pressure selling with the convenience of home sales? The answer reached by both Congress and the Texas Legislature is the same: Pass a law that requires that door-to-door salespeople give you a chance to change your mind. In Texas this law is called the **Home Solicitation Sales Act.** To see this law, as well as all other Texas consumer laws, go to www.peopleslawyer.net.

The books seemed like a good idea, but now I don't want them. . . .
Help!
"Door-to-door sales give you time to change your mind."

Dear Mr. Alderman:
The other day I was sitting at home when the doorbell rang. A nice-looking man, well dressed, asked if he could come in and talk to me about a program that could help my kids in school. I said OK, and after about an hour I agreed to buy the complete set of books. He promised it would help my kids in school and that it was approved by the school board. Right after he left I talked with my neighbor and

*found out what he said was true, but the school library would lend
the books to my kids for free. I really don't want the books. What can
I do? He was so nice and persuasive that I couldn't say no. I guess I
learned a lesson: Don't talk to door-to-door salesmen.*

You may not have learned the lesson you think. The lesson you should
have learned is that *under the law you have three days to change your
mind and get out of a contract entered into in your home.* Both Texas and
federal law provide that a door-to-door merchant must give you a three-
day cooling-off period to change your mind. Based on what you say in
your letter, I believe the salesman has violated the law; you should be able
to cancel the sale and not have to pay.

So what should you do? If you paid cash you may have a problem. Try
to get in touch with the company and demand your money back. Federal
law lets you promptly dispute and refuse to pay an unlawful transaction.
If you paid by check, go to the bank at once and stop payment. If the
check has already been cashed, you are in the same position as if you
paid cash. If you used a credit card, contact the credit card company, tell
it you are not paying the bill, and explain why. The credit card company
stands in the shoes of the merchant and can't collect because the merchant has violated the law. If you don't get your money back, contact
the district attorney's office and the attorney general's office to report
the company and the salesperson. You can also take steps to recover
your money, and if you are successful in court, you can recover under
the Deceptive Trade Practices Act, because any violation of the Home
Solicitation Sales Act is automatically a violation of the Deceptive Trade
Practices Act. Look over Chapter 10, and you will see how to get substantial damages.

*Be careful when dealing with door-to-door salespeople, and don't pay
cash or with a check unless you are absolutely sure you want the goods.
And remember, under the law all door-to-door contracts must have the
following printed on them:*

NOTICE OF CANCELLATION

(enter date of transaction)

You may cancel this transaction without any penalty or obligation within three business days from the above date.

If you cancel, any property traded in, any payments made by you under the contract or sale, and any negotiable instrument executed by you will be returned within 10 business days after receipt by the merchant of your cancellation notice, and any security interest arising out of the transaction will be canceled.

If you cancel, you must make available to the merchant at your residence, in substantially as good condition as when received, any goods delivered to you under this contract or sale; or you may, if you wish, comply with the instructions of the merchant regarding the return shipment of the goods at the merchant's expense and risk. If you do not agree to return the goods to the merchant or if the merchant does not pick them up within 20 days of the date of your notice of cancellation, you may retain or dispose of the goods without any further obligation.

To cancel this transaction, mail or deliver a signed and dated copy of this cancellation notice or any other written notice, or send a telegram to (**Name of merchant**) at (**Address of merchant's place of business**) not later than midnight of (**Date**).

I hereby cancel this transaction.

(**Date**)

(**Buyer's signature**)

CHAPTER 9

Employment

For most of us nothing is more important to our economic well-being than keeping a job. Those of you who have lost jobs know how devastating it is, and those who have not can imagine what it would be like. Unfortunately, it seems that I have been receiving more and more questions from people who have lost their jobs, or are afraid they may—questions such as "When and how can I be fired?" and "What are my rights if I am fired?" As you will see, Texas is not an employee-friendly state.

I don't have a contract. When can I be fired?
"Probably whenever the boss wants."

Dear Mr. Alderman:
I have worked at the same job for nearly two years. I have never had a contract and really didn't think I needed one. It is a small company, and everyone has always trusted everyone else to be fair. Recently, one of my friends came into work and was told, "Go home. You're fired." As far as I know he was doing a good job, and there was no reason to fire him. I think the boss just decided the company could get along without him. Now I am afraid I am next. What are my rights? Am I safe as long as I do my job well and don't violate any company rules?

Texas is basically an "employment-at-will" state. This means you can be fired at will and you can quit at will. Unless you have a contract or a union agreement, the company can fire you with no notice, for no reason at all. The other side of that coin is you can quit the same way. Although many states have changed this doctrine, the employment-at-will doctrine governs in Texas, at least for now. I should point out, though, that this rule is not absolute. The Texas Supreme Court has found at least one exception (you can't be fired for failing to perform an illegal act), and it may be willing to find others. Also, a contract may be found in many ways, and you may have an implied or oral contract with the company that would prohibit it from firing you without cause. Generally, however, you can be fired just because the company doesn't want you there.

One final point must be mentioned. In all cases, laws can change, and it is important that you make sure the advice I give you is up to date. In the case of employment law, though, it is even more important you do so because this is a rapidly changing area of law. If a problem arises, you may want to contact an attorney to make sure there hasn't been a recent development in this area.

I think I was fired because of my age. Isn't there a law?
"The law prohibits certain discrimination."

Dear Mr. Alderman:
I am sixty-two years old, and while I don't think that is very old, my boss does. She is only thirty-four and thinks I am too old to be deal-ing with customers. Yesterday, she told me to work in the stock room or quit. I do my job well, and the only reason she wants me in the back is because of her image of the store. Is this legal? I have worked hard all my life, and it doesn't seem fair.

It doesn't seem fair, and it doesn't seem legal. Under federal law it is illegal to discriminate on the basis of race, color, religion, sex, or national origin. It is also unlawful to discriminate based on age and against anyone over the age of thirty-nine. The major exception to this is when the employer can establish that for the particular task age is a legitimate qualification.

If you feel you are being discriminated against because of your age, contact the U.S. Equal Employment Opportunity Commission (EEOC) at EEOC, General Inquiries, (800) 669-4000, www.eeoc.gov.

Can I be forced to take a drug test?
"Probably."

Dear Mr. Alderman:
I work at a small company that manufactures parts used in engines. My job is to box the finished product, and in the six years I have worked here I have never had any problems performing my job well. I know this may not sound too good, but the job is so simple I could do it in my sleep or drunk (which I may have been on occasion). Last week the company said everyone had to take a drug test. If we refused we would be fired. Is this legal? I don't use drugs, but it doesn't seem fair. Don't I have some kind of constitutional right not to have to take this test?

As of right now, a private employer in Texas probably has the right to force employees to take a drug test and to fire them if they don't. This is the result of the employment-at-will doctrine discussed in the first letter. Because you can be fired without a reason, it follows that you can also be fired for nearly any reason—including your refusal to take the test. This issue is in the courts, however, and some states have laws preventing this kind of drug testing. But as of right now, you may want to take the test or risk losing your job.

The same rule would not apply, however, if you were employed by a public employer such as the post office or state motor vehicle department. In the case of a public or governmental employer, the constitutional right of privacy protects you. Drug testing can usually only be done under certain limited circumstances. Without getting too detailed, governmental entities may only drug test if they can justify who is going to be tested (e.g., someone who will endanger himself or others if impaired); when the testing is done (e.g., because there was a reasonable suspicion the person may have been using drugs); how the tests were performed (e.g., the most accurate test was used); and what was done with the result (e.g., testing will be authorized more readily if the person is rehabilitated, not fired).

Can I be forced to take a lie detector test?
"Probably not."

Dear Mr. Alderman:
I applied for a job and was asked to take a lie detector test. I refused and was told to look elsewhere. I don't have anything to hide, but I just don't trust those things. Is this a common practice? Do I have any legal rights?

What happened to you is probably illegal. Under federal law—the Employee Polygraph Protection Act—it is basically illegal for an employer to ask an employee or prospective employee to take a lie detector test. It is also illegal to refuse to hire or fire someone because he or she refused to take the test. The law provides both criminal and civil penalties for an employer who violates the law.

There is, however, a limited exception to this law. An employee may be asked to submit to a lie detector test if it is part of an ongoing investigation regarding economic loss or theft to the employer. If the employer has a reasonable suspicion that an employee was involved, a lie detector test may be given. The only other exception is with respect to government entities. They are not subject to this law.

This law is enforced by the Secretary of Labor and can be used by individuals in private lawsuits. I suggest you either file a complaint with the U.S. Department of Labor, www.dol.gov/whd/polygraph, or consider a private lawsuit if you feel you have been harmed as a result of what may be an illegal practice.

The union negotiates my contract, but I am not a member. Isn't Texas a right-to-work state? "It is, but the union still negotiates your contract."

Dear Mr. Alderman:

I work for a medium-size company in West Texas. About two years ago, there was a vote in the company about joining a union. I voted no and did not join. Most of the employees voted yes. I was told that because Texas is a right-to-work state, I would not have to join the union and would not have to pay dues.

Last week, the union, which I did not join, voted to reduce the number of overtime hours employees are allowed to work. The company has agreed. Now, I am losing money. How can this happen? How can a union I don't even belong to make contracts for me? What happened to my right to work?

In a right-to-work state, an employee does not have to join a union or pay union dues as a condition of employment. "Right-to-work" means the right to work without joining a union. Nevertheless, if a majority of the employees vote to be represented by a union, then the union is the exclusive bargaining representative of all the employees, even those employees who are not members or who voted against union representation. Likewise, the union has a duty to represent, in contract negotiations and grievances, the interests of all employees. This is sometimes referred to as "majority rule with minority rights." The bottom line is, the union negotiates for you even though you are not a member.

I work with chemicals. Do I have a right to know what they are? "Probably yes."

Dear Mr. Alderman:

I work for a small company that cleans ships. In the course of my employment I use a chemical supplied to me in an unmarked drum. I have been told to always wear gloves and to be careful not to spill it on myself.

I never really thought about what was in the drum until I went to the doctor and he asked if I had been working with any dangerous chemicals. I told him I didn't know, and he said, "Find out." When I asked my boss what was in the drum he said, "Don't worry. Just wear gloves and be careful." I tried to push for an answer, but he got mad. How can I find out what is in the drum? I am afraid I will be fired if I insist on knowing.

Under the **Occupational Safety Health Act (OSHA)** an employer has a duty to disclose to employees if they are working with hazardous chemicals. This law, enforced by the U.S. Department of Labor, has a list of dangerous chemicals, and if you are working with any of these chemicals, you must be told. On the other hand, if the substance you are working with is not on the list, your employer has no duty to tell you.

Your employer's actions in not telling you indicate one of two things. Either the chemical you are working with is not on the list and is probably not dangerous, or he is violating the law. If you are still concerned, I suggest you contact the U.S. Department of Labor, www.osha.gov/workers, and ask for an investigation. You also should know that the law protects you if you are fired for trying to find out. An employer can't just fire employees who insist on their legal rights. For more information visit www.dol.gov.

I just quit. Can my former boss stop me from going into business for myself?
"Perhaps."

Dear Mr. Alderman:
For the past five years, I have been in the sales business. I am no longer satisfied working for a large company and want to work for a smaller one, where I have more of a future. Because my background is basically in one field, the companies I am interested in are all in competition with my present employer.

I have been told that if I leave, I will not be able to work for any competing company in the southwestern states. My employer told me my contract has a covenant-not-to-compete clause that prevents me from working for someone else. Can this be true? I thought I had the right to work for whomever I wanted. Can I be prevented from earning a living?

I cannot give you a specific answer to your question because it will depend on what your contract says and all the facts surrounding your employment. I can tell you there are such things as "covenants not to compete," and they are enforceable.

Under Texas law, an employer has the right to enter into an agreement with an employee that prevents the employee from competing with the employer after the employee terminates employment. Because of the harshness of such clauses, they are only enforceable if they are ancillary to another enforceable contract (such as an employment contract), and if they are reasonable. This means the geographical area and scope of the limitation must not be overbroad. The test is a balance between the employer's right to be protected against unreasonable competition from a former employee and the employee's right to work. Based on what you say in your letter, the clause may be unreasonable because it prohibits you from working within a very broad geographic area. Usually, the limited area is much smaller. For the clause to be enforceable, your employer would also have to show that, due to the nature of the business and the knowledge you obtained while working for the employer, the restriction is reasonable. If a lawsuit were to develop, the court would have the right to limit the clause to a reasonable geographic area.

Generally, the courts do not favor overbroad covenants not to compete. They do, however, serve a legitimate purpose when applied to situations in which employees receive special training and knowledge that could be used in a competitive way against the employer. In these cases, the law enforces such agreements as long as they are reasonable.

Am I entitled to leave if I have a child?
"You may be."

Dear Mr. Alderman:
I am three months pregnant. I told my employer I would need some time off when the child was born. He told me I could have a few weeks maximum. I thought it was the law that I had to be given three months of leave.

Since 1993, the **Family and Medical Leave Act** generally provides that eligible employees may take family or medical leave for up to twelve weeks during any twelve-month period. *Unpaid leave* may be taken for any of the following reasons: (1) birth of a child; (2) adoption of a child or placement of a foster child; (3) to care for a child, spouse, or parent with a serious health condition; or (4) the employee's own serious health condition. Upon termination of the leave, you must be reinstated to the same or an equivalent position. Your employer must also maintain health coverage during the leave period, just as though you had continued working.

To be eligible to take a leave, you must satisfy two requirements. First, you must have been employed for at least one year. Second, you must have worked at least 1,250 hours during the previous twelve-month period. In other words, even some part-time employees are protected by this law.

This law, however, does not apply to all employers. Because of the burden this law could place on small employers, it is limited to larger employers. The law applies only to employers with fifty or more employees for each working day during twenty or more workweeks in the current or preceding calendar year. Both part-time and full-time employees count for purposes of meeting this requirement.

If you think you are protected by this law, you should speak with your employer. If you still cannot resolve the problem, you can either consult a private attorney about a civil lawsuit or complain to the U.S. Department of Labor, www.dol.gov/whd/fmla/index.htm. This is the government office that enforces the Family and Medical Leave Act.

Can my company require a see-through purse?
"Probably."

Dear Mr. Alderman:
My employer requires that employees carry plastic see-through bags as purses. Is this legal? I do not like everyone knowing what I have in my purse.

Under the law, employers generally may impose whatever restrictions they want on employees. I do not see anything illegal about see-through purses. While you and I may not agree with the approach, your employer appears concerned with employee theft. Although the law may give your employer the right to require see-through purses, if you object, you have the right as an employee to find employment elsewhere.

Do I have to wear a funny uniform?
"You have to if you want to keep your job."

Dear Mr. Alderman:
I work for a company that requires me to wear a funny-looking uniform. I know it is important for workers to be neat and tidy, but can I be forced to wear a silly uniform?

Unfortunately for you, the answer is yes. A company has the right to require employees to wear whatever uniforms it wants. You, of course, also have the right to quit and go to work for someone that does not require uniforms.

Can my company tell me when to take my vacation?
"Yes."

Dear Mr. Alderman:
I work for a company that forces all of its employees to take vaca-
tions when the company wants, not when we want. Can it do this?

The company can do this unless you have a contract saying it cannot. Under the law, a company does not even have to give employees vacation time. Once the company decides to do so, it will be governed by whatever agreement it has with the employees. If, when you were hired, you were told vacations could be taken anytime, or if the employee handbook states so, you would have this right under your contract with the company. On the other hand, if this has been the policy from the time you were hired, there probably is nothing you can do.

How long do I have to work to get a vacation?
"As long as your employer wants."

Dear Mr. Alderman:
I just started a new job. My employer tells me that I have to work two
years before I am entitled to any paid vacation. Is this legal? This
seems like a very long time without a vacation.

There is no requirement in the law that employers give their employees any paid vacation time. I agree this is a long time, but if your employer wants you to work two years before a paid vacation, it has the legal right to do so. On the other hand, you have the right to look for another job with better benefits. I suggest that you ask your employer to reconsider. If he does not, you should consider looking for another job.

Who pays unemployment benefits?
"Employers pay an unemployment tax."

Dear Mr. Alderman:
I was recently fired. I filed for unemployment benefits and my
employer objected, saying I quit. We are going to have a hearing
and I am confident I will win. I don't understand, however, why my
employer cares. Doesn't the money for unemployment benefits come
from the state?

Although you file a claim for unemployment benefits with a state agency, the Texas Workforce Commission, unemployment benefits are, in effect, insurance benefits, and employers pay the insurance policy premiums. The reason that your employer cares is that the unemployment tax that funds the benefits plan is not a set rate. The amount of tax that an employer pays depends, at least in part, on the number of claims filed by employees. In other words, a company that does not fire anyone pays a lower tax rate than a company that fires a large number of employees.

Do I have free speech rights at work?
"You can say what you want, but you still may be fired."

Dear Mr. Alderman:
I was fired for simply "speaking my mind" at work. How can this happen in this country? Whatever happened to the right of free speech? Can I sue my employer?

Unfortunately for you, the right of speech does not give you the right to say whatever you want at work *without consequences*. The Constitution's right of free speech applies to the government's attempt to restrict an individual's speech. It does not have anything to do with a private employer's right to fire an employee.

For example, if the government tried to pass a law that said you could not express your opinion on the President, it would be an unconstitutional restriction on free speech. On the other hand, a private employer can have a policy that employees will not discuss politics in the office. If you were to violate this policy, you could be fired.

Can my employer search my locker?
"Unreasonable search and seizure laws do not apply to private employers."

Dear Mr. Alderman:
My employer has enacted a new policy enabling it to search an employee's locker. Isn't this unconstitutional under the Fourth Amendment?

The Constitution's prohibitions against unreasonable search and seizure apply to the government and governmental entities. For example, the police may not engage in an unconstitutional search. The prohibitions of the Constitution, however, are not extended to private employers. Your employer is free to require you to allow your locker to be searched, and you are free to quit or be fired if you do not want to allow him to do so.

Can my employer deduct from my check?
"Probably not."

Dear Mr. Alderman:

My employer recently deducted $10 from my paycheck because I didn't follow one of his rules. I know I should follow rules, but I don't think it is fair to take money from my paycheck without warning. Is this legal?

No. Under the law, employers generally do not have the right to deduct money from your paycheck. An employer may deduct from an employee's wages only if the employer

- is ordered to do so by a court
- is authorized to do so by law
- has written authorization from the employee

Based on what you say in your letter, none of these three events occurred. This means your employer had no right to penalize you in this manner. I suggest you speak with your employer about paying you the wages you are owed. You also may want to speak with the Texas Workforce Commission, the agency that enforces the **Texas Payday Law.** You can contact the commission at (512) 463-2222 or www.twc.state.tx.us. For more information about the Texas Payday Law, ask for "An Employer's Survival Guide to the Texas Payday Law," or visit www.twc.state.tx.us/jobseekers/texas-payday-law.

Finally, I should point out that even if an employer has the right under state law to deduct from a paycheck, he may not do so if it reduces an employee's pay below minimum wage.

Can I be required to take a blood test?
"Probably not."

Dear Mr. Alderman:
Can my employer require me to take an HIV blood test?

Texas employers generally cannot require a blood test. If, however, the employer can show that knowledge of the employee's HIV status is related to the employee's job performance, the employer may be able to require the test. The employer must show, however, there is a reasonable basis for believing that no HIV-positive person could perform the job with safety or efficiency.

Can I force my employer to pay for a course I took?
"Yes, if he requested it."

Dear Mr. Alderman:
My employer told me that if I took a certain course he would reim-
burse me for the tuition costs. I took the course and gave him the
$395 receipt. Now he says the course was for my own benefit, and he
won't pay. What are my legal rights?

In my opinion, you have a legal right to be reimbursed by your employer.
Based on what you say, there probably is a contract. Even if there is not,
there is a legal doctrine known as "promissory estoppel" that would allow
you to recover based on your reliance on his promise. The real question, however, is a practical one. Do you want to anger your employer
by attempting to assert your legal rights? I suggest you weigh your legal
rights and the practical consequences and determine what is in your best
long-term interest.

Can I be sued if I give a negative recommendation
about a former employee?
"The law helps protect you."

Dear Mr. Alderman:
I was asked to give a recommendation about a former employee.
The employee did not do a very good job and was always late for
work. That is the reason I let him go. I was afraid to tell the prospec-
tive employer about this, however, because I don't want to be sued. I
have heard so many stories about former employees suing when they
receive a negative recommendation. What is the law in this area?

There has never been a law that allows an employee to sue a former employer
simply because the employer gives a negative recommendation. Liability in
such cases is usually based on the fact that the recommendation was not just
negative; it was also false and known to be false by the employer.

A Texas law enacted in 1999 recognizes the employer's right to make
a truthful recommendation regarding a former employee and protects
employers who act in good faith. Under this law, an employer who dis-
closes information about a former employee is immune from any liability
unless "it is proven by clear and convincing evidence that the information
disclosed was known by that employer to be false at the time the disclosure was made or that the disclosure was made with malice or in reckless
disregard for the truth or falsity of the information disclosed."

This law provides substantial protection for employers for two reasons. First, it requires the employee to show that the employer either had knowledge of the falsity of the information, or acted with malice or reckless disregard for the truth. Second, it raises the standard of proof that the employee must meet to a standard of "clear and convincing" evidence. This is a higher test than that usually used in civil trials.

It is impossible to prevent a person from filing a lawsuit against another person. This law, however, does as much as possible to make it clear that employers who report truthful information about former employees have no liability if the information prevents the employee from getting another job.

How do I get my wages?
"File a wage claim with the Texas Workforce Commission."

Dear Mr. Alderman:
I worked for a local store for more than a year and recently left to be with my children. When I left I was owed wages for two weeks. I still have not been paid. What can I do? Do I have to file a claim in justice court?

You can file a claim in justice court, but you also have another alternative. File a wage claim with the Texas Workforce Commission under the Texas Payday Law. You can get the forms you need to file your claim at www.twc.state.tx.us, or you can call (800) 832-9243. Be sure to act quickly, because a wage claim must be filed within 180 days of when the wages should be paid. If the Commission determines your wages were wrongfully withheld, your employer may be fined, or even charged with a crime.

Can I be fired if I file a worker's compensation claim?
"No, the law protects you."

Dear Mr. Alderman:
I was injured at work. I was going to file a claim for worker's compensation, but a friend said my employer might fire me if I do. Can I really be fired for this?

Under the law, it is unlawful to retaliate against an employee for filing a worker's compensation claim. You could be entitled to substantial damages if you were unlawfully terminated.

Can my employer just cut my hours?
"Employees are not guaranteed a minimum number of hours."

Dear Mr. Alderman:
My employer just notified us that our hours were being cut back from
thirty-six a week to thirty. It was my understanding that a full-time
employee must work at least thirty-two hours. Is this the law?

As a general rule, the employer determines the hours and wages for the
employees. Generally, the difference between a "full-time" and a "part-
time" employee is that full-time employees receive benefits. Although
most employers consider thirty-five to forty hours to be "full-time," there
is no required number of hours you must work. Unless you have a union
agreement or an employment contract, the only limits are that the employer
pays at least minimum wage, and overtime for more than forty hours in
a week. In my opinion, your options are to try and negotiate a better deal
with your employer, accept his proposal, or look for another job.

How do I keep health insurance after I lose my job?
"It is called COBRA."

Dear Mr. Alderman:
I was just laid off. My employer has no idea when, or if, I will be
rehired. I remember reading that I can keep my insurance after los-
ing my job. How do I go about doing this?

The law you are referring to is the Consolidated Omnibus Budget Rec-
onciliation Act, commonly referred to as COBRA. COBRA applies to
private-sector employers with twenty or more employees. Basically, it
allows anyone who voluntarily or involuntarily (except for gross misconduct) stops working to continue benefits for a period of eighteen months
by paying the same group premium your employer was paying.

If your employer fits the COBRA category and you had employer-
provided health insurance, your employer must explain to you that you are
entitled to elect temporary continuation of the same group coverage you
had the day before you were terminated. You then have sixty days to sign
up for COBRA or lose your eligibility.

COBRA coverage can be expensive; however, it provides insurance
while you look for another job or seek other coverage. It also eliminates
problems with preexisting coverage and allows you to be "continuously
insured," which helps when you obtain other health insurance. To find out

more about COBRA, check out the U.S. Department of Labor's website, www.dol.gov.

Can I extend COBRA coverage?
"In case of disability, COBRA may be extended."

Dear Mr. Alderman:
I lost my job and filed for COBRA medical coverage. Shortly after I filed, I became disabled and I am afraid I may not work for a while. Is it possible to extend my COBRA coverage?

As the letter above indicated, COBRA coverage is generally available for a period of eighteen months. Disability, however, can extend the eighteen-month period of continuation coverage. To qualify for additional months of COBRA continuation coverage, you must:

- Have a ruling from the Social Security Administration that you became disabled within the first sixty days of COBRA continuation coverage; and
- Send the plan administrator a copy of the Social Security ruling letter within sixty days of receipt, but prior to expiration of the eighteen-month period of coverage.

If these requirements are met, the entire family qualifies for an additional eleven months of COBRA continuation coverage. Plans can charge 150 percent of the premium cost for the extended period of coverage.

Will COBRA help if I am divorced?
"Yes, divorced spouses and dependent children may continue coverage under COBRA."

Dear Mr. Alderman:
My husband has filed for divorce. I do not work and have two young children. I plan on getting a job, but am scared our health insurance coverage will end when the divorce is final. I have read about COBRA. Does it apply to me?

First, if you are getting divorced, health care insurance is one of the subjects you should talk to your attorney about. Your husband may be responsible for continuing coverage. Under COBRA, however, covered spouses and dependent children may continue their plan coverage for a limited time when they would otherwise lose coverage due to a divorce. A covered employee's spouse who would lose coverage due to a divorce may elect continuation coverage under the plan for a maximum of thirty-six months. You must notify the plan administrator of the divorce within sixty days after the divorce is final. After being notified of a divorce, the plan administrator must give notice, generally within fourteen days, to the qualified beneficiary of the right to elect COBRA continuation coverage. Divorced spouses may call their plan administrator or the EBSA toll-free number, 866-444-EBSA (3272), if they have questions about COBRA continuation coverage.

Can an employer require workers to speak English only?
"In some cases, yes."

Dear Mr. Alderman:
I have a friend who has a catering business. She hires many bilingual employees. In the course of her business, she requires that employees speak only English. She does this so that she knows that the employees understand how to prepare food and her instructions to them. She was told that she could not require them to speak English during work. Is this true?

An employer does not have an absolute right to require workers to speak English only. English-only rules implemented for the purpose of safe and efficient operation of the business, however, are lawful. The EEOC's policy guidance in this area of the law provides that situations justifying an English-only rule include communications with customers, coworkers, or supervisors who only speak English, and work assignments in which the use of a common language is necessary to the promotion of efficiency. It seems to me that instructions regarding food preparation and service would fall within the justification requirement. For more information, visit www.eeoc.gov/eeoc/publications/immigrants-facts.cfm.

False & Deceptive Acts

Texas has a law that every consumer should know by name, the **Texas Deceptive Trade Practices Act.** It is a very beneficial consumer protection law and, as you will see, it covers a lot more than you might think. Nearly every transaction you make, from buying a house to selling a toaster at a garage sale, falls within the scope of this law.

The Deceptive Trade Practices Act lists thirty-four things considered false, misleading or deceptive, and unlawful. Basically, anything someone does that has the potential to deceive is prohibited by the law; and more important, the law is a no-fault statute.

No-fault means that in most cases you don't have to intend to violate the law—or even know you are violating the law—to be held responsible. For example, someone thinks a car is in excellent shape and, without any intent to hurt you, says, "This car is in excellent condition." If it turns out the car was in poor condition, the seller is liable under this law. It doesn't matter that the seller had no idea there was anything wrong with the car.

One last point: the Texas Deceptive Trade Practices Act is often amended by the legislature. To stay current with this law, or any consumer law, visit my website www.peopleslawyer.net.

What is the Deceptive Trade Practices Act?
"The consumer's best friend."

Dear Mr. Alderman:
I have watched you on television, and you always talk about some great law that helps consumers. I think it is a deceptive practices law. Could you please tell me about this law and what it covers?

The Texas Deceptive Trade Practices Act is our state's primary consumer protection law. *Anyone who violates the Deceptive Trade Practices Act may be liable for up to three times your damages plus all your court costs and attorney's fees.* The following list identifies all the things made unlawful under this law. The list may sound a bit technical, but that is merely because I have used the same language the law uses:

1. Passing off goods or services as those of another;
2. causing confusion or misunderstanding as to the source, sponsorship, approval, or certification of goods or services;
3. causing confusion or misunderstanding as to affiliation, connection, or association with, or certification by, another;
4. using deceptive representations or designations of geographic origin in connection with goods or services;
5. representing that goods or services have sponsorship, approval, characteristics, ingredients, uses, benefits, or quantities which they do not have, or that a person has a sponsorship, approval, status, affiliation, or connection which he does not;
6. representing that goods are original or new if they are deteriorated, reconditioned, reclaimed, used, or secondhand;
7. representing that goods or services are of a particular standard, quality, or grade, or that goods are of a particular style or model, if they are of another;
8. disparaging the goods, services, or business of another by false or misleading representation of facts;
9. advertising goods or services with intent not to sell them as advertised;
10. advertising goods or services with intent not to supply a reasonable expectable public demand, unless the advertisements disclosed a limitation of quantity;
11. making false or misleading statements of fact concerning the reasons for, existence of, or amount of price reductions;
12. representing that an agreement confers or involves rights, remedies, or obligations which it does not have or involve, or which are prohibited by law;
13. knowingly making false or misleading statements of fact concerning the need for parts, replacement, or repair service;
14. misrepresenting the authority of a salesman, representative, or agent to negotiate the final terms of a consumer transaction;
15. basing a charge for the repair of any item, in whole or in part, on a guaranty or warranty instead of on the value of the actual repairs made or work to be performed on the item without stating separately the charges for the work and the charge for the warranty or guaranty, if any;
16. disconnecting, turning back, or resetting the odometer of any motor vehicle so as to reduce the number of miles indicated on the odometer gauge;
17. advertising of any sale by fraudulently representing that a person is going out of business;

18. advertising, selling, or distributing a card which purports to be a prescription drug identification card issued under Section 4151.152, Insurance Code, in accordance with rules adopted by the commissioner of insurance, which offers a discount on the purchase of health care goods or services from a third party provider, and which is not evidence of insurance coverage, unless:

   A. the discount is authorized under an agreement between the seller of the card and the provider of those goods and services, or the discount or card is offered to members of the seller;

   B. the seller does not represent that the card provides insurance coverage of any kind; and

   C. the discount is not false, misleading, or deceptive;

19. using or employing a chain referral sales plan in connection with the sale or offer to sell of goods, merchandise, or anything of value, which uses the sales technique, plan, arrangement, or agreement in which the buyer or prospective buyer is offered the opportunity to purchase merchandise or goods and in connection with the purchase receives the seller's promise or representation that the buyer shall have the right to receive compensation or consideration in any form for furnishing to the seller the names of other prospective buyers if receipt of the compensation or consideration is contingent upon the occurrence of an event subsequent to the time the buyer purchases the merchandise or goods;

20. representing that a guarantee or warranty confers or involves rights or remedies which it does not have or involve, provided, however, that nothing in this subchapter shall be construed to expand the implied warranty of merchantability as defined in Sections 2.314 through 2.318 and Sections 2A.212 through 2A.216 to involve obligations in excess of those which are appropriate to the goods;

21. promoting a pyramid promotional scheme, as defined by Section 17.461;

22. representing that work or services have been performed on, or parts replaced in, goods when the work or services were not performed or the parts replaced;

23. filing suit founded upon a written contractual obligation of and signed by the defendant to pay money arising out of or based on a consumer transaction for goods, services, loans, or extensions of credit intended primarily for personal, family, household, or agricultural use in any county other than in the county in which the defendant resides at the time of the commencement of the action or in the county in which the defendant in fact signed the contract; provided,

however, that a violation of this subsection shall not occur where it is shown by the person filing such suit he neither knew or had reason to know that the county in which such suit was filed was neither the county in which the defendant resides at the commencement of the suit nor the county in which the defendant in fact signed the contract;

24. failing to disclose information concerning goods or services which was known at the time of the transaction if such failure to disclose such information was intended to induce the consumer into a transaction into which the consumer would not have entered had the information been disclosed;

25. using the term "corporation," "incorporated," or an abbreviation of either of those terms in the name of a business entity that is not incorporated under the laws of this state or another jurisdiction;

26. selling, offering to sell, or illegally promoting an annuity contract under Chapter 22, Acts of the 57th Legislature, 3rd Called Session, 1962 (Article 6228a-5, Vernon's Texas Civil Statutes), with the intent that the annuity contract will be the subject of a salary reduction agreement, as defined by that Act, if the annuity contract is not an eligible qualified investment under that Act; or

27. taking advantage of a disaster declared by the governor under Chapter 418, Government Code, by:
    A. selling or leasing fuel, food, medicine, or another necessity at an exorbitant or excessive price; or
    B. demanding an exorbitant or excessive price in connection with the sale or lease of fuel, food, medicine, or another necessity;

28. using the translation into a foreign language of a title or other word, including "attorney," "lawyer," "licensed," "notary," and "notary public," in any written or electronic material, including an advertisement, a business card, a letterhead, stationery, a website, or an online video, in reference to a person who is not an attorney, in order to imply that the person is authorized to practice law in the United States;

29. delivering or distributing a solicitation in connection with a good or service that:
    A. represents that the solicitation is sent on behalf of a governmental entity when it is not; or
    B. resembles a governmental notice or form that represents or implies that a criminal penalty may be imposed if the recipient does not remit payment for the good or service;

30. delivering or distributing a solicitation in connection with a good or service that resembles a check or other negotiable instrument or

invoice, unless the portion of the solicitation that resembles a check or other negotiable instrument or invoice includes the following notice, clearly and conspicuously printed in at least 18-point type: "SPECIMEN-NON-NEGOTIABLE";

31. in the production, sale, distribution, or promotion of a synthetic substance that produces and is intended to produce an effect when consumed or ingested similar to, or in excess of, the effect of a controlled substance or controlled substance analogue, as those terms are defined by Section 481.002, Health and Safety Code:

   A. making a deceptive representation or designation about the synthetic substance; or

   B. causing confusion or misunderstanding as to the effects the synthetic substance causes when consumed or ingested; [or]

32. a licensed public insurance adjuster directly or indirectly soliciting employment, as defined by Section 38.01, Penal Code, for an attorney, or a licensed public insurance adjuster entering into a contract with an insured for the primary purpose of referring the insured to an attorney without the intent to actually perform the services customarily provided by a licensed public insurance adjuster, provided that this subdivision may not be construed to prohibit a licensed public insurance adjuster from recommending a particular attorney to an insured; or

33. a warrantor of a vehicle protection product warranty using, in connection with the product, a name that includes "casualty," "surety," "insurance," "mutual," or any other word descriptive of an insurance business, including property or casualty insurance, or a surety business.

34. owning, operating, maintaining, or advertising a massage establishment, as defined by Section 455.001, Occupations Code, that:

   A. is not appropriately licensed under Chapter 455, Occupations Code, or is not in compliance with the applicable licensing and other requirements of that chapter; or

   B. is not in compliance with an applicable local ordinance relating to the licensing or regulation of massage establishments.

As stated before: Anyone who commits any of these thirty-four acts or practices has violated the law, and you may have the right to recover substantial damages. But don't count on having to sue. Once someone knows that you know about this law, you will be amazed by how cooperative folks can become—and how quickly you can settle your dispute.

To find out who the law applies to and how to use it, read on.

Who can use the Deceptive Trade Practices Act?
"Nearly everyone, including a small business."

Dear Mr. Alderman:

I own a small business called Bob's Repair Shop. I run the business part-time out of my garage, repairing lawnmower motors and other small engines. The other day I bought some replacement parts from a dealer who told me the parts were as good as the ones I usually buy. They weren't . . . and as a result, three engines I fixed needed extensive repairs. I believe what the salesman told me wasn't true—the parts were nowhere near good as new. I want to know: Can I use the Deceptive Trade Practices Act to sue?

You sure can! The act applies to any "consumer," and the term is defined to include any individual, partnership, corporation, or governmental entity. The only exception is a business consumer with more than $25 million in assets. I assume from your letter that you are running your business as a sole proprietorship, and therefore, you would sue as an individual. If it is a partnership or corporation, you can still use this law, but you will have to sue in the name of your business.

The other requirement of the law is you must have purchased (or tried to purchase) goods or services. This obviously applies to you—as you bought parts from the dealer. About the only time the law doesn't apply is when someone makes representations in connection with free gifts. For example: If the local burger restaurant had a promotion and promised you could win a new car, free, with no purchase required, and that car was, in fact, not new, you could not sue under this law because you did not try to purchase the car—it was a gift.

Depending on how much money is involved, you may not need a lawyer. You can represent yourself in justice court if your damages are $10,000 or less. To find out the procedures you should use to sue under the Deceptive Trade Practices Act, read the next few letters. As you will see, the act is easy to use.

To whom does this act apply?
"Nearly everyone."

Dear Mr. Alderman:

I just bought a television for $150 from someone at a garage sale. When I looked at it, the girl told me it was less than a year old and in good condition. It turns out it is three years old and needs a lot of *work. Does the Texas law about false statements apply here, and can I get three times my damages?*

Under the Texas Deceptive Trade Practices Act, you can sue anyone, including an individual not in business, if he or she violates the law. In your case, making a false representation about the television violates the law. If you can prove the statement was made knowingly and was false, you will be entitled to three times your damages. In this case, your damages are the difference between the value of a one-year-old television and a three-year-old television.

The law protects consumers, and this means whenever you sell anything, you must be careful. You may not think about it, but whenever you have a garage sale or place an ad in the paper, you are governed by this law. Unless you are willing to stand by your word, be careful when you say something is in excellent condition or good as new.

Advice: If you are selling something, make sure the buyer knows you are just giving your opinion, unless you are willing to stand by your word. As the seller in the next letter discovers, you may be in trouble—even if you are acting innocently and in good faith.

What if I didn't know it wasn't true?
"Tough luck!"

Dear Mr. Alderman:
I am a geologist. I have never been in the business of selling boats, and I have never sold one before. About one month ago, I decided to sell my small outboard motorboat. I took it to my mechanic, who said he would put the engine in excellent shape. I paid him $500, and he told me it was "good as new." I put the boat, with the engine, in my front yard with a "For Sale" sign. Someone I didn't know stopped and asked me about it. I told him the motor was in "excellent condition," "perfect condition," and "just like new." As far as I knew, these statements were true, and were what the mechanic told me. What I didn't know was my mechanic did not do the work. The buyer has now written me a letter telling me he wants $450 (the cost of having the engine repaired). He says unless I pay he is going to sue me under the Deceptive Trade Practices Act and may recover three times the $450. What should I do? Does this law apply to me?

The law applies to anyone who sells goods or services. This includes you— even though you are not in business. The Texas Deceptive Trade Practices Act is very broad. It protects consumers regardless of who deceives them.

The law is clear that you do not have to intend to deceive or trick someone. Your honesty or good faith does not matter. The law simply states it is unlawful to misrepresent the nature of goods. You stated that the boat engine was in excellent condition, and it wasn't. That violates the act. The buyer will be entitled to three times his damages, however, only if he shows you made the misrepresentation knowingly.

The best advice I can give you is to try to settle this with the buyer. Then contact the mechanic and tell him you expect a reimbursement. If he refuses, you have a claim against him under the Deceptive Trade Practices Act. Next time, be careful.

Remember: Whenever you sell anything, you are responsible for whatever you say. If you are not sure, don't say it, or make it clear that it is just your opinion or based on what you know. For example, the seller would have no liability had he said, "The mechanic told me it was now in excellent condition."

Is there a law regarding construction defects?
"Yes, and it preempts the Deceptive Trade Practices Act."

Dear Mr. Alderman:
I am a small independent contractor. I heard that the legislature passed a law that protects us when we are sued under the Deceptive Trade Practices Act. Is there such a law, and if there is, what does it say?

You are right. There is a law that offers contractors additional protection when they are sued based on construction defects. The law is called the Residential Construction Liability Act, or RCLA. This law is important to both consumers and contractors because the consumer who does not comply with the provisions of this law may collect substantially less in damages.

The law applies to any action to collect money from a contractor based on a "construction defect," unless it is a personal injury action. Under the law, you must give written notice by certified mail to the contractor at least sixty days before filing suit, specifying in reasonable detail the defects that are the subject of the complaint. For thirty-five days after receiving this notice, the contractor has the right to inspect the defective property. Within forty-five days after receiving notice, the contractor may make a written offer of settlement to the consumer. The offer may include an agreement to repair the defects or have them repaired. The repairs must be made within forty-five days, if the offer is accepted.

The most important aspect of this law is that it substantially limits your damages in a suit against a contractor. For example, your economic damages are limited and you possibly may not recover damages for mental anguish. There are also special limits on damages when the consumer fails to accept the contractor's offer of settlement. If the consumer unreasonably rejects the settlement offer, he may not recover an amount in excess of the reasonable costs of the repairs, and may only recover attorney's fees incurred up to the time the offer was rejected. In other words, before filing a claim under the Deceptive Trade Practices Act or any other law, you must give a contractor an opportunity to repair the defects, and if it does or offers to do so, you proceed with a lawsuit at your peril.

Here is a quick example of how the law works: Suppose Tom hires a builder to repair his garage. After the work is completed and paid for, Tom discovers the siding was not of the quality represented by the contractor. Tom wants to file suit under the Deceptive Trade Practices Act for misrepresentation. Tom must first give the contractor sixty days notice of his complaint. He must then allow the contractor to come and look at the problem. If the contractor subsequently writes to Tom that it will change the siding at no cost, Tom must accept the offer, or else if he sues, his damages will be limited to what it will cost to make the change. He also will not recover his attorney's fees for the lawsuit.

How much should I pay to obtain a homestead exemption? "Nothing."

Dear Mr. Alderman:
I received a letter stating that I may be entitled to a property tax refund. It looks like it is from the tax office, but I am not sure. The letter states that I could be entitled to get money back if I agree to pay the agency a fee to do the paperwork. How much should it cost to get the paperwork done?

You can obtain a homestead exemption form from your local tax appraisal district and fill it out yourself, *at no cost*. It is a simple one-page form that requires just basic information about you and your home. Your county appraisal district probably has the forms online.

There are, however, agencies that solicit homeowners to enter into contracts for the preparation of these forms. Under Texas law, a person may not deliver a written advertisement to you offering, for a fee, to assist you with designating your property as a homestead unless there is a specific conspicuously printed disclaimer on the advertisement stating that the document is an advertisement for services and not an official document of the state of Texas.

A person who solicits a homeowner to pay a fee for the service of applying for a property tax refund from a tax appraisal district on your behalf must, before accepting money from you or signing a contract with you for the person's services, disclose to you the name of the tax appraisal district or other governmental body that owes the homeowner a refund. If a person fails to provide the disclaimer on an advertisement, or to provide the required disclosure, it is a violation of the Deceptive Trade Practices Act, and is subject to action by the consumer protection division.

What can I do about a "free" prize that wasn't really free? "The Deceptive Trade Practices Act may help."

Dear Mr. Alderman:
I won a contest from a radio station. The prize was jewelry stated to be worth $10,000. I had the jewelry appraised at $5,400. A second appraisal said $2,700 was more like it. The station sent a Form 1099 to the IRS for $10,000, and my taxes on this free prize came to more than it was actually worth. Do any laws prohibit such false advertising by a radio station?

First, as you found out, whenever you win a prize you must pay income taxes on the value of the prize. The question is, then, what is the value? I should point out that the value indicated on Form 1099 is not necessarily the value you have to use for taxes. The IRS requires that you pay taxes on the fair market value. This is generally what a willing buyer would pay a willing seller.

In your case, your estimates are as good an indication of this amount as is the 1099. You may want to protest the 1099 from the station and insist it reissue one with a corrected amount. Additionally, if you sell the item you won, the IRS will usually use that amount as the value on which you are required to pay taxes.

The question you ask, however, is a good one. Are there laws regulating false advertising of contests? The simple answer is yes. False, misleading, or deceptive advertising is unlawful under the Texas Deceptive Trade Practices Act. The attorney general enforces this law and could bring an action against any radio station that advertised falsely. The real issue under this law would be whether you may use this law.

To recover under this law, you must be a "consumer." This basically means you must "seek or acquire" something by "purchase." The free prize would not qualify unless you were required to do something to win. For example, if you had to purchase a product, count songs, send in an entry, or allow the station to use you for publicity purposes, then, in my opinion, the prize had strings attached and was not free. On the other hand, if you just called in and were given the prize, you probably do not have a claim under this law.

The seller didn't say anything. Am I out of luck?
"There is a duty to speak."

Dear Mr. Alderman:

I must have bought a junker. It is a 2009 car, and I paid more than $1,000 for it. As soon as I got it home, I found out the transmission was so bad that the car would not run for more than a few miles. I took it to the repair shop and learned it would cost nearly $800 to fix. The shop couldn't imagine how a car dealer wouldn't have known it. When I went back to the used car dealer, he admitted he knew the car needed a new transmission, but he said, "You didn't ask about the transmission, and I didn't tell you about it. . . . What you saw is what you bought." Is this the law? The car isn't worth more than a few hundred dollars in this condition. It seems to me the law should require someone to tell you when there is something wrong.

The law is just what you think it should be. Under the Texas Deceptive Trade Practices Act it is unlawful for a person to fail to disclose known defects if "such failure to disclose such information was intended to induce the consumer into a transaction which the consumer would not have entered into had the information been disclosed."

In your case, if you can show that the seller didn't disclose the information because he knew you wouldn't pay the same price if you knew the car didn't work, the dealer would be violating the law. It doesn't matter that you didn't ask any questions. Your failure to inquire is not a defense to this law.

If the seller has violated the Deceptive Trade Practices Act, you could be entitled to up to three times your damages. In your case your damages would be how much it will cost you to get the car into the condition it should have been in when you bought it: $800. If you prevail in court, you will also be entitled to any court costs or attorney's fees you incur.

The best advice I can give you is to contact the seller, certified mail, return receipt requested, and tell him you want your car fixed or money damages. Let him know you know your rights under the Deceptive Trade Practices Act, and unless you can settle things, you will pursue your legal rights.

Does a private seller have to disclose defects?
"All sellers must make the same disclosures."

Dear Mr. Alderman:
I bought a used car from an individual. I have discovered that the seller intentionally covered up some major problems. I told him I thought he had an obligation to tell me about the problems and he said that as an individual selling a car he didn't have any legal obligation to disclose anything. What are my legal rights?

As discussed above, the Texas Deceptive Trade Practices Act protects buyers whenever a seller acts in a misleading or deceptive manner, breaches a warranty, or acts unconscionably. One of the acts specifically listed as deceptive is the knowing failure to disclose information about the goods being sold. Of particular importance to your question, this law applies to all sellers, including individuals not in business.

Under this law, a seller who knowingly fails to disclose facts or takes steps to conceal them may be liable for up to three times your damages plus court costs and attorney's fees. In your case, damages will be either what it will cost to get the car properly repaired or the difference between what you paid and what the car was worth.

The contract said "as is." Am I out of luck?
"Not necessarily, under the Deceptive Trade Practices Act."

Dear Mr. Alderman:
I bought a used car. It was advertised in the paper as being in "excellent condition." When I looked at the car, the owner (he was not a dealer) assured me the car ran well and was in great shape mechanically. I relied on what he told me and bought it. Before I got it home it broke down. The mechanic says the car is a piece of junk and is in terrible mechanical condition. When I asked for my money back, the seller told me to read the contract we had. I did, and it says the car was sold "as is." Am I out of luck? I guess it was my own fault for not carefully reading the contract.

In some cases, buying something "as is" does mean you are out of luck. But if, when signing the contract, a seller makes a false statement of fact about a product and you, in fact, rely on the misrepresentation to purchase the product, my opinion is the seller is liable under the Deceptive Trade Practices Act. Saying something is sold "as is" does have the legal effect of eliminating many warranties, but it does not necessarily change the Deceptive Trade Practices Act.

I suggest you talk to the seller and let him know that you know the law. Be sure he understands you relied on what he said, and that is why you signed the contract. As you probably already know, the Deceptive Trade Practices Act applies to any seller, even one not in business, and you could be entitled to three times your damages if you sue. I also should point out that the Texas Supreme Court has said the good faith, intent, or knowledge of the seller who made the statement is irrelevant. If a misrepresentation is made, the Deceptive Trade Practices Act has usually been violated. The owner assured you the car was in excellent condition, and it was not. Small print in a contract may not change the effect of the Deceptive Trade Practices Act.

What can I do about something I paid for but never received? "That may be unconscionable and unlawful."

Dear Mr. Alderman:

I made arrangements with an auto repair shop to rebuild my car's motor. I made payments until I had paid $750 in advance. The deal was that after I paid the $750, the mechanic would do the work. So far he has done nothing. I have tried numerous times to get him to make the repairs or give me my money back, and he won't. I don't know anything about cars, and every time I ask a question, I get the runaround.

Fortunately for you, the Deceptive Trade Practices Act protects you against someone taking unfair advantage of you. Under the law, it is unconscionable for someone to "take advantage of the lack of knowledge, ability, experience, or capacity" to a grossly unfair degree. In my opinion, the merchant is taking advantage of your lack of knowledge and ability, and this would violate the Deceptive Trade Practices Act.

I suggest you let the mechanic know you know about this law and that you promptly want your money back or your car repaired.

The real estate agent didn't tell me the former owner of the house died of AIDS. Doesn't this have to be disclosed? "Not under the law."

Dear Mr. Alderman:

I just bought a new house. Right after I moved in I found out the former owner of the house had died of AIDS in the house. I don't want to sound like a crazy person, but I am afraid of getting the disease.

I probably would not have bought the house if I had known about this. I thought the Texas Deceptive Trade Practices Act required that sellers disclose things like this. Do I have any legal rights?

First, from everything I have heard or read, there is no possibility of you contracting AIDS from living in a house where someone with the disease died. Hopefully, you will be able to enjoy the house and not worry about its prior occupants.

As far as your legal rights, you probably have none in this situation. You are right that the Deceptive Trade Practices Act (DTPA), as well as the new real estate disclosure law discussed in the next letter, requires a seller to disclose material facts to you if he knows these facts would matter. Under the law, a seller would probably have an obligation to tell you about the prior occupant's death. But the legislature has passed a law that preempts the DTPA and allows people to remain silent with respect to AIDS. This law is consistent with federal laws that prohibit discrimination against persons with AIDS. The bottom line is that under present law there is no liability for the failure to disclose information regarding AIDS or related complexes to a prospective home buyer.

No one told me the appliances didn't work. Do I have any rights? "Yes! There is a real estate disclosure law."

Dear Mr. Alderman:
I bought a new house—actually a new used house. Everything appeared in good condition. The seller never told me everything worked, but I assumed it did. Shortly after we moved in, we discovered serious problems with the air conditioning unit. We didn't think to ask about this because it was winter when we bought the house. Are we just out of luck?

Even though you may have rights under the Deceptive Trade Practices Act, you also are entitled to a full disclosure by the seller. Under the law, a seller of residential real estate must give you written notice that contains certain required information. Although the notice does not have to be in any specific form, what follows is a copy of the form suggested by the legislature. If you did not receive such disclosures, you have the right to terminate the contract. You also may have a claim under the Deceptive Trade Practices Act. As a practical matter, however, my guess is once the seller finds out about this, he will promptly negotiate a fair settlement with you. A copy of this form may be downloaded from the Texas Real Estate Commission, www.trec.texas.gov.

Example of the type of real estate disclosure statement required by law.

SELLER'S DISCLOSURE NOTICE

CONCERNING THE PROPERTY AT _____

(Street Address and City)

THIS NOTICE IS A DISCLOSURE OF SELLER'S KNOWLEDGE OF THE CONDITION OF THE PROPERTY AS OF THE DATE SIGNED BY SELLER AND IS NOT A SUBSTITUTE FOR ANY INSPECTIONS OR WARRANTIES THE PURCHASER MAY WISH TO OBTAIN. IT IS NOT A WARRANTY OF ANY KIND BY SELLER OR SELLER'S AGENTS.

Seller ____ is ____ is not occupying the Property.

If unoccupied, how long since Seller has occupied the Property? ___

---

1. The Property has the items checked below:

Write Yes (Y), No (N), or Unknown (U).

___ Range	___ Oven	___ Microwave
___ Dishwasher	___ Trash Compactor	___ Disposal
___ Washer/Dryer Hookups	___ Window Screens	___ Rain Gutters
___ Security System	___ Fire Detection Equipment	___ Intercom System
___ TV Antenna	___ Cable TV Wiring	___ Satellite Dish
___ Ceiling Fan(s)	___ Attic Fan(s)	___ Exhaust Fan(s)
___ Central A/C	___ Central Heating	___ Wall/Window Air Conditioning
___ Plumbing System	___ Septic System	___ Public Sewer System
___ Patio/Decking	___ Outdoor Grill	___ Fences
___ Pool	___ Sauna	___ Spa
___ Hot Tub	___ Pool Equipment	___ Pool Heater
___ Automatic Lawn Sprinkler System		
___ Fireplace(s) & Chimney (Wood-burning)	___ Fireplace(s) & Chimney (Mock)	
___ Gas Lines (Nat./LP)	___ Gas Fixtures	

Garage:
___ Attached   ___ Not Attached   ___ Carport

Garage Door Opener(s):
___ Electronic   ___ Control(s)

Water Heater:
___ Gas   ___ Electric

Water Supply:
___ City   ___ Well   ___ MUD   ___ Co-Op

Roof Type: _____

Age: _____ (approx.)

Are you (Seller) aware of any of the above items that are not in working condition, that have known defects, or that are in need of repair?

___ Yes   ___ No ___ Unknown

If yes, then describe. (Attach additional sheets if necessary):

_____

_____

_____

2. Are you (Seller) aware of any known defects/malfunctions in any
   of the following? Write Yes (Y) if you are, write No (N) if you are
   not aware.

___ Interior Walls	___ Ceilings	___ Floors
___ Exterior Walls	___ Doors	___ Windows
___ Roof	___ Foundation/Slab(s)	___ Basement
___ Walls/Fences	___ Driveways	___ Sidewalks
___ Plumbing/ Sewers/Septics	___ Electrical Systems	___ Lighting Fixtures

Other Structural Components (Describe):

_____

_____

If the answer to any of the above is yes, explain. (Attach additional
sheets if necessary):

_____

_____

3. Are you (Seller) aware of any of the following conditions?
___ Active Termites   ___ Previous Structural or Roof Repair
    (includes wood-destroying insects)
___ Termite or Wood Rot Damage
___ Hazardous or Toxic Waste
___ Asbestos Components
___ Previous Termite Damage
___ Urea Formaldehyde Insulation
___ Previous Termite Treatment
___ Radon Gas   ___ Lead-Based Paint
___ Previous Flooding   ___ Aluminum Wiring
___ Improper Drainage   ___ Previous Fires
___ Water Penetration   ___ Located in 100-Year Floodplain
___ Unplatted Easements
___ Present Flood Insurance Coverage
___ Landfill, Settling, Soil
___ Subsurface Structure or Pits
___ Movement, Fault Lines

If the answer to any of the above is yes, explain. (Attach additional sheets if necessary):

_____

_____

4. Are you (Seller) aware of any item, equipment, or system in or on the property that is in need of repair? ___ Yes (if you are aware) ___ No (if you are not aware). If yes, explain (attach additional sheets if necessary):

_____

_____

5. Are you (Seller) aware of any of the following?
Write Yes (Y) if you are aware, write No (N) if you are not aware.
___ Room additions, structural modifications, or other alterations or repairs made without necessary permits or not in compliance with building codes in effect at that time.
___ Homeowners' Association or maintenance fees or assessments.
___ Any "common area" (facilities such as pools, tennis courts, walkways, or other areas) co-owned in undivided interest with others.

___ Any notices of violations of deed restrictions or governmental ordinances affecting the condition or use of the Property.

___ Any lawsuits directly or indirectly affecting the Property.

___ Any condition on the Property that materially affects the physical health or safety of an individual.

If the answer to any of the above is yes, explain. (Attach additional sheets if necessary):

_____

_____

_____

_____

_____   _____
Date   Signature of Seller

The undersigned purchaser hereby acknowledges receipt of the above notice.

_____   _____
Date   Signature of Purchaser

What are treble damages?
"Good news for you."

Dear Mr. Alderman:
I have heard you speak about the Deceptive Trade Practices Act and the fact that it allows you to recover "treble damages." Just what does this mean?

The Deceptive Trade Practices Act is designed to do two things: first, to compensate consumers for their losses and, second, to deter people from engaging in false or deceptive practices. To deter wrongdoers, the law enables you to collect what may be viewed as punitive damages, damages designed to punish the wrongdoer and not just to compensate you for your loss.

Under the law, you may recover *up to* three times your damages—"treble damages." To recover these additional damages, you must show that the person you sued acted "knowingly." This means he knew or should have known what he did was false, misleading or deceptive, or breached a warranty.

For example, suppose someone sells you a car and says it is in excellent condition when it is not. Because the statement is false, you have a claim under the Deceptive Trade Practices Act. You would only be entitled to up to a total of three times your damages, however, if you could show the seller knew, or should have known, that the car was not in excellent condition when he said it was. In other words, an innocent misrepresentation does not result in treble damages.

The possibility of treble damages is what lends teeth to the Deceptive Trade Practices Act. *Once a person knows he may have to pay a large sum if he loses in court, he is more likely to treat you fairly and try to settle.* Make sure the seller is aware that you know the law and how much his damages may be. My guess is you usually will be able to work out an agreeable settlement.

How do I use the Deceptive Trade Practices Act? "It's simple."

Dear Mr. Alderman:

I have heard about the consumer protection law in Texas called the Deceptive Trade Practices Act. From what I have been told, this could be just the law to help me with a problem I'm having with my mechanic. I was just wondering—is there anything special I have to do to utilize this law? Can I go to justice court? I only want the $300 he took from me.

The Deceptive Trade Practices Act allows a consumer to recover damages—and if the act was committed "knowingly," up to a total of three times his or her damages—plus court costs and attorney's fees, if any. But if you are going to use this law there are a few steps you must follow.

First, remember you cannot go to justice court if you are asking for more than $10,000. If the amount you are seeking is more than $10,000, you probably will need an attorney to file suit in county or district court. In your case, this does not present any problem.

Next, once you decide to use this law, you must give written notice of your problem at least sixty days before you file your claim in court. The notice must give the specific nature of the claim in reasonable detail and the amount of economic damages, damages for mental anguish, and attorney's fees if any. The following letter could be used as a model:

Mr. C. Consumer
435 Central Dr.
Consumer, TX 77597

Dear Mr. Merchant:

On Wednesday, June 16, I brought my car into your shop to be repaired. I told you to tune it up, and you stated it would cost $49.95. This is the same amount advertised in the paper the day before. When I picked up my car you charged me $349.95. You told me the $49.95 was for American cars only. This was not stated in the ad or told to me before I agreed to have work done.

I feel your conduct in stating one price and charging another is a false and deceptive practice under the Texas Deceptive Trade Practices Act. I have been damaged in the amount of $300.

Under the law I must give you sixty days' notice of my complaint prior to filing a claim. Unless I receive a satisfactory settlement from you within that period, I intend to pursue my claim in justice court. I should point out that if you acted with knowledge of your false representation, I may be entitled to up to three times my damages.

Thank you for your expected cooperation.

Sincerely yours,
Consumer

The purpose of the notice requirement is to give the other party a chance to settle the case without costly litigation. Under the law, if the other side offers a settlement and you refuse it, and if then the court awards substantially the same amount offered in the settlement, collection of your damages and attorney's fees could be substantially limited. *If you are offered a settlement substantially the same as what you asked for, you should accept.*

If you do not give the proper notice, the other side may be able to delay the proceedings, so make sure to send your notice certified mail, return receipt requested, so you have proof it was sent. And be sure to include a description of what you think the person has done that violates the law and exactly how much your damages are.

One final comment: Should you see an attorney? The simple answer is: It is up to you. If the amount is less than $10,000, justice court is simple to use and quick. But an attorney may increase your potential for recovery and may know of damages you are entitled to that you overlooked. But litigation with an attorney takes a longer time and costs money. You must balance all these factors and make the decision yourself. You may want to talk with an attorney before going to justice court, just to get an idea of how he or she could help.

Where can I go for help with a consumer problem?
"The Texas Consumer Complaint Center."

Dear Mr. Alderman:
I have a problem with a car dealer that I have been unable to resolve. I think I have done all I can to resolve things myself. I would rather not file in justice court. Is there an organization that might be able to help me?

The Texas Consumer Complaint Center at the University of Houston Law Center may be just what you are looking for. Founded in 2006, the Center has staff attorneys and law students to help consumers resolve disputes. The Center has helped thousands of consumers resolve their problems and saved them millions of dollars. There is no guarantee they will be able to help you, but it will not be for lack of trying. The best way to contact the Center is to visit its website, www.texasccc.com, or you can call (713) 743-2168.

CHAPTER 11

Immigration

Few areas of law have sparked as much public interest and controversy as immigration law. Immigration law determines who has the right to live and work in the United States. As you might imagine, this area of law is of great concern to many people, and is rapidly changing. The following questions and answers are based on the law as of the publication date of this book. My suggestion is that after reading the question and answer, you check with one of the organizations listed after the next question to verify that the law has not changed.

What should I do to see if I can legally stay in the United States?
"Contact an attorney or an agency accredited
by the Department of Justice (DOJ)."

Dear Mr. Alderman:
I have come to Texas illegally from Honduras and now want to stay here. However, I have been told that if I am discovered I will be deported. I have been here almost ten years and have a good job, and my wife is here legally. I am thinking of quitting my job because I am afraid of being caught. Is there anything I can do to stay here legally? Is there any organization that can help me?

Several laws may provide you with an opportunity to remain in the United States. For example, depending on your wife's immigration status, you may be entitled to remain here. The first thing you should do is see an attorney or an immigration counselor at one of the agencies accredited by the U.S. Department of Justice (DOJ) in Texas. Here is a list of some of the organizations designated on the Department of Justice website: www .justice.gov/eoir/recognized-organizations-and-accredited-representatives -roster-state-and-city.

LIST OF RECOGNIZED LEGAL SERVICES PROVIDERS IN TEXAS

The following organizations and attorneys provide free or low-cost legal services and/or referrals for services to indigent individuals in immigration removal proceedings.

Dallas/Fort Worth

Catholic Charities
9461 Lyndon B. Johnson Freeway, Suite 128
Dallas, TX 75208
(214) 520-6590
https://catholiccharitiesusa.org/members/catholic-charities-of-dallas

249 W. Thornhill Dr.; P.O. Box 15610
Fort Worth, TX 76115
(817) 534-0814
https://catholiccharitiesusa.org/members/catholic-charities-of-fort
-worth

Human Rights Initiative of North Texas, Inc.
2801 Swiss Ave.
Dallas, TX 75204
(214) 855-0520
http://www.hrionline.org

Mosaic Family Services
12225 Greenville Ave., Suite 800
Dallas, TX 75243
(214) 821-5393
http://mosaicservices.org

El Paso

Diocesan Migrant and Refugee Services
2400 A. E. Yandell
El Paso, TX 79903-3617
(915) 532-3975
http://dmrs-ep.org

United Neighborhood Organization (UNO)
8700 Boeing Dr.
El Paso, TX 79925
(915) 755-1161

Las Americas Refugee Asylum Project
1500 E. Yandell Dr.
El Paso, TX 79902
(915) 544-5126
http://las-americas.org

Harlingen

ProBAR (South Texas Pro Bono Asylum Representation)
222 E. Van Buren Ave.
Harlingen, TX 78550
(956) 425-9231
(888) 425-9231 if calling from the PISPC Detention Center
www.americanbar.org/probar

Casa de Proyecto Libertad
113 N. 1st St.
Harlingen, TX 78550
(956) 425-9552
(800) 477-9552 if calling from the PISPC Detention Center

South Texas Immigration Council
107 N. 3rd St.
Harlingen, TX 78550
(956) 425-6987

South Texas Immigration Council
4 E. Levee St.
Brownsville, TX 78520
(956) 542-1991

Texas RioGrande Aid, Inc.
316 South Closner St.
Edinburg, TX 78539
(956) 393-6200
www.trla.org

Houston

Carecen Central American Refugee Center
6006 Bellaire Blvd., Suite 100
Houston, TX 77081
(713) 665-1284

International Services of the YMCA Greater Houston Area
Pro Bono Asylum Program
6300 Westpark, Suite 600
Houston, TX 77057
(713) 339-9015
www.ymcahouston.org/locations/ymca-international

Catholic Charities, Cabrini Center
2900 Louisiana St.
Houston, TX 77006
(713) 526-4611
https://www.catholiccharities.org/supporting-refugees-immigrants/
    st-frances-cabrini-center-for-immigration-legal-assistance

Central American Refugee Center
6006 Bellaire Blvd., Suite 100
Houston, TX 77081
(713) 665-1284

Tahirih Justice Center
1717 St. James Place, Suite 450
Houston, TX 77056
(713) 496-0100
www.tahirih.org/locations/houston

San Antonio, Austin, and Laredo

**Refugee and Immigrant Center for Education
and Legal Services (RAICES)**
1305 N. Flores St.
San Antonio, TX 78212
(210) 222-0964
www.raicestexas.org

American Gateways
One Highland Center
314 Highland Mall Blvd., Suite 501
Austin, TX 78752
(512) 478-0546
www.americangateways.org

**Immigration & Human Rights Clinic,
Center for Legal & Social Justice**
2507 NW 36th St.
San Antonio, TX 78228
(210) 436-3011

Immigration Clinic of the University of Texas School of Law
727 E. Dean Keeton St.
Austin, Texas 78705-3299
(512) 232-1292
https://law.utexas.edu/clinics/immigration

Catholic Charities/Archdiocese of San Antonio, Inc.
202 West French Place
San Antonio, TX 78212
(210) 222-1294
http://ccaosa.org

Asociacion Pro Servicios Sociales, Inc.
406 Scott St.
Laredo, TX 78040
(956) 724-6244
http://apsslar.org

I have heard that the INS no longer exists. Is that true?
"INS is part of the Department of Homeland Security (DHS)."

Dear Mr. Alderman:
I told my roommate that I was going to apply with the INS to obtain
a green card. My roommate told me that the INS no longer exists. Is
this true? If so, where do I go to obtain the necessary forms to apply
for a green card? Where do I file my application?

The Immigration and Naturalization Service (INS) no longer exists by that name. It has been incorporated into the U.S. Department of Homeland Security (DHS). The old INS was responsible for protecting the borders as well as adjudicating applications for benefits, such as green cards and citizenship applications. Those functions have now been divided up among three different agencies within the Department of Homeland Security. United States Citizenship and Immigration Services (USCIS) handles all applications for benefits such as work permits, green cards, and citizenship applications. Border protection is now handled by U.S. Customs and Border Patrol Protection (CBP). The removal of undocumented aliens or others present illegally within the United States is handled by U.S. Immigration and Customs Enforcement (ICE). DHS information may be found at www.dhs.gov. The website for seeking benefits with the USCIS is www.uscis.gov. The websites for the enforcement branches are www.ice.gov and http://cbp.gov.

What does someone from another country need to visit this country?
"A visa."

Dear Mr. Alderman:
I have a friend in another country who wants to visit me for a while.
I have heard all the complaints about illegal aliens, and I want to
know what she has to do to comply with the law while she lives with
me.

Basically, to enter the United States from another country you must have
the permission of the United States. This permission is called a "visa."
Your friend can obtain a visa from the American consul. Because she is
only coming to visit you temporarily, she can obtain a nonimmigrant visa.
These are issued to people who plan on staying in the United States temporarily. For example, a nonimmigrant visa can be used by a businessperson
who is coming temporarily to work for his company, a student who will be
attending school, or a tourist, such as your friend.

I should point out that a tourist visa authorizes your friend to stay here,
but not to work here. She also must return home after the visa expires,
unless she has it extended or changes her status to an immigrant visa. For
some countries (Canada, Japan, western European countries, and a few
others) there is no need for a visa because the United States has agreements with these countries to permit their citizens to enter under a "visa
waiver" program.

What is a green card?
"The right to stay in the United States."

Dear Mr. Alderman:
I am an American citizen and have never paid much attention to
immigration laws. Now that I own a small business, I have been told
I shouldn't hire any aliens unless they have green cards. Just what is
a green card?

The law prohibits you from hiring an alien who is not properly documented. For example, a worker with a worker's visa would be properly
documented and could be hired to work for you. A visa is the document
given to aliens who are here temporarily.

If an alien wants to reside in the country permanently and wants the right
to come in and go out of the United States, he or she must obtain an Alien
Registration Receipt Card. Although this card is no longer green, its common name is still "green card." Not everyone, however, can get a green card.

There are limited means of obtaining a green card. They include: a) application by a U.S. citizen or lawful permanent resident (immediate) family member; b) application by employer for a professional or skilled worker; c) application by one granted asylum; and d) diversity visa (lottery).

The most common way of obtaining a green card is by having a family relationship with someone in this country. For example, if you are a spouse, child, parent, brother, or sister of an American citizen or are engaged to an American citizen, you can become a permanent resident if your U.S. citizen family member applies for you. To do this, the person you have the relationship with must file an application with the Department of Homeland Security or the American embassy of the country where the alien lives. You also can obtain a green card if you are the spouse or child of a person with a green card. In this case, the relative who is a permanent resident of the United States must file the application. Although it is less common, permanent resident status can also be obtained if you have a job that this country considers a priority or skilled position. Skilled or professional workers may be eligible to remain in this country as permanent residents if an employer files a petition for them.

Also, the Immigration Act of 1994 allows 55,000 immigrants from certain countries to come to the United States as permanent residents without the need to meet the above requirements. The countries are those that have sent the fewest immigrants to this country in the past. The DHS can give you the list of countries whose citizens are considered "diversity immigrants." This process is commonly called the visa "lottery" program. Check out www.uscis.gov/greencard/diversity-visa.

How should an application for a green card be filed?
"Generally it is filed by mail or online with a DHS Service Center."

Dear Mr. Alderman:
I am a United States citizen. Recently I went to the local DHS office to file an application to bring my parents here from India to live with me. I was told that the application had to be filed by mail. Is this true? If so, where?

While the local DHS office still gives out forms, answers questions, and accepts certain applications, most applications for permanent residence (green cards) are filed with DHS Service Centers. There are located in Vermont, Nebraska, California, Washington D.C., and Texas. The Texas Service Center handles family-based visa petitions filed by those living in Texas. The application and all supporting documents may be sent by mail, or may be filed online at www.uscis.gov/tools. The service center then adjudicates the application and forwards it to the appropriate American consulate or DHS office for the interview and completion of the process.

How can I get a "permiso" or work permit for employment?
"Not everyone is eligible."

Dear Mr. Alderman:

I came from Mexico several years ago and have been working here for several years without a work permit or social security card. My employer has told me that I must present a work permit from the Department of Homeland Security or he will have to let me go. What can I do to get a work permit?

Not everyone is authorized to work in the United States. There are limited classes of people eligible to obtain a work permit. In order to obtain a work permit you must generally have some lawful status in the United States or have an application pending to legalize immigration status. For example, if a person is here legally as a student he or she may be able to obtain a work permit from DHS. Individuals who have applied for asylum, adjustment of status, or other means of legalizing their status can often get a work permit during the period that the application is pending. However, if the person is here illegally (without any immigration papers) and there is no application pending to make that person's status lawful, he cannot get a work permit. For more information, visit www.uscis.gov/working-united-states/temporary-nonimmigrant-workers.

How can I become a citizen?
"Generally you must first get a green card."

Dear Mr. Alderman:

I am a student from Cameroon completing my university studies here on a student visa. I would like to become a citizen of the United States. How can I accomplish this?

Generally, you can only be naturalized as a U.S. citizen after you have had lawful permanent residence (a green card) for several years. For most individuals, the requirement is five years. Those married to United States citizens need to wait only three years after becoming lawful permanent residents. There are other requirements to becoming a naturalized U.S. citizen as well. These include a basic understanding of U.S. history and government; the ability to speak, read, and write basic English; and good moral character.

Does divorce change my immigration status?
"Not if you have been married more than two years."

Dear Mr. Alderman:
My husband and I are Canadian citizens living in Texas legally with
green cards. We are divorcing. We have lived in Texas for nine years.
How will the divorce affect our green card status? Will the Canadian
legal system and immigration be involved? What will be the DHS
implications of a divorce?

As long as you have been married for two years after obtaining the green
card there is no problem. The only time a problem arises is when DHS
suspects fraud. There may be a presumption of fraud by the DHS if the
divorce takes place within a short period, defined as within two years, of
obtaining lawful permanent resident status, the green card. Outside of that
there should be no problem. Your divorce should have no impact on your
immigration status.

I have to go to Immigration Court and cannot afford a lawyer.
Will the court provide one for me?
"No!"

Dear Mr. Alderman:
I have been notified that I must go before the immigration judge for a
removal (deportation) hearing next month. I am not employed and I
cannot afford a lawyer. Will the judge appoint one for me?

No. There is a right to an attorney in immigration court proceedings, but
not at government expense. The judge will not be able to provide you with
free legal representation. However, the court does have a list of charitable
or "pro bono" organizations that may be able to provide you with representation free of charge or at a nominal fee. The judge will generally give
this list to indigent immigrants appearing in court without lawyers. Also,
if this is your first time in court, the judge will generally give you time to
get an attorney. See the list after the first question in this chapter for nonprofit agencies. Even if you do not have an attorney, be sure to appear in
court and ask for time to obtain one. Failure to appear generally results in
a removal (i.e., a deportation) order.

What is a notary?
"Not a lawyer or a 'notario.'"

Dear Mr. Alderman:
I am from Mexico, and I wanted legal advice in Dallas, where I live.
I went to a notary public, where the notary said for $500 he would
help me with my problem. What is a notary public? Is it a "notario"
(lawyer)?

In Mexico and other Spanish-speaking countries, a "notario" performs many of the same functions as an attorney. In the United States, a notary public is not an attorney and cannot hold himself out as a lawyer to represent you in court or in other legal proceedings. Basically, all a notary public does is attest to signatures or certify that you signed a document, and perform other clerking services. Nearly anyone can become a notary public just by paying a small fee.

If you need legal services, see an attorney ("abogado" or "licenciado"). If you think the notary public misrepresented himself or engaged in unauthorized legal work, you should report him to the district attorney's office, the attorney general, or the state bar of Texas, (800) 932-1900. The unauthorized practice of law is a crime.

And by the way, notaries usually charge very little for their services. Beware of anyone charging a high fee for performing his or her duties as a notary public.

I am afraid to go home. What can I do?
"You may be entitled to asylum."

Dear Mr. Alderman:
I am from El Salvador, and fled to the United States because my
brother was killed by a government soldier and I heard they were
looking for me too. Is there any way I can stay in the United States,
at least until things get better in my country and it is safe for me to
return?

You should seek assistance from an immigration attorney or the counseling agencies listed on the preceding pages. If you have reason to believe you may be harmed, you may be eligible for asylum "because of persecution on account of race, religion, nationality, membership in a particular social group, or political opinion." These are highly technical terms, but an attorney or qualified immigration counselor could help you apply for asylum if you qualify. You are entitled to certain rights and a hearing. You may even be eligible to work in the United States. Even more than other persons, however, you should be careful not to commit a crime or break a law, because any immigration hearings will include a record of your time and behavior while in the United States.

I am a U.S. citizen, but I am still asked for ID. Is this legal?
"All people must show they are eligible to work."

Dear Mr. Alderman:
I am a citizen, but notice my union won't hire anybody without ID or a green card. Is this legal? I am a third-generation American, and I resent having to prove I am legal.

Employers must screen all new employees (those hired since November 6, 1986) to determine if they are eligible to work. However, they must ask the same questions and require the same papers of everyone, not just people who may look Hispanic or who speak with accents. There are no sanctions for employers who hired undocumented employees before November 6, 1986, but there may be penalties for people hired after that date. All employees must be treated equally in the hiring process.

Does my child have to have a Social Security
number to stay in school?
"No!"

Dear Mr. Alderman:
My daughter brought home a letter from school that said all school-children must have Social Security numbers and that we should fill out forms to get a Social Security number. I'm afraid not to get one because they might not let my daughter stay in school. What can I do?

No child has to have a Social Security number to enroll in school. Even undocumented children can attend public schools if their parent resides in the school district. Recent tax law changes affect who may be eligible for a tax deduction, but you are not required to take any action that exposes you or your children to possible deportation. As with any such case involving immigration, you should consult an attorney or reputable immigration counseling center.

I should also note that immigration enforcement actions may not occur at schools. In general, DHS has explained that immigration enforcement actions may not occur at or in "sensitive locations." Sensitive locations include schools, such as known and licensed day-care centers, preschools, and other early learning programs; primary schools; secondary schools; post-secondary schools up to and including colleges and universities; as well as scholastic or education-related activities or events. Also protected are school bus stops that are marked and/or known to the officer during periods when children are present at the stop.

I am a small employer. Must I comply with the immigration law? "Probably yes."

Dear Mr. Alderman:
I have a small business, delivering documents for local firms. I employ five to ten people. The other day someone told me I could get in trouble if I didn't comply with the immigration law. I don't have anyone working for me who is not a permanent resident or U.S. citizen; do I still have to bother with this law?

Yes. The law applies to nearly everyone who employs someone to perform work, labor, or services in return for wages. Under the law you must complete a Form I-9 for:

- *Persons hired on or after November 6, 1986.* For these employees, you must complete a Form I-9 within three business days of the date of hire. (If you employ the person for less than three days, you must complete Form I-9 before the end of the employee's first working day.)
- *Note:* If you employ people for domestic work in your private home on a regular (such as weekly) basis, these requirements also apply to you.

You do not need to complete Form I-9 for:

- Persons hired on or before November 7, 1986.
- Persons hired after November 6, 1986 who left your employment before June 1, 1987.
- Persons you employ for casual domestic work in a private home on a sporadic, irregular, or intermittent basis.
- Persons who provide labor to you and who are employed by a contractor providing contract services (e.g., employee leasing).
- Independent contractors or individuals providing labor to you if they are employed by a contractor providing contract services (for example, employee leasing or temporary agencies).

Form I-9 is designed to verify that people are eligible to work in the

United States. The form is easy to complete, and information is available to help you. To get more information and a copy of the form and more information, visit www.uscis.gov/i-9.

Note: You can be fined if you do not comply with this law—and don't try to get around it by not hiring anyone you think may be unauthorized to work here. Under the law it is also unlawful for a business with four or more employees to discriminate against any individual because of that person's national origin or citizenship status. In other words, ask for papers from everyone you hire, not just minority workers.

Are sanctuary cities now banned in Texas?
"A new law bans sanctuary cities."

Dear Mr. Alderman:
I heard that Texas has now banned sanctuary cites. Is this true? What does it mean?

A new law, referred to as SB 4, bans so-called sanctuary cities by punishing jurisdictions that do not fully cooperate with federal immigration officials. Under this law, law enforcement agencies, including campus police, may not "adopt, enforce, or endorse a policy under which the entity or department prohibits or materially limits the enforcement of immigration laws." For example, it prohibits a policy prohibiting officers from asking people about their immigration status. Police can ask about immigration status not just during an arrest, but also while detaining someone for any purpose. Some have argued that the law gives a green light to police officers in the state to investigate a person's immigration status during a routine traffic stop, leading to racial profiling, baseless scrutiny, and illegal arrests of citizens and noncitizens alike presumed to be "foreign" based on how they look or sound.

The law also requires all sheriffs and police chiefs to honor ICE detainers, which are requests that suspected undocumented immigrants be held in the county jail until federal agents can pick them up. Should police leaders fail to "enforce immigration law," they can be removed from office and charged with a crime; their jurisdictions can also face a steep civil fine. Defenders of the law say it is intended to protect public safety by banning so-called sanctuary cities, which regulate how their police conduct immigration checks.

As you might expect with a law of this nature, lawsuits have been filed to stop its enforcement. One way of staying current with this law is to subscribe to my News Alert, www.peopleslawyer.net.

Does a new law make it harder for immigrants to get a driver's license?
"Yes."

Dear Mr. Alderman:
I have heard there is a new law that might make it difficult for immigrants to get a driver's license. Is this true?

Under a law called the REAL ID Act, each applicant for a driver's license will have to present proof that he or she is one of the following: a U.S. citizen; a lawfully admitted temporary, permanent, or conditional resident; an asylee; or a refugee. In addition, individuals who have been granted Temporary Protected Status (TPS), deferred action, or have pending applications for permanent residence or asylum are eligible to apply for a driver's license if they have proof of their immigration status. Individuals who have only temporary legal status or pending applications for lawful status will receive a driver's license marked "temporary DL." The Texas Department of Public Safety may not accept foreign documents except passports as proof of identification. The temporary DL is valid only for the period of the individual's lawful status in the United States. To see how Texas intends to comply with the REAL ID Act, visit www.dps.texas.gov/DriverLicense/federalRealIdAct.htm.

If I just graduated from college, can I work in the U.S.?
"Foreign national graduates can work in the U.S., in some cases."

Dear Mr. Alderman:
I am a foreign national attending school in Texas. I will graduate next spring. I have been told that I can stay in the U.S. to work. Is this correct?

In some cases, a foreign national who graduates from a U.S. college or university may work for a year in the U.S. following graduation. To be eligible, the school must approve Optional Practical Training (OPT), and U.S. Citizenship and Immigration Services must issue an Employment Authorization Document. The student must work in his or her field of study, and cannot be unemployed for more than ninety days after granted OPT. In some cases, a student with a degree in science, technology, engineering, or mathematics may work for twenty-nine months, but only if the employer has registered with the Department of Homeland Security for the E-Verify program.

CHAPTER 12

Landlord & Tenant Rights

Landlord-tenant law is centuries old, and for most of that time, it has been very one-sided. Landlord-tenant law historically has favored the landlord. But there have been some changes, and while you may not have all the rights you would like, you are not without recourse when something goes wrong.

Two laws in particular give you rights against the landlord when he doesn't properly maintain the apartment or doesn't return your security deposit. To see the text of all Texas landlord-tenant laws, visit my website at www.peopleslawyer.net.

The most important part of any landlord-tenant relationship is the lease. Read yours carefully before you sign. If you don't like something in the lease, don't sign until the landlord agrees to remove it.

Do I need a lease?
"No, but it can help."

Dear Mr. Alderman:
I just moved to the city. I found an apartment I liked and told the landlord I would take it. He said, "Fine. You can move in on the first." When I asked for a lease he told me not to worry—he never uses them, and I could just pay monthly. Now I am worried. Is it legal to rent an apartment without a lease? What if he just throws me out?

A landlord-tenant relationship is created by an agreement called a lease. This agreement can be oral or written, and can be as informal or formal as the parties want to make it. *There is no requirement that you have a formal lease to rent an apartment.*

If you do not have a written lease, the law implies a lease for at least as long as the period between rent payments. For example, if you agree to pay rent once a month, the law says you have a month-to-month lease. This means neither you nor the landlord may terminate the agreement without giving at least one month's notice to the other. If you were paying rent once a week, your agreement would be weekly, and one week's notice of termination would be required.

In your case, you can have an implied lease with your landlord; however, it is only a month-to-month agreement. This means you can only leave or be evicted after thirty days' notice. You may have an oral lease for a period of up to one year, but if you want an agreement for more than one month, you should have a written lease. A written lease eliminates a dispute as to the length of your lease, and allows you to spell out all the terms of your agreement. This is a good way to avoid problems that might arise concerning who is obligated to do what—for example, who pays for utilities or repairs.

As far as your question about the landlord just throwing you out, read the next letter.

If I am late with my rent, can my landlord just throw me out? "No. You can be evicted only after a court hearing and only by a constable or sheriff."

Dear Mr. Alderman:
I was laid off, and I don't have enough money to pay my bills. I am already one month late in my rent. I just received a notice from my landlord to vacate. It says if I am not out in three days, he will have me evicted. I have a place to move to, but it won't be ready for a week. Does the landlord have the right to throw me out in the street in three days?

Under the law a landlord cannot personally evict a tenant. You may only be evicted after (1) the landlord commences a legal proceeding against you; (2) you have an opportunity to appear in court; (3) the judge orders you to leave; and (4) you do not leave. Even then the eviction must be carried out by a constable or sheriff pursuant to a court order.

If your landlord were to throw you out, he would be responsible for any damages you suffered and may even be liable for criminal and civil penalties. I suggest you talk to your landlord and tell him you are moving out in a few days. It will take the landlord at least that long to have you evicted legally, and he may prefer just to cooperate.

I should emphasize one point. Even though you are moving out, you are still responsible for the rent you owe, including rent for the period remaining on your lease after you move, if the landlord cannot find another tenant. Your landlord has the right to sue to try to collect this money.

When can I move out?
"Read your lease."

Dear Mr. Alderman:

My company just transferred me to another city. When I gave my landlord a thirty-day notice, he told me my lease still had six months left. I told him I was transferred, and there was no way I could stay. He told me if he couldn't rent the apartment to someone else, I would have to pay the six months' rent. This does not seem fair. Don't I have the right to move if I am transferred?

This may not be what you want to hear, but unless your lease says so, you do not have the right to move out if you are transferred, and you may be responsible for rent for the remainder of the lease term. *A lease is a binding legal agreement, and you are controlled by its terms. As a general rule, you may only terminate a lease early for reasons permitted by the lease.* For example, if your lease says you may terminate by giving thirty days' notice if you are transferred, you are all right. But if the lease is silent as to early termination, you may not terminate early just because you have been transferred. If you do terminate early you will be responsible for all the damages the landlord incurs, including rent for the period he cannot lease the apartment to someone else.

If you do not have a lease agreement, the law will imply one for the period of time between rent payments. For example, if you pay rent once a month, the law will create what is called a month-to-month tenancy. This type of arrangement can be terminated by either the tenant or the landlord for any reason by giving one month's notice. A lease protects you by ensuring the landlord does not terminate the lease or raise the rent, but it also protects the landlord by obligating you for the entire period of the lease. *If you think you may have to terminate your lease early, make sure there is a clause permitting you to do so. Otherwise, you may end up owing rent on two apartments.*

I was sexually assaulted. Can I break my lease?
"Yes, if you follow the law."

Dear Mr. Alderman:

I have lived in my apartment complex for three months. Someone recently broke into my apartment and sexually assaulted me. Now I am so scared that I can't continue to live here. I want to move. The landlord told me I signed a lease and cannot get out early. What can I do? I cannot afford to pay for two apartments.

As a general rule, a tenant may not terminate a lease due to circumstances beyond the control of the landlord. In the case of sexual assault or domestic violence, however, there is an exception to this general rule. Under a change in the law effective January 2010, a tenant who is a victim of domestic violence or a sexual assault, or a parent or guardian of a victim of sexual assault, may terminate a lease and have no liability for future rent. To take advantage of this law, the assault must have occurred on the premises or at any dwelling on the premises within the preceding six months, and the tenant must provide specific documentation of the assault from a health or mental care services provider or a protective order. The tenant who complies with this law has no liability for future rent but may remain responsible for any delinquent rent or other sums owed prior to termination, depending on the language of the lease. The tenant will not owe past-due rent if the lease did not contain language informing the tenant of the right to terminate the lease in certain situations involving domestic violence, sexual assault, or abuse.

I suggest you speak again with the landlord and make sure he knows about this law. A landlord who does not let you terminate your lease could be liable for actual damages, attorney's fees, and a penalty of one month's rent and $500.

What if I don't get my security deposit back?
"There's a law."

Dear Mr. Alderman:
My apartment was a dump. The landlady never fixed it, and as soon as my lease was up, I moved. Now my landlady refuses to return my security deposit. I have called her and written many times, and she just won't respond. Don't Texas tenants have any rights?

Your landlady may not wrongfully keep your security deposit. If she does, you may be entitled to three times your deposit plus an additional $100 and any court costs or attorney's fees you may incur.

A law known as the **Texas Security Deposit Law,** which may not be waived or changed by your lease, requires a landlord to return a security deposit within thirty days after the tenant moves out or give the tenant written notice, with an itemized list of deductions, explaining why the deposit is being kept.

Remember, you are only entitled to have your deposit returned if you complied with your lease, left the apartment in good condition, and left a forwarding address. For example: If you move before your lease is up, you may not be entitled to the return of the deposit. A landlord can also deduct the costs of cleaning the apartment if you left it damaged. *No damages may be deducted, however, for ordinary wear and tear.*

If you were current in your rent and gave a forwarding address, and your landlady has not returned your deposit within thirty days or sent written notice to you why it was not returned, you should send her a certified letter, return receipt requested, to make certain she has your forwarding address. You should also tell her that should you not get your deposit back soon, you will take advantage of the security deposit law. You can use the following letter as a model. (Send this letter certified mail, return receipt requested, thirty days after you move out if your security deposit has not been returned.)

If you still do not receive your deposit or written notice, consider justice court. Under the law, a landlord who acts in bad faith in not returning your deposit may be liable for three times the deposit plus $100 in additional damages. *If the landlord does not return your money or give you a written explanation, the burden will be on the landlady to prove she did not act in bad faith.* The burden is also on the landlady to prove any deductions, such as money taken out for cleaning, were reasonable. If your landlady does not provide you with a written description of the deductions, she may forfeit the right to deduct from the security deposit or bring a suit against you for damages. If you had to sue to recover the deposit, your landlady would also be liable for your attorney's fees.

The Texas Security Deposit Law is one of the few landlord-tenant laws that really help the tenant. It is my experience that once the landlord knows you know about this law, he or she quickly returns your deposit. Just sending the form letter should be enough to retrieve your money.

Landlady's Name
Street Address
City, State, Zip

Dear Landlady:

On (<u>fill in date</u>) I moved out of the apartment I was renting from you. As our lease agreement provided, I gave proper notice, left a forwarding address, and left the apartment in good condition. I was also current in my rent.

When I moved in, I paid a security deposit of (<u>amount</u>). You have not returned my deposit, as the law requires. Under the law, a landlady must refund a security deposit or send written notice of the reason(s) it is being withheld within thirty days after the tenant vacates the property.

Unless I receive my security deposit from you within a reasonable time, I intend to go to justice court. I should tell you that if I do go to court, I may be entitled to three times the amount of my deposit plus $100.

Thank you for your expected cooperation in this matter. If you need to reach me, my present address is: (<u>street address</u>).

Sincerely,
(sign your name)

**I am a commercial tenant.
Does the security deposit law apply to me?
"There is a similar law that protects you."**

Dear Mr. Alderman:

I am a small business owner. After having several problems in my retail space, I decided to move locations at the end of my lease. It's been nearly three months and I have yet to receive my security deposit from my old landlord. I know there is a law protecting residential tenants, but I don't know if this applies to me. Am I protected?

Just as with residential leases, a similar law protects commercial tenants from having their security deposits wrongfully withheld by their landlords. The Texas Commercial Security Deposit Law requires that the landlord refund a security deposit no later than the sixtieth day after the date the tenant moves out and provides a forwarding address.

If a landlord has wrongfully withheld a commercial tenant's security deposit in bad faith, the tenant may be entitled to recover three times the portion of the deposit withheld, plus $100 and any attorney's fees. Even if the landlord has retained the security deposit to pay for damages, the landlord is still required by law to provide you with a written description and an itemized list of all deductions. On this same note, the landlord is not allowed to deduct for normal wear and tear.

If a landlord does not provide the tenant with a written description of the deductions, he may forfeit the right to deduct from the security deposit or bring a suit against the tenant for damage, and be liable for the tenant's attorney's fees.

If your landlord has not provided you with a list of deductions and you have already given him a forwarding address, my advice is to send a certified letter to him informing him that you know what the law is in Texas, and that you would like your security deposit back. As I have said so many times before, once a landlord knows you know your legal rights, he usually complies with the law.

What if my landlord won't fix my apartment?
"Keep paying rent."

Dear Mr. Alderman:
Nothing in my apartment works right. It seems every day something else breaks, and it always takes the landlord weeks to fix it. Even though the problems are small, it is still an inconvenience. Last week, for example, I had to use a wrench to turn the stove on and off. Right now six things are wrong, and it has been one week since I reported them. What I would like to do is just not pay my rent until everything is fixed. My landlord keeps saying he will fix it but never does. What do you recommend?

The first thing I should point out is, unless your lease says so, your landlord does not have a general obligation to repair the property. Texas law, however, requires a landlord to repair conditions that materially affect physical health or safety. This law is discussed in the next letter, and it doesn't seem to apply to your problem. Small inconveniences, such as problems with a door or a drawer in the kitchen, or the knobs on an appliance, probably are not the responsibility of the landlord unless he has agreed to make these repairs.

So what should you do? First, read your lease. See if the landlord has undertaken to repair your apartment. If he has, you should contact him in writing and request that he make the necessary repairs. If he still refuses, you can make them yourself and recover the costs from him in justice court. You cannot, however, deduct the amount from your rent unless the landlord agrees.

Even if the lease does not say anything about repairs, your landlord may still be responsible if he has otherwise agreed to make repairs. From what you say, the landlord has repaired the apartment before and seems to understand this is his obligation. Assuming you can show he has agreed to make repairs, then he would be responsible just as if it were in the lease.

The law generally does not impose an obligation on the landlord to repair your apartment, *and in most cases you must continue to pay rent regardless of whether your apartment needs repairs.* But there is an exception to this general rule. As the next letter shows, if the condition is serious enough, the law makes the landlord repair it and lets you move or deduct from your rent if he doesn't.

What can I do if the apartment is in such bad shape I can't live in it? "The warranty of habitability applies here."

Dear Mr. Alderman:
I need help! The roof in my apartment leaks, and the landlord won't fix it. The leak keeps getting worse, and now when it rains I have to go somewhere else to sleep. Is there any way I can force the landlord to fix this place? I don't want to move because moving is so expensive.

First of all, do not stop paying rent. Under the law, even if you have a claim against your landlord for not maintaining your apartment, you are not excused from paying rent until you take the necessary steps. *If you stop paying rent, your landlord could have you evicted.* Here is what you have to do to withhold rent or get damages.

Texas law requires that a landlord make a reasonable effort to repair or remedy any condition that materially affects the health or safety of an ordinary tenant once the tenant gives the landlord *written notice* of the problem. This law imposes an obligation on the landlord to make sure your apartment is "habitable." If the landlord does not comply with this law, you may be entitled to withhold rent and have the repairs made yourself, to get a rent reduction and a penalty of one month's rent plus $500, or to terminate the lease and move out.

A landlord is liable to a tenant under this law if:
(1) the tenant has given the landlord notice to repair or remedy a condition by giving that notice to the person to whom or to the place where the tenant's rent is normally paid;

(2) the condition materially affects the physical health or safety of an ordinary tenant;

(3) the tenant has given the landlord a subsequent written notice to repair or remedy the condition after a reasonable time to repair or remedy the condition following the notice given under subdivision (1) or the tenant has given the notice under subdivision (1) by sending that notice by certified mail, return receipt requested, by registered mail, or by another form of mail that allows tracking of delivery from the United States Postal Service or a private delivery service;

(4) the landlord has had a reasonable time to repair or remedy the condition after the landlord received the tenant's notice under subdivision (1) and, if applicable, the tenant's subsequent notice under subdivision (3);

(5) the landlord has not made a diligent effort to repair or remedy the condition after the landlord received the tenant's notice under subdivision (1) and, if applicable, the tenant's notice under subdivision (3); and

(6) the tenant was not delinquent in the payment of rent at the time any notice required by this subsection was given.

Although the law allows the tenant to make repairs and deduct from the rent, this remedy is available only in the following situations:

(A) The landlord has failed to remedy the backup or overflow of raw sewage inside the tenant's dwelling or the flooding from broken pipes or natural drainage inside the dwelling.

(B) The landlord has expressly or impliedly agreed in the lease to furnish potable water to the tenant's dwelling and the water service to the dwelling has totally ceased.

(C) The landlord has expressly or impliedly agreed in the lease to furnish heating or cooling equipment; the equipment is producing inadequate heat or cooled air; and the landlord has been notified in writing by the appropriate local housing, building, or health official or other official having jurisdiction that the lack of heat or cooling materially affects the health or safety of an ordinary tenant.

(D) The landlord has been notified in writing by the appropriate local housing, building, or health official or other official having jurisdiction that the condition materially affects the health or safety of an ordinary tenant.

Here is how the law works: First, you must give your landlord written notice of the problem with your apartment. I recommend you send this notice via certified mail, return receipt requested. Explain the problem, and tell the landlord it materially affects your health and safety. Next, under the law, the landlord has a reasonable time to repair the problem. What is reasonable depends on the facts of the situation, but a leaking roof is serious, and I would say a few days is a reasonable time. Under the law, there is a presumption that seven days is reasonable, but you may show why it should be shorter.

If your apartment is not repaired within a reasonable time, and you did not send your notice by certified mail, you must give the landlord a second notice that unless the condition is repaired you will terminate the lease, repair the condition yourself, or bring a civil action for damages. If you terminate the lease, you will be entitled to a refund of any rent paid for the period after you move out. If you want to stay there but want damages, you can sue by yourself in justice court for up to $10,000 in damages, or, if your situation meets one of the requirements set out above, you can have the repairs done yourself and withhold the cost from your rent.

In summary:

1. Texas law imposes an obligation on landlords to make a reasonable effort to repair any condition that materially affects the physical health or safety of a reasonable tenant.

2. You must give the landlord notice of the condition and a reasonable time to repair it. You should send this by certified mail.

3. If it is not repaired, and you did not send your notice by certified mail, you must give the landlord a second notice that if it is not repaired you will either terminate the lease, seek damages, or have the repairs made and the cost deducted from your rent.

4. If the landlord doesn't repair the condition, you have the right to move out, have the condition repaired, sue and force a rent reduction, or recover damages of a month's rent plus $500. If you have to hire an attorney, the landlord must pay your attorney's fees if you win.

Here are some form letters you can use to show your landlord you are serious and that you know the law. Send the following letter after your landlord hasn't made the repairs. Send it certified mail, return receipt requested. Be sure to keep a copy.

Landlord
Landlord Street
City, Texas 77000

Dear Landlord:

On (<u>fill in date</u>) I discovered that [state nature of problem, e.g., my roof was leaking].

This condition materially affects the health and safety of an ordinary tenant. I have in no way caused or contributed to this condition.

Please repair this condition immediately. If you need more information or would like to arrange for a repair person to enter my apartment, I can be reached during the day at (phone number) and in the evening at (phone).

Thank you for your expected cooperation in this matter.

Sincerely yours,
Your Name
SEND VIA CERTIFIED MAIL

After you send this letter, you must wait a reasonable period of time. If the letter was sent by certified mail, no additional notice is necessary.

If after a reasonable period of time repairs are not made and *your first letter was not certified*, send the following letter. Send it certified mail, return receipt requested. Be sure to keep a copy.

Landlord
Landlord Street
City, Texas 77000

Dear Landlord:

On (<u>fill in date</u>) I wrote you concerning (<u>state nature of problem</u>). I have attached a copy of that letter.

It has now been more than a reasonable time to make repairs, and you have not fixed it. As I told you in my earlier letter, this condition materially affects my physical health and safety.

Unless the repairs are made to my apartment immediately, I intend either to terminate the lease, seek damages for your failure to repair, or have the condition repaired and withhold the cost from my rent. I should advise you that, under the law, I may be entitled to a refund of any rent already paid if I terminate, or a penalty of one month's rent plus $500 and court costs and attorney's fees if I seek damages.

I hope it will not be necessary for me to take any further action. Thank you for your expected cooperation.

Sincerely yours,
Your Name

Can we move out early?
"Not without paying rent."

Dear Mr. Alderman:

We left our apartment a half-month early. We did not pay rent for the last half of the month because the pool was never usable and we didn't live there. Now the owner is suing us for the rent and for cleaning. How can we owe rent for the time when we didn't live there and when things didn't work?

You owe rent because you signed a lease. Under the terms of the lease you were obligated to pay rent until the lease was terminated. It doesn't matter if you moved out early.

The fact that the pool didn't work probably did not give you the right to move out and terminate the lease. You may have been able to claim damages against the landlord for not providing services as promised. In my opinion, however, the defective pool is not a sufficient basis to terminate the lease early and end your obligation to pay rent.

You may want to assert a counterclaim against your landlord, however, for the difference of what the apartment was worth with the pool and what it was worth without it. That difference is how much you lost by being unable to use it.

I can't live in my apartment. Do I still have to pay rent?
"Yes."

Dear Mr. Alderman:
I rented an apartment with a roommate. We both signed the lease. Recently we got into a fight. I am afraid to go back to the apartment. I have even filed criminal charges against him. Now the landlord tells me I am still responsible for the payment of rent through the lease term if my roommate does not pay. Is this correct? Why should I pay rent when I can't live there?

The reason is that the problem is between you and your roommate, not the landlord. Ask yourself why the landlord should risk losing money because you and your roommate had a fight. The bottom line is that you signed the lease and the terms of the lease control. If the lease does not allow you to terminate under such circumstances, you remain responsible for the rent. The only exception to this rule is when there is domestic violence or a sexual assault.

As a practical matter, however, you may not owe rent for that long. First, you have as much right as your roommate to live there. You should try to discuss this matter with your roommate and see if either he will agree to move out or he will agree to pay the rent in full. If he moves out, you will owe the rent; however, you will also have use of the apartment. If your roommate pays in full you will owe nothing. If he does not pay, the landlord will probably evict him. You will then owe rent only until the apartment is rented to someone else.

Finally, your landlord may be willing to help you resolve this matter. Your landlord may be willing to talk to your roommate to see what can be worked out.

My apartment promised security, and there is none.
"Landlord may be responsible if you are injured."

Dear Mr. Alderman:
I rented a new apartment. I chose one based on the agent's assurance that there was good security. In fact, there is none. All the complex has is a guard who never leaves his house at the entrance to the complex. I am concerned for my safety and want to know my rights.

First, I should point out that landlords have no obligation to provide additional security. Basically, all the law requires is locks on doors and windows, peepholes in the door, lights in common areas, and fences and latches at pools.

A landlord may, however, be required to provide additional security in two instances. First, a landlord is responsible if he acts negligently. Negligence generally means not acting as a reasonable person would. For example, suppose the landlord knows about a security problem, such as strangers walking around the complex, and takes no steps to either eliminate it or report it to the police. The landlord could be found to have acted negligently if he did not do what a reasonable person would have. If a reasonable person in the same position would have investigated, hired security, or reported it to the police, the landlord's failure to act would be negligence.

The landlord may also be responsible under the Deceptive Trade Practices Act if he made any misrepresentations about security. This law, discussed in Chapter 10, is a powerful consumer protection law that also applies to renting apartments.

As far as I am concerned, if the agent told you there was good security, and there is none, the agent and the landlord have violated the Deceptive Trade Practices Act. This law would allow you to recover economic damages if you were injured or your apartment was robbed as a result of the failure to provide the promised security, and it may also provide you with a basis to terminate your lease.

Your best bet may be to talk with the landlord and let him know you know about this law and expect the security you were promised. Hopefully you can negotiate a settlement you are happy with. You may not get security, but you may get him to let you move out without breaching your lease.

Am I entitled to a peephole I can use?
"Yes."

Dear Mr. Alderman:
The peephole in my apartment door is so high I can't see out of it. I am 5' 4" tall. Am I entitled to have the landlord lower it?

The law requires that a landlord install a door viewer, or peephole, at the tenant's request. The door viewer "must allow a person inside the dwelling to view a person outside the door." In my opinion, this means that it be of "reasonable" height, permitting the ordinary person to see out of it. I believe 5' 4" is an average height for a woman. I suggest you ask the landlord to lower it.

My landlord lied to me. What can I do?
"The Texas Deceptive Trade Practices Act applies."

Dear Mr. Alderman:
I just moved into a new apartment. When I looked at the model, the rental agent told me that when new tenants move in, the apartment is painted, and the rugs are shampooed. I was scheduled to move in on Saturday and went to look at the unit on Wednesday. It had not even been cleaned, let alone painted. The agent again told me not to worry, that it would be painted by the time I moved in on Saturday. On Saturday, I arrived with my furniture, and the unit was clean but not painted. Also, the rugs were not shampooed. The owner had changed his mind and wasn't going to paint anymore. What are my rights?

Any time someone leases anything, including an apartment, the Texas Deceptive Trade Practices Act applies. Under this law (discussed in Chapter 10), it is unlawful to misrepresent the qualities or characteristics of something. For example, telling a tenant an apartment will be painted when it will not be is a misrepresentation. As far as I am concerned, the landlord has violated the Deceptive Trade Practices Act by not providing an apartment as represented. I should also point out that because the agent is the authorized employee of the owner, the owner is liable for the agent's representations.

I suggest you reread Chapter 10 and then send proper notice to the landlord demanding that your unit be painted and the rugs shampooed as promised, or that you be reasonably compensated. A fair amount would be how much you would have to pay someone else to perform these services. If the landlord does not comply and you have to go to court to collect, the law entitles you to up to three times your damages plus any court costs and attorney's fees involved. As a practical matter, it is unlikely you will end up in court. Usually, these problems are resolved once the other side knows you know your rights.

Can I sublease?
"Not without consent."

Dear Mr. Alderman:
I have a simple question to ask: Do I have the right to sublease my apartment? I have seven months left on my lease, and I am getting married. What I would like to do is sublease to a friend for the remainder of my lease term.

You may not like this answer, but the law is clear: *You may not sublease unless your lease expressly gives you this right or the landlord agrees.* Under the law, a tenant does not have the right to sublease. This right can only be given to you by your landlord. I suggest you read your lease carefully to see what it says about subleasing. If it is silent, then you do not have the right to sublease. Even if your lease does not give you the right to sublease, your landlord may still agree to it. You should talk to him and try to get him to agree. You also should remember that even if he does agree, you will be responsible for the rent if your subtenant doesn't pay.

Can my landlord come into my apartment and take my property if I don't pay rent? "Maybe."

Dear Mr. Alderman:
I admit it; I should pay my rent, and it is my own fault I was late, but does my landlord have the right to come in and take my TV and stereo when I am late? I came home last night, and there was a note telling me as soon as I paid I could have the property back. I plan on paying the rent tomorrow, but I want to know if what my landlord did was legal.

The answer is that it is legal if all the steps of the law have been followed. What your landlord is doing is asserting what is called a "landlord's lien." This allows the landlord to peacefully enter your apartment and take your property until you pay the rent. If you do not pay, he has the right to sell the property. But to assert this lien certain requirements must be met.

First, the right to assert this lien must be underlined or printed in conspicuous bold print in your lease. Read your lease carefully. If the lien does not appear, the landlord has no right to take your property, and doing so would, in effect, be theft—entitling you to substantial damages. Second, a landlord may only take certain property under this lien. Here is a list of what the law says the landlord may not take:

1. wearing apparel;
2. tools, apparatus, and books of a trade or profession;
3. schoolbooks;
4. a family library;
5. family portraits and pictures;
6. one couch, two living room chairs, and a dining table and chairs;
7. beds and bedding;
8. kitchen furniture and utensils;

9. food and foodstuffs;
10. medicine and medical supplies;
11. one automobile and one truck;
12. agricultural implements;
13. children's toys not commonly used by adults;
14. goods the landlord or the landlord's agent knows are owned by a person other than the tenant or an occupant of the residence; and
15. goods the landlord or the landlord's agent knows are subject to a recorded chattel mortgage or financing agreement.

If the landlord has taken any of this property he has violated the law. Finally, the landlord must leave you a note telling you what he took and what you need to do to get it back (the note must also tell you how much you owe in back rent).

The bottom line is, although a landlord may have the right to take your property pursuant to a landlord's lien, the requirements of the law are often not met, and the landlord is acting wrongfully. If you feel your landlord has acted wrongfully, speak with him and try to get your property back. If you can't, you should consider justice court or an attorney. Under the law, a landlord who violates the provision of the lien law is responsible for all the tenant's damages and one month's rent or $500—whichever is greater—plus attorney's fees.

My landlord has locked me out. Help!
"There is a law."

Dear Mr. Alderman:
I lost my job and got behind in my rent. Last night when I got home, my landlord had changed the locks on the door of my apartment and told me to get off the property until I come up with some money. I don't have any way to get the money I owe him, and I just want to get my things and leave. How long can he hold all my property?

As discussed in the prior letter, unless a landlord has a landlord's lien and acts according to state law he can't hold your property at all. *In fact, it is illegal for a landlord to just lock you out, no matter how much money you owe.* Under the law a landlord has the right to change the locks on your doors if your written lease allows this, but he must give you notice he intends to lock you out five days before changing the locks. The notice must also tell you that you have the right to receive a new key to come and go, twenty-four hours a day. Once the lock is changed, he must give you notice of where a key may be obtained, and give you a new key whenever you want. He also can't stop you from removing your property and moving out. As I said before, only if he has a landlord's lien can he hold your property.

I suggest you speak with your landlord and make it clear you know the law, and you expect to be immediately given a key to your apartment. If your landlord does not, he could be ordered to allow you to reenter the apartment and could be liable for your actual damages, plus a civil penalty of $1,000 and one month's rent.

I don't have a lease. Can I be locked out for not paying rent?
"Without a written lease, a landlord cannot lock you out."

Dear Mr. Alderman:
I am a month-to-month tenant. I do not have a formal written lease with my landlord. I went out of town for a few days near the end of last month. I forgot to pay this month's rent before I left. When I got back I found that my landlord had changed the lock on the door of my apartment. I paid him the rent and got the new key but I just know this can't be legal. How much will I be able to recover from the landlord for this conduct?

As I explain in the prior letter, it is legal for a landlord to lock you out if the landlord follows the proper procedures and makes a key available. Under the law, if you fall behind with rent your landlord may change the lock to your apartment's door only if your written lease contains a provision giving him that right. In your case, you do not have a written lease and the landlord, therefore, does not have the right to deny you access to your apartment, even if you do not pay rent. If the landlord prevents you from entering your apartment, he may be liable to you for actual damages, one month's rent plus a $1,000 penalty, and attorney's fees.

Do I have to live in an apartment complex with children?
"Yes, unless the complex is for persons over age fifty-five."

Dear Mr. Alderman:
I live in a nice apartment complex just outside town. I have lived here for five years, and it has always been for adults only. Recently, several families with children moved into the complex, and the whole mood has changed. The complex is no longer the quiet place it once was. I am awakened on weekend mornings by the sound of motorized toys in the courtyard.

I complained to the manager and he said there is nothing he can do; the law requires that he rent to people with children. Is this the law? Don't I have the right to live where I want?

Under amendments to the federal **Fair Housing Act,** it is illegal to discriminate against families with children with respect to housing. This means a landlord must rent to anyone, regardless of whether he or she is married, single, or has children. The only restrictions that may be placed are those that apply to all tenants. For example, the number of occupants per unit may be limited. It can't be limited, however, to adults.

There is a major exception to this law, however, that may help you. If a complex has 80 percent or more units occupied by at least one person over age fifty-five, it is not required to take children. If you are over fifty-five it may be a good idea to look for one of the "seniors only" complexes. Seniors only is now another way of saying no children.

One last point. Just because apartments cannot discriminate against children or families with children does not mean you have to have your peace and quiet disturbed. If the children are getting up very early and making a lot of noise, the manager has the right to insist they be kept quiet. I suggest you speak with the manager and ask him to take steps to ensure the children comply with the same rules and regulations as everyone else.

I was refused an apartment because the landlord said my wheelchair would ruin the carpet. Is this legal? "No. You can't discriminate against the handicapped."

Dear Mr. Alderman:
I am disabled, confined to a wheelchair. I just found the perfect apartment and when I went to sign the lease was told by the landlord that I would have to look elsewhere. He told me, "Your wheelchair will ruin my carpet." Is this legal? I thought new laws protected the disabled. I realize my chair may do some damage, but I am willing to pay for it.

You are correct about the law. The Fair Housing Act prohibits discrimination against a disabled person. "Disabled" is defined to include a physical or mental impairment that substantially limits one or more of such a person's major life activities; a person who has a record of such impairment; or a person who is regarded as having such an impairment.

Based on what you say, the landlord has acted illegally. Under the law he could be subject to civil penalties of up to $10,000. You can enforce this law privately, with the assistance of an attorney, or you can contact the

Department of Housing and Urban Development, www.hud.gov. At a minimum, I would contact the landlord and let him know what the law is. Hopefully he was just uninformed and will now take steps to comply with the law.

Can my landlord ask for more security deposit?
"If it is a new lease, yes."

Dear Mr. Alderman:
I live in an apartment and have a six-month lease. This is the third such lease I have signed. Every time a lease is up, my landlord asks me to sign a new one. Each time I sign a new lease, however, my landlord raises my security deposit by $20. Is this legal?

If you have a lease, the terms of your agreement with your landlord are governed by the lease and cannot be changed without your consent. In other words, during the lease period your security deposit could not be raised. When your lease expires, however, both you and the landlord are free to either renew the lease on its present terms, terminate the agreement, or write a new agreement.

For example, at the end of your lease, the rent could be raised or lowered, or the six-month term could be increased or decreased. Similarly, if your landlord wants additional security, he may ask for it. Of course, if you don't want to pay it you have the right to insist there not be additional security, and if the landlord refuses to give notice and move. The amount of the security deposit is a matter to be negotiated by you and the landlord.

Is there a limit on how much my landlord may raise my rent?
"Unless your lease says otherwise, there is no limit on
how much rent a landlord may charge."

Dear Mr. Alderman:
My lease is up next month. I would like to renew the lease for another year. My landlord wants to raise my rent more than 25 percent. Is this legal? Aren't there some limits on how much I may be charged?

Basically, the only limits on the amount of rent a landlord may charge are those imposed by the marketplace. In other words, when there is a scarcity of apartments, landlords may charge high rents, and tenants do not have much choice. On the other hand, when an abundance of units are available, landlords usually do not raise rents because tenants will move to other apartments. I suggest you try to negotiate a lower rent. If you cannot, your choices are to agree to what the landlord has proposed or move to another apartment.

Can I be forced to pay a high re-letting fee?
"Yes, if your lease says so."

Dear Mr. Alderman:
I broke my lease. The lease says I must forfeit my security deposit
and pay a re-letting fee equal to 80 percent of one month's rent. This
seems very high. Is there a limit on how much a landlord may charge
as a re-letting fee?

As far as I am concerned, the re-letting fee is a matter of contract between
you and your landlord. If you signed the lease agreeing to pay the fee, it
is enforceable. The fee would be invalid only if it was so high as to be
"unconscionable." In my opinion, less than one month's rent is not an
unreasonably high amount.

Is there a limit on how much a landlord may ask for a pet deposit?
"You may agree to any amount."

Dear Mr. Alderman:
Is there any legal limit on how much a landlord may ask for as a pet
deposit?

No, this is a matter of agreement between you and the landlord. A landlord
has no obligation to allow a tenant to have pets. The landlord may require a
pet deposit in any amount. If you do not want to pay it, rent somewhere else.

My landlord turned off my electricity. What can I do?
"Landlords may not disconnect utilities."

Dear Mr. Alderman:
My landlord is supposed to provide electricity for my apartment.
Recently he stopped paying the bill, and the power company cut it
off. What are my legal rights?

Texas law provides that a landlord may not disconnect electric service, even
if a tenant becomes delinquent with rent. Prior law allowed a landlord to
disconnect electrical service to a dwelling in delinquent rent situations if the
landlord was responsible for paying the electric bill to the utility company
and gave proper notice to the tenant before disconnecting the service.

Under the current law, a landlord may interrupt utility service only for
bona fide repairs, construction, or an emergency. If a landlord wrongfully
interrupts service, the tenant may terminate the lease or remain in the

apartment and collect an amount equal to the tenant's damages, one month's rent, or $500—whichever is greater. The law also allows the tenant to file a claim in justice court, requesting that the justice of the peace issue an order requiring that service be restored immediately. If it is necessary to hire an attorney, the tenant may also recover reasonable attorney's fees.

Can my landlord come into my apartment?
"It depends on your lease."

Dear Mr. Alderman:
My landlord came into my apartment to exterminate without giving me prior notice. When he came in, my dog escaped. I spoke with the landlord and told him I didn't want him in my apartment when I was not home and that I was concerned that the next time my dog got out I wouldn't be able to find her. Well, it happened again, and now my dog is lost. Do I have any rights?

Your landlord's right to enter your apartment depends on the lease you signed. As a first step, I suggest you carefully read your lease. If your lease doesn't say otherwise, then the landlord probably does not have the right to enter your apartment whenever he wants. He probably may enter, however, at reasonable times to check the condition of the property, or to perform necessary services such as extermination. A landlord who wrongfully enters an apartment should be responsible for any damage that results.

I should point out, however, that even if your landlord has the right to enter your apartment, he must act "reasonably." In my opinion, letting your dog escape after you warned him of this danger would be negligence. In this case, the landlord would be responsible for the value of the dog and any other damages you suffered as a result of the loss.

What are a landlord's rights if a tenant didn't
pay the last month's rent?
"You may be entitled to three times the rent."

Dear Mr. Alderman:
I am a landlord. Is there anything I can do to make my tenants pay the last month's rent? They tell me to just keep the security deposit, but then I have nothing to cover damages.

As I discuss in the beginning of this chapter, a landlord who does not properly return a tenant's security deposit may be liable to the tenant for three times the deposit plus $100.

Conversely, under the law a tenant who tells a landlord to use the security deposit for the last month's rent is liable to the landlord for three times the rent withheld plus attorney's fees. My guess is if you let your tenants know about the law, they will pay the last month's rent.

How do I get a tenant to leave?
"File eviction papers."

Dear Mr. Alderman:
I rent out a house. The tenants, who are on a month-to-month tenancy, have not paid rent in two months. They will not pay rent or move out. How do I get them to move?

As I discussed above, a landlord cannot just lock tenants out or personally evict them. To evict the tenants, you must give them one more written notice to move. Let them know if they do not leave, you will take steps to have them evicted. To evict them, go to the local justice of the peace and file a Forcible Entry and Detainer, commonly called an eviction suit. This is the device you use to evict them. The clerk of the court will probably be able to help you fill out any necessary forms.

How may a landlord compute the charges for water?
"There are a number of ways."

Dear Mr. Alderman:
One year ago I rented an apartment. All utilities were included in my rent. Now that my lease is up my landlord says I am going to have to start paying for water. He says that the amount will be based on the number of people living in my apartment. Is this legal? I am out of town a lot and it doesn't seem fair. Doesn't the landlord have to charge me based on my actual use?

As far as the law is concerned, a landlord has several options when it comes to charging for water. First, the landlord may do what was done in your first lease and include water in the rent and not bill separately. Second, the landlord may not include water at all and have the tenant make arrangements with the water company. Finally, the landlord may take the approach your landlord is now taking and allocate the water bill among all the tenants. If the landlord does this, the law controls how the amount may be divided. Also, whatever method the landlord chooses must be spelled out in your lease.

The fairest way for a landlord to allocate water is to submeter each unit and charge the tenant only for the water that tenant uses. The law, however, does not require submetering and allows the landlord to allocate the water bill in other ways. The Texas Commission on Environmental Quality has rules about how the amount may be allocated.

Under these rules, the landlord may not charge tenants for any amount not attributable to tenants' use. For example, the landlord may not charge tenants for general fees charged by the utility company, or for water for common areas, such as pools or landscaping. After making the necessary deductions, the landlord may allocate the bill among all the tenants under a number of systems. First, he may divide the bill by the total number of occupants and then charge each occupant his or her pro rata share. The landlord may also modify this formula to reflect the fact that some units have more than one occupant, or use a formula based on the number of occupants per bedroom. The law also allows the landlord to establish a formula based on a combination of the square footage of the unit and the number of occupants.

The bottom line is that the landlord has a number of options regarding how a tenant is billed for water; however, which method is chosen must be disclosed in the lease and cannot be changed during the lease without the tenant's consent.

The house I rent was foreclosed. Do I have to move?
"Yes, but probably not for 90 days."

Dear Mr. Alderman:
For the past few years I have been renting a house from an individual. A month after I signed a new lease, the bank foreclosed on the house. The buyer at the foreclosure sale told me he wants to move in and I must get out. He gave me written notice to move out in a month. What happens if I can't find another place?

When there is a foreclosure of rental property, the new owner is generally not subject to the lease. In this case, however, you have some additional time. Under a federal law called the "Protecting Tenants at Foreclosure Act," a person who buys foreclosed residential property occupied by a tenant of the previous owner must honor the lease term. If the lease has less than ninety days left, the new owner must give you at least ninety days' prior notice to move. I suggest you let the new buyer know about this law. In many cases the new buyer may offer you "cash for keys" and compensate you if you agree to move earlier than required.

Can I pay my rent in cash?
"Yes, and the landlord must give you a receipt."

Dear Mr. Alderman:
I do not have a lease with my landlord. I pay rent every month. I usually pay with cash, but I am concerned because my landlord does not give me a receipt. If a dispute arises, how can I prove I paid my rent?

Under the Texas Property Code, unless you have a written lease that says otherwise, the landlord must accept rent payments in cash or by check or money order. If the landlord receives a cash payment, he must provide the tenant with a written receipt, and enter the payment on a record book maintained by the landlord. I suggest you ask for a receipt the next time you pay and let the landlord know the law requires you receive one.

Can my landlord tow my car for being parked illegally?
"Only if you have signed an agreement or lease with the policies."

Dear Mr. Alderman:
I just moved into a new apartment building. After about a week I came home and found my car had been towed. The landlord told me that because my car was not in running condition it had been towed. I knew the battery was dead but didn't have a chance to jump-start it. Is this legal? I had no idea there was a rule about nonrunning cars.

A landlord has the right to establish rules and regulations about parking, but you must be given notice of these rules before you sign your lease. The law provides that the landlord must give you a copy of the rules or policies, and that you must either sign a copy of the rules, or they must be included in the signed lease agreement. If they are included in the lease, they must be marked "Parking," and be capitalized, underlined, or printed in bold print. A landlord who tows a tenant's car without proper notice is liable for the cost of towing and storage plus an additional penalty of $100. The landlord could also be liable for any damage the towing company caused to your car.

I suggest you let the landlord know you know the law and that you expect him to reimburse you for the costs of the tow. If he does not, consider justice court.

Is my oral agreement with my roommate enforceable?
"Yes, most agreements do not have to be in writing."

Dear Mr. Alderman:
My ex-roommate agreed to pay half the utility bills, even though the
bill was in my name. She paid every month except the last two. I do
not have anything in writing. Can I still go to justice court?

You can go to justice court and there is no need for a written agreement.
Most agreements, including the one between you and your ex-roommate,
do not need to be in writing to be legally enforceable. If you can prove she
promised to pay half the bill, you can recover in justice court. If you have
proof that she paid for previous months that is a pretty good indication you
had an agreement.

I should point out that before going to justice court you should try to
resolve the matter with your roommate yourself. You may want to send a
certified letter explaining your position, suggesting that settling things will
be much less expensive and time-consuming than justice court.

Is a cosigner responsible if the lease is renewed?
"A cosigner is liable only for the original term of the
lease unless agreed otherwise."

Dear Mr. Alderman:
I cosigned a lease for my son when he got his first job. I assumed it
was for one year. Now, three years later, the landlord has told me that
my son did not pay his rent and I owe it. Is this right? How long am
I bound for?

As you probably know, a cosigner or guarantor has the same responsibility as the person for whom he cosigns. In many cases, a lease gives the
tenant the right to renew the lease, and until recently, the cosigner would
be bound for any renewal. Under current law, however, the law limits a
guarantor's liability to only the original lease term, unless a written agreement is made that the cosigner guarantees any renewal of the lease and the
amount of the guarantor's liability does not increase.

Be sure to read any lease carefully before you cosign. To protect against
future liability, cross out or delete any provision that obligates you to
future renewals of the lease.

How do I get my deposit back after being rejected for an apartment?
"You may be entitled to three times the deposit if you have to sue."

Dear Mr. Alderman:
I filled out an application to lease an apartment. I paid a $300 deposit
and was told it would be refunded if I was not accepted. The landlord
said he would do a credit check and get back to me in a few days.
After two weeks, I called to see what was going on. The landlord told
me he was rejecting my application and would send me my deposit. A
month later I still have not received my money. What can I do?

Under the law, a landlord who does not accept an applicant within seven
days is deemed to have rejected the application. Once a landlord rejects an
applicant, he must notify the applicant and return the deposit to the address
the applicant provided him. In your case, my opinion is that the landlord
has violated the law by delaying too long in notifying you that your application was rejected, and failing to return your deposit.

The law provides that a landlord who in bad faith refuses to return a
deposit is liable for three times the deposit, plus $100 and any reasonable
attorney's fees. In my opinion, the landlord's conduct is in "bad faith"
because you gave him two opportunities to comply with the law, and he
still failed to do so.

I suggest you send the landlord a certified letter, telling him you know
the law and that you expect he will promptly return your deposit. My guess
is you will get a check by return mail. If you do not, consider justice court.

Can I sue to force the landlord to make repairs?
"Yes, and the suit may be brought in justice court."

Dear Mr. Alderman:
I gave my landlord proper notice, by certified mail, to repair the air
conditioning in my apartment, and after more than a week he still
refuses to fix it. It is sometimes over 90 degrees in my apartment. Can
I sue him to force him to make the necessary repairs?

As discussed above, if a landlord does not repair a condition dangerous to
health or safety after receiving proper notice from the tenant, the tenant
may terminate the lease, have the condition repaired and sue for the costs,
and sue for a penalty of one month's rent plus $500. In some extreme
cases, the tenant may make repairs and deduct from the rent the cost of
the repairs.

Until recently, a tenant could sue a landlord in justice court only for monetary damages. You could not, however, sue to "force" him to make repairs. Effective January 1, 2010, however, the tenant now has the right to sue in justice court for an order directing the landlord to make the necessary repairs, or reducing the rent in proportion to the reduced value of the property resulting from the condition until the condition is repaired. My guess is letting the landlord know you will exercise this option will get the situation remedied.

I don't know where my landlord lives. How do I sue? "You serve the agent for service."

Dear Mr. Alderman:
I want to sue my landlord. I know his name because he signed the lease but have no other information. The clerk told me I need an address to serve him with the petition if I want to sue. How do I find out where he lives?

You are correct that to sue someone you need to provide the court with a location where the party can be served with notice of the lawsuit. You do not, however, need his address. Under the law, you may serve what is called the "agent for service." If you were given written notice of the name and address of the management company that manages the property, the management company is the sole agent for service and may be served. If you were not given such notice, you may serve the landlord, if he provided you in writing his name and business street address, or you may serve the management company, the on-premises manager, or rent collector.

CHAPTER 13

Lawyers

This book was written to provide some basic legal information that can help you resolve everyday disputes. As I said in the introduction, once someone knows you know your legal rights, you usually can settle the matter in an amicable manner.

Unfortunately, however, some disputes cannot be resolved by the involved parties, and justice court cannot be used. When you find yourself in this position, you have no choice but to hire a lawyer to assist you. Many letters I receive ask questions about how to find a good attorney and what to do if you have a problem with the one you hire. Here are some answers to the more common concerns.

How do I find a lawyer?
"There are lots of ways."

Dear Mr. Alderman:
I never thought I would have any legal problems, but now I need a lawyer. How do I find one I can trust?

As with any professional, there is no "best way" to find a lawyer. I suggest you take the same approach you would if you were looking for a doctor, architect, or accountant.

The best way to start may be to talk with friends and family. See if anyone has used an attorney he or she liked. If so, this person may be able to help or refer you to someone else. You also should look at advertisements for lawyers. Treat these ads like those for any other service. Look for an advertisement that gives you useful information in a way you think is consistent with a good, trustworthy lawyer.

You also should consider calling a referral service operated by the State Bar of Texas or your local bar association. Look online or in the phone book to see if your city or county bar association operates a referral service. The State Bar of Texas operates a statewide referral service, www .texasbar.com or (800) 252-9690.

Once you get some names of attorneys, speak with several before you make a decision. Remember, you may have to work with this person for a long time. Be sure to find someone you can easily communicate with and with whom you feel comfortable.

What does it mean to be board certified?
"The lawyer demonstrated special competence."

Dear Mr. Alderman:
I noticed that some attorneys say they are "certified by the Texas Board of Legal Specialization," but most do not. What does this mean? Why would anyone hire an attorney who was not certified?

Any lawyer who has passed the Texas State Bar Exam is licensed to practice law and may practice in any area. For example, I am a member of the State Bar. That means I may represent a person with any sort of legal problem.

Under Texas law, however, any attorney who specializes in a particular area of law may choose to take an exam and become "board certified." This is a special certification an attorney may seek in any one of nearly twenty areas of law. If the lawyer passes the exam and complies with other requirements, he or she will be certified in that specialty. Within the Texas legal community, board certification means an attorney has substantial, relevant experience in a select field of law, as well as demonstrated and tested special competence in that area of law. The process is voluntary and can only take place after an attorney has been in practice for five years, with a minimum of three years' experience in the specialty area.

Being board certified means the attorney has chosen to demonstrate excellence in an area of law. But most attorneys do not choose to put in the additional time and effort to obtain certification, even though they may have the expertise. In fact, fewer than 10 percent of the attorneys in Texas are board certified. Many very good attorneys have chosen not to become certified. For example, I am not board certified.

My advice is to consider the fact that someone is board-certified as a plus when you evaluate an attorney. I would not, however, consider it a negative factor if an attorney were not certified. Evaluate any lawyer you talk with based on his or her qualifications and how well he or she relates to you. Board certification is just one of many factors to consider.

I have a problem with my lawyer. What can I do?
"The State Bar wants to know."

Dear Mr. Alderman:
I hired an attorney to help me with a problem. He took my money,
and I can't get him to even talk to me. I am afraid he has spent the
money, and I am out of luck. What can I do?

The answer to your question will depend on whether your lawyer engaged in professional misconduct or malpractice. The most important difference is that the Texas Bar Association regulates professional misconduct that violates the rules of professional conduct established by the State Bar of Texas. On the other hand, the bar does not regulate "malpractice," defined as not acting as a reasonably competent attorney would when handling a matter, and you would have to bring a private lawsuit.

Essentially, the rules of professional conduct require that an attorney act ethically. This means handling the client's case in a professional manner, keeping funds separate, and communicating with the client before making any important decisions. In your case, it sounds like your attorney has violated this code of ethics.

Fortunately, the State Bar of Texas closely regulates the lawyers it licenses. If a lawyer violates any rules of professional conduct, the bar association may begin an investigation into the alleged violation and may discipline the lawyer. The punishments range from a simple reprimand to termination of the license to practice law.

How do you decide whether your claim involves professional misconduct? You don't have to. When you file a complaint with the bar association, one of the first things it does is determine if the complaint has been properly filed.

I suggest you contact the bar association and get a copy of its free booklet about attorney complaints. You can obtain information by calling (800) 932-1900 or visiting "For the Public" at www.texasbar.com. The bar association also has a video on its website explaining how to file a grievance.

CHAPTER 14

Mail-Order, Telephone & Online Sales

Mail-order, telephone, and online sales are big business. Today you can buy everything from food and clothing to furniture and a car from catalogs and online. You can shop in the privacy of your home or office, with no high-pressure salesperson looking over your shoulder. For the busy worker, catalogs and websites have replaced department stores and shopping malls.

But shopping at home has one big drawback: You don't see what you are buying, you can't try it on, and you don't receive it as soon as you pick it out. When you go into a store and buy a pair of jogging shoes, you pick out the style and size you want, try them on, pay for them, and off you go. You are on your way home to use them.

But when you buy the same pair of jogging shoes by phone, through the mail, or online, you must first pay and then wait until they arrive. And two bad things can happen: (1) They may never arrive; or (2) They may not be what you thought they were. These are the risks inherent in shopping by mail or online; you must pay first and then wait for the goods—goods you cannot examine until they arrive, if they arrive at all. However, the next few letters will show you shopping by mail, phone, or Internet does not have to be risky. Laws ensure you can enjoy the convenience of shopping at your home or office, without the risk of never receiving what you paid for.

What can I do if the goods never arrive?
"Next time, use a credit card."

Dear Mr. Alderman:
I saw an ad in a magazine for a Wizard Roach Remover, guaranteed to keep roaches out of my house for two months. I sent the company $19.95 plus postage more than five weeks ago. I still have not received my roach killer, and the company won't answer my letters.

216

It did cash my check, though. What can I do to get my money back? The company is in Iowa.

I have some good news and some bad. The bad news is you may be out of luck unless the company voluntarily sends your money back. The good news is you can avoid this problem in the future by taking advantage of a federal law, the Fair Credit Billing Act.

First, as to what you can do now. As the next letter discusses more fully, under the law a mail-order company can only wait thirty days to send your goods. In your case it has already delayed beyond this period. The problem is that to enforce any of your rights against the company you will have to sue, and even if you used justice court in Texas, you probably could not collect unless the company has assets or an office here. In other words, you are probably out of luck because it will cost you more to enforce your rights in Iowa than you lost in the deal. You may take steps to prevent this from happening to others by contacting the Better Business Bureau, the Federal Trade Commission, and the attorney general's office and telling them of your problem.

So what can you do to avoid this in the future? Use a credit card whenever you order by mail. Under the Fair Credit Billing Act, the credit card company cannot collect for items you ordered but never received. If you had paid for your goods with a credit card, you could simply contact the credit card company, dispute the charge, and tell the company there is a billing error and that you are not going to pay your bill. Here is what you should do to protect yourself.

When the goods don't arrive:

When many consumers find mistakes on their bills, such as charges for goods they never purchased or that never arrived, they pick up the phone and call the company to correct the problem. You can do this if you wish, but phoning does not trigger the legal safeguards provided under the law. To be protected under the Fair Credit Billing Act, you must send a separate written billing error notice to the credit card company. Your notice must reach the company within sixty days after the first bill containing the error was mailed to you. Send the notice to the address provided on the bill for billing error notices (and not, for example, directly to the store, unless the bill says that's where it should be sent). In your letter, you must include the following information: your name and account number; a statement that you believe the bill contains a billing error; the dollar amount involved; and why you believe there is a mistake—the goods never arrived. It's a good idea to send it by certified mail, return receipt requested. That way you'll have proof of the dates of mailing and receipt. If you wish, send photocopies of sales slips or other documents, but keep the originals for your records.

What must the credit card company do?

Your letter claiming a billing error must be acknowledged by the credit card company within thirty days after it is received, unless the problem is resolved within that period. In any case, within two billing cycles (but not more than ninety days), the creditor must conduct a reasonable investigation and either correct the mistake or explain why the bill is believed to be correct.

What happens while the credit card company investigates?

You may withhold payment of the amount in dispute, including the affected portions of minimum payments and finance charges, until the dispute is resolved. You are still required to pay any part of the bill not disputed, including finance and other charges on undisputed amounts.

While the Fair Credit Billing Act dispute settlement procedure is going on, the creditor may not take any legal or other action to collect the amount in dispute. Your account may not be closed or restricted in any way, except the disputed amount may be applied against your credit limit.

What happens once the credit card company determines you never received the goods?

If your bill is found to contain a billing error (the goods didn't arrive), the creditor must write you explaining the corrections to be made on your account. In addition to crediting your account with the amount not owed, the creditor must remove all finance charges, late fees, or other charges relating to that amount.

The credit card company must follow these procedures or it will violate federal law. If you feel the credit card company has not complied with the law, you should report it to the Federal Trade Commission, www.ftc. gov, or the Consumer Financial Protection Bureau, www.consumerfinance .gov/complaint.

How long do I have to wait for delivery?
"Thirty days."

Dear Mr. Alderman:
Three months ago I ordered a new bathing suit. It cost more than $40. I still have not received the suit, and it is almost fall. The company keeps telling me it will arrive any day. What can I do? I want my money back, not a bikini to wear in the winter.

Under federal law a seller must deliver the goods within the time promised. If no time is stated in your agreement, there is a presumption that thirty days is reasonable. *If your bathing suit has not arrived within thirty days, the company must notify you of when it will be delivered and let you cancel if you change your mind.*

Based on your letter, it appears the company has violated the law and you have the right to cancel and get your money back. I suggest you write the company once more via certified mail, return receipt requested, and say you want to cancel your order. If you do not receive your money back, contact the Federal Trade Commission, www.ftc.gov, and report that the company has violated the mail-order rules.

You should also know that the company, by violating the federal law, may have violated the Texas Deceptive Trade Practices Act as well. This means the attorney general could take action against the company and you could file suit in justice court for three times your damages. The problem with filing suit is the company is probably far away, and collecting anything will be difficult.

So what can you do? Read the letter right before this one, and next time make sure you use a credit card.

What happens when the wrong thing arrives?
"Protect yourself."

Dear Mr. Alderman:

I ordered a woman's size 12 jacket from a company in New York. It arrived three weeks later as a man's size 42. I sent it back to the company and was told I would be sent a new one. The company has not sent a new jacket, and it has cashed my check for $150. What can I do? I don't think the company is even in business anymore.

If you read the letter right before this one, you know a federal law requires companies to deliver goods or give you a refund within thirty days. The problem is that even though you are entitled to your jacket or your money back, it will be difficult, if not impossible, for you to collect. Having legal rights is meaningless unless the company you have rights against is solvent and in a location convenient for you to sue in.

So what do you do? First, report the company to the Federal Trade Commission for violating federal mail-order laws. Then, if the company has a local office, advertises, or owns property in Texas, you can sue in justice court. From your letter, though, it sounds like the company has disappeared with your money, and now you should be concerned with making sure this never happens again.

In the future, to protect yourself, make sure you use a credit card whenever you order by mail. As discussed above, if you don't receive what you ordered, the Fair Credit Billing Act lets you withhold payment from the credit card company. To find out just how this law works, read the first letter in this chapter.

I didn't order this. What can I do?
"Accept the gift."

Dear Mr. Alderman:

The other day I arrived home and found a box on my doorstep. It was from a company in Nebraska I had never heard of. Inside was all sorts of junk: toys, stationery, ashtrays, and trinkets. The letter that came with the stuff said it was sent to me on approval and I could keep it for only $49.95 or send it back. The post office wants $5 to send the junk back, and I don't want to pay it. It doesn't seem right that I get stuck because of this stupid company. Is there anything I can do?

You are in luck. Texas and federal law provide that you may treat unsolicited merchandise as a gift. *If you did not order the goods* (but be careful, because you may have signed something a long time ago agreeing to accept such orders on approval), *you can do whatever you want with them.* I think that to be polite you should write the company a letter, thank it for the gift, and tell it you will be glad to receive other gifts in the future. If you do not want to keep the merchandise, you may want to tell the company that if it will send you postage, you will return the merchandise. Of course, if you want, you can simply throw the box away.

The only requirement that must be met before the goods can be treated as a gift is they must not be ordered or solicited by you. To make sure you didn't order them, you may want to write the company via certified mail, return receipt requested, and ask for proof that you ordered the goods. Tell the company that unless it can show you that you did in fact order the goods, you will keep them as you are permitted to do by law.

The Texas law is a short one, so I thought I would let you see what it says:

Sec. 602.002 ACTIONS AUTHORIZED ON DELIVERY OF UNSOLICITED GOODS. Unless otherwise agreed, a person to whom unsolicited goods are delivered:
(1) is entitled to refuse to accept delivery of the goods; and
(2) is not required to return the goods to the sender.

Sec. 602.003. CERTAIN UNSOLICITED GOODS CONSIDERED GIFT.

(a) Unsolicited goods that are addressed to or intended for the recipient are considered a gift to the recipient.

(b) The recipient may use or dispose of goods described by subsection (a) in any manner without obligation to the sender.

Sec. 602.004. MISTAKEN DELIVERY. A person who receives unsolicited goods as the result of a bona fide mistake shall return the goods. The sender has the burden of proof as to the mistake.

Remember: This law applies only to unsolicited merchandise. If you authorize a company to send you merchandise on approval, you do not have the right to keep it, and you must bear the cost of returning the item.

CHAPTER 15

Miscellaneous Problems

Most legal problems can be categorized, and fit into one of the chapters in this book. But not everything fits neatly into the categories I have chosen to discuss. This chapter contains the many questions I receive that deal with problems outside of the other chapter headings—for example, questions about neighborly problems.

My neighbor's tree fell on my car. Who's responsible? "Why did the tree fall?"

Dear Mr. Alderman:
Last week there was a severe thunderstorm. The wind blew down my neighbor's tree, and part of the tree landed on my car. The damage to my car will cost approximately $1,500 to repair. I have insurance, but it has a $500 deductible. I talked with my neighbor, but he refuses to pay and says it wasn't his fault. Do I have any rights? Can I force him to pay?

Your neighbor may not have to pay for the damage to your car, even though it was his tree. *Under the law your neighbor is only responsible to you if he was negligent in caring for the tree, and that is why it fell.* In other words, if the tree was healthy and blew down in an unusually strong wind, your neighbor would probably not have any liability. But if the tree was diseased and your neighbor knew it, and took no steps to prune it or cut it down, he could be responsible for the damage if the tree fell during a regular storm—one that did not blow over healthy trees.

People have a duty to their neighbors to keep their property in a way that will not injure their neighbors. If your neighbor was negligent in the care of his property, he is responsible for the damage caused. But your neighbor is not responsible for an act of God that could not have been prevented, even by the most careful person.

What can I do about my neighbor's tree?
"Trim it carefully."

Dear Mr. Alderman:

My neighbor's tree hangs over my garage and is close to my roof. I am afraid a strong wind will blow the tree onto my property and damage it. Do I have the right to cut the overhanging branches down? Can I force my neighbor to cut it? Who will be responsible if the tree damages my property?

Problems with neighbors' trees can be among the most difficult to resolve, both legally and practically. Because the tree is on your neighbor's property, you do not have the right to cut it down. You also do not have the right to cut the overhanging branches; if you injure the tree, you could be responsible. The best suggestion may be to speak with your neighbor and let him know about the problem. Explain that the branches are a hazard to your property and that you would like him to cut them down. If you are willing to do it, tell him so. If he still refuses to work with you, he could be liable for any damage that occurs due to the overhanging branches. As I said in the previous letter, the owner of a tree is negligent—and therefore responsible—if he does not take reasonable steps to protect you and your property from harm. In my opinion, not cutting overhanging branches after being warned of a danger is negligence.

What happens if the neighbor's kid is hurt playing on my property?
"You are probably not responsible."

Dear Mr. Alderman:

I don't want to sound like someone who doesn't like kids—I do—but the neighbor's children are worrying me. They seem to find my roof an exciting place to play, and just last week, I caught two nine-year-olds on the roof. They climb up from the fence and then wander around wherever they like. What I need to know is whether I am in trouble if they get hurt up there. I have done everything I could to stop them, but they keep coming back.

If you have done everything a reasonable person would do to keep the children off your roof, you probably will not be responsible if one of the children is injured. *The law only imposes a duty on you to take ordinary care to protect the trespassing children from injury.* This means taking reasonable steps to keep them off your property and not leaving unusually dangerous conditions where the children play.

For example, if the children climb over a fence to get to your property, you probably are not responsible if they fall and injure themselves. But if you were to leave a gun outside, where you knew the children played, you could be responsible if one of them was shot. The test is what a reasonable person would do in a similar situation.

There is one exception to this general rule you should know about. A doctrine known as "attractive nuisance" places a greater duty on a landowner when there is a condition known to be attractive to children. For example, we all know children like swimming pools. If you have a pool in your yard, the law presumes you know children will try to use it and imposes an obligation on you to take extra steps to keep them out. While a person generally does not have a duty to fence his property to keep out trespassers, an owner with a pool may be required to do so.

Do I have to pay for damage caused by my child? "Probably not."

Dear Mr. Alderman:
My eleven-year-old son and some of his friends were playing base-ball in the lot near our house. I am not sure exactly what happened but apparently my son hit a ball that broke a neighbor's window. Now the neighbor says we must pay to have the window replaced. I intend to pay to be a good neighbor, but I was wondering what my liability is. Am I responsible for damage my son causes?

Being a good neighbor is always the best approach, but as far as the law is concerned you probably have no liability. Generally, parents are not responsible for wrongs committed by their children. There are, however, a few exceptions.

First, a parent is responsible if the damage occurred as a result of the failure to properly supervise the child. For example, if the kids were playing in the backyard and you did not take reasonable steps to make sure they did not hit a ball into a neighbor's window, you could be responsible. You cannot just sit back and watch them hit balls into the neighbor's house and then say, "Kids will be kids." Parents are also responsible for certain intentional acts committed by their children.

Under the law, a parent is responsible for property damage caused by willful and malicious acts committed by a child between the ages of ten and eighteen. If your child intentionally threw the baseball at the window, you would be responsible for the damage. A parent's liability under this law, however, is limited to $25,000.

The bottom line is that your decision to pay is probably the best one. Sometimes being a good neighbor is more important than exercising your legal rights.

How can I stop my neighbor's barking dog?
"There may be a law."

Dear Mr. Alderman:

Why is it the smallest dogs seem to make the most noise? My neighbor has a small dog that barks all day when she is gone. My neighbor leaves the dog outside, and it stands at my fence and barks. It is driving me crazy. This would be bad enough, but she lets the dog out every morning at 6 a.m. When the dog wants back in, about five minutes later, it just starts barking. I have talked to my neighbor and she says there is nothing she can do—dogs will be dogs. I don't want to get into an argument with her about who is right and who is wrong until I know my rights. Does a neighbor have the right to force someone to stop their dog from barking like this?

I have been surprised by the number of people who have contacted me about barking dogs. Unfortunately, I don't have a simple answer. However, two areas of law may help you.

Under general legal principles, you cannot use your property or maintain it in a manner that is a nuisance to others. If the barking dog is seriously disrupting your enjoyment of your property, you may be able to sue your neighbor to force the dog to stop. The test, however, would be whether a reasonable person would be seriously disturbed by the dog. For example, if the dog barked occasionally during the day, something all dogs do, you probably would not have any basis for objection. On the other hand, if it barked all night, your neighbor would probably be maintaining a nuisance. If the dog is a nuisance you can bring a lawsuit to stop it.

Before you consider a lawsuit, though, you should see if there are any local laws or ordinances directly on point. The first thing I suggest you do is contact your local governing body. Many cities and counties have laws regulating barking dogs, and you could get them to enforce the law. If there are no specific laws or ordinances, you will have to bring a civil action, a costly and often time-consuming thing to do.

The best advice I can give you is to try to talk to your neighbor and work it out. You may be right legally, but it will be difficult to prove and enforce.

The neighbor's dog bit me. Must the neighbor pay?
"It depends."

Dear Mr. Alderman:
My neighbor has a large, vicious dog. The dog is always chasing my
children and has bitten one of them before. Last week the dog got
out of his fence and bit my son, doing severe damage. The doctor
bills were expensive, and our insurance didn't cover them. I asked
my neighbor to pay the bills and he said no. I told him I would sue
and he said, "Go ahead. An owner isn't legally responsible for what
a dog does." Is this true? How can a person let his dog bite people
and not have to pay the bills?

Based on what you say in your letter, I think your neighbor is wrong. In
some states a pet owner is "strictly liable" for injuries caused by a pet. This
means if a dog bites someone, the owner must pay for the damages regardless of whether the owner did anything wrong. Unfortunately, Texas has
not yet adopted a rule like this, and in Texas you must show that the owner
was "negligent;" that is, the owner had reason to know the dog would bite
and didn't take reasonable steps to protect you. In many cases this means
the dog must either have bitten someone previously or be known to have
vicious tendencies.

In your case the dog had chased and bitten people before and the owner
should have known the dog was vicious. If the owner did not take reasonable steps to protect you—for example, by keeping the dog well penned—I
believe the owner should be responsible. If the amount is low enough for
you to go to justice court (look at Chapter 16 to learn more about this real
"People's Court") you can sue without an attorney.

One final point: In many cases, the breed of dog, for example a pit bull,
is known to be vicious. In my opinion, owners of this kind of dog are held
to a higher standard and should be responsible when the dog bites, even if
the dog never bit before. While the owner of a poodle may not have to take
steps to protect you from injury, the law probably imposes a higher duty on
the owner of a dog whose breed is known to be vicious.

My neighbor's dog got my dog pregnant.
Is my neighbor responsible?
"Yes. Owners are responsible for the consequences
of their dogs' acts."

Dear Mr. Alderman:

I have a strange problem. I came home to find my neighbor's dog engaged in intercourse with my dog in my backyard. My dog is chained up in our fenced backyard. My neighbor's dog had been running loose and dug under my fence. My dog is pedigreed, and we want to breed her. To protect our dog, and to not have to deal with a litter of mutt puppies, we terminated the pregnancy. I asked my neighbor to help pay the costs, and he refused, saying he was not responsible for the misdeeds of his dog. Is he?

Don't think your problem is that strange or unusual. These things do happen. In fact, in a case in Florida, the owner of a Rottweiler successfully sued the owner of a Chihuahua for impregnating his dog under similar circumstances.

As far as I am concerned, your neighbor should be responsible if he did not take proper steps to ensure that his dog did not run wild and break into your yard. If your city has a leash law that was broken, your neighbor should be responsible because he did not comply with this law. If there is no such law, you must show that your neighbor knew his dog was running wild and that there was a likelihood the dog would take advantage of other dogs in heat. Generally, owners are responsible for conduct such as you describe.

I should point out, however, that the neighbor may not be responsible if he did everything he could to keep the dog locked up, and it was not his fault the dog got out. For example, if the dog was locked in the backyard and someone else opened the gate and let the dog out, your neighbor probably would not be responsible.

Finally, as you might guess, it can be very hard to prove the case of the promiscuous poodle. The best advice may be to speak with your neighbor again and try to work things out.

My car was vandalized at a restaurant. Is the restaurant responsible? "Possibly."

Dear Mr. Alderman:

The other night, I went to dinner with my boyfriend. We parked the car in front of the restaurant, and when we came out we found that the front window had been smashed and the tape deck stolen. We talked to the manager of the restaurant, and he said the restaurant was not responsible. Is that true? It doesn't seem right. It provides the parking lot. Doesn't it have to provide security?

There is no simple answer to your question. Legally, the restaurant is only liable if it has been negligent—that is, if it did not take reasonable care to protect your property. For example, ordinarily a restaurant does not have to provide security. This means if there is an incident of vandalism, the restaurant probably would not be responsible. But once a restaurant—or any other establishment, for that matter—knows there may be problems or that it is located in a high-crime area, its obligations change. Now the restaurant must take reasonable steps to protect its customers. If it does not, it will be responsible. For example, if every restaurant in that neighborhood had lights and security guards in the parking lot, and this restaurant did not, it probably would be liable because it was negligent. On the other hand, if it does the same thing as everyone else has done to protect you and vandalism still occurs, it probably is not liable.

The simple fact that your property is damaged while in a parking lot is not enough to make the restaurant owner responsible. To recover, you will have to show that the restaurant did not take reasonable steps to protect your property. What is reasonable will depend on how high the risk of vandalism is, how much knowledge the owner has of the risk, and what others do under similar circumstances. If you feel an owner did not act reasonably to protect you, you should consider a claim for negligence in justice court.

My stolen property ended up in a pawn shop. Can I get it back? "Yes!"

Dear Mr. Alderman:
I was robbed. The thief took all my jewelry and electronic equipment. Now I found out the police caught him and know where he pawned my property. Can I get my property back from the pawn shop? What if it has been sold? It seems like this is my property and I ought to be entitled to it.

You are right. It is your property, and under the law you can get it back from whomever has it. If a thief steals your property, anyone who receives it is subject to your title. This means the pawnbroker, or anyone who purchased it from the pawnbroker, will have to return it to you. Of course, you will have to prove the property is yours. That is why it is a good idea to keep serial numbers and photographs of all your valuables.

The apartment next door has an unfenced pool. What can I do?
"There is a law."

Dear Mr. Alderman:
We live close to a small apartment complex. The apartments have a
swimming pool in the middle of the complex. It does not have a fence,
and the door to the courtyard is always open. I am afraid my young
son will play in the pool and drown. What can I do to get the complex
to fence in the pool? I checked with the city and learned the pool is
within city building codes.

Texas has a law governing swimming pool enclosures. Under this law, pools owned by an apartment complex or a property owners' association must be properly enclosed. Basically, to comply with this law, a pool must have a fence at least 48 inches high around it. The pool also must have a gate that is self-closing and self-latching. (In addition, your municipality may have its own laws.)

This law may be privately enforced by a tenant, homeowner, or any other interested party. Many government agencies, including the attorney general's office, the local health department, and the city or county attorney's office, also can bring an action to enforce it. If the apartment complex has not taken steps to comply with the new law, I suggest you speak with the manager and then contact the appropriate officials to have them require compliance. I should point out that failure to comply could result in civil penalties of up to $5,000.

Do I have the right to take my neighbor's trash?
"It depends on your neighbor's intent."

Dear Mr. Alderman:
I often pick things out of the trash left on the curb in my neigh-
borhood. Recently someone saw me and told me to leave it alone
because it was his property. Is this correct? Who owns the trash left
for the trash collector?

Good question. I think the answer is the person who left the trash probably owns it unless it was his or her intent to abandon it.

Under the law, a person may abandon title to personal property. For example, if I no longer want something, I can leave it at a junkyard, and it would no longer be mine. Anyone who came along would have the right to pick it up and claim ownership of it.

The question is whether people intend this when they leave trash on the curb for the trash collector to pick up. My guess is that in most cases, people do intend to abandon the property, and you, therefore, would have the right to take what you wanted.

On the other hand, a person could intend to leave the garbage only for the trash collector. In this case it would belong to that person until picked up. You, therefore, would not have the right to just take the property.

The intent of the person who placed the property on the street controls ownership. If your neighbor says to leave it alone, you should.

Is a homeowner liable for injury caused by a contractor? "Usually not."

Dear Mr. Alderman:
I hired a contractor to add a room to my house. He has hired several subcontractors to perform the work. I trust the contractor, but I do not know anything about the subcontractors he has hired. What is my liability if one of the workers is injured?

As a general rule, a property owner is not liable for injury to an employee of a contractor or subcontractor who is working on his or her property.

Texas law provides that the property owner is liable only if he exercises some control over the manner in which the work is to be performed, other than the right to order the work to start or stop, or to inspect progress or receive reports. It also must be shown that the property owner had actual knowledge of the danger or condition resulting in the injury. In other words, you are not responsible for any worker's injury simply because you own the property.

Can someone just come and drill a well in my backyard? "Maybe, if they own the mineral rights."

Dear Mr. Alderman:
I am buying a new house and some land. I was told that if I didn't own the mineral rights someone might have the right to come in and drill a well on my property. Is this correct? How do I make sure I own the mineral rights?

First, you are correct that someone might enter your property and drill for oil if they own the mineral rights for your property. They also may not have to reimburse you for any damage done to your property.

The simple way to avoid this problem is to make sure that when you purchase the property you also purchase the mineral rights. If nothing specific is said about mineral rights, you will own them as part of the property. If the seller specifically reserves mineral rights, or someone else already owns them, you are buying the property subject to the risk of future exploration on your property.

Who has to pay for the fence between yards?
"Maybe no one."

Dear Mr. Alderman:
The fence between my backyard and my neighbor's is falling down. He says I have to pay to replace it because it is on my property. I told him I thought we should share the expense. Before I talk to my neighbor I would like to know what the law is. Who is responsible for paying for the fence?

As far as the law is concerned, neither of you has an obligation to build a fence or to pay for one to be built. Unless you live in a subdivision where there are deed restrictions requiring a fence, or a town that has enacted a fencing ordinance, Texas law does not require fences be built. My suggestion is to talk to your neighbor and see if you can't come up with a satisfactory way of dividing the costs. If he refuses to pay, however, the only way you can build a fence is at your own expense.

Can I recover mental anguish damages for the death of my dog?
"Probably not in Texas."

Dear Mr. Alderman:
My dog was run over by a neighbor who wasn't looking where he was going and lost control of his car. He has offered to replace the dog but I think we should be entitled to much more. The dog was five years old and part of our family. Shouldn't we be entitled to something for the pain and suffering and mental anguish we have gone through?

As you recognize, for many people the dog is a part of the family. Under Texas law, however, dogs are treated as nothing more than personal property. As a general rule, you cannot recover mental anguish damages for the loss of property. All you are entitled to is what it will cost to replace the dog.

In some states, the courts or legislatures have allowed limited mental anguish damages for the loss of a pet. Until the Texas legislature acts or the Texas Supreme Court reverses an 1891 decision, however, pets in Texas will be treated no differently from a chair, and damages for mental anguish will not be allowed.

Is my friendly poker game illegal?
"Probably not."

Dear Mr. Alderman:
My friends and I play poker each week. We make pretty small bets and no one ever wins or loses more than about $50. Is this illegal gambling? Could we be arrested?

As a general rule, gambling is illegal in Texas. There is an exception, however, for gambling such as your poker game conducted in a private place. As long as you do not pay for the right to gamble—in other words, the "house" does not take a share—what you are doing is not illegal.

Who gets a ticket for not wearing a seat belt?
"The passenger and the driver."

Dear Mr. Alderman:
I was curious. I know that under Texas law you must wear a seat belt when driving or riding in a car. Who gets the ticket when a passenger in a car doesn't wear a seat belt? Is it the passenger or the driver?

You are correct that Texas law requires all passengers and the driver to wear a seat belt when riding in a car equipped with seat belts. Under the law, anyone over the age of fifteen who does not wear a seat belt may receive a misdemeanor traffic ticket. In addition, the driver of the car may be ticketed if he or she allows a child under the age of seventeen to not wear a seat belt. As the next letter shows, children under the age of eight are also subject to different rules regarding child safety seats.

When does a child have to ride in a safety seat?
"Any child under the age of eight may be required to be restrained in a safety seat."

Dear Mr. Alderman:
I saw a neighbor pull into his driveway with a young child sitting in the front seat without a safety seat. I made a joke about how it wasn't

really safe, and he said his daughter was large for her age and could wear a seat belt. Is this the law?

Under a relatively new law, whether a child must be secured in a safety seat when a car is operated depends on both the age and the size of the child. The law says that any child under the age of eight must be secured in a safety seat system, *unless* the child is taller than 4'9". Once the child reaches that height the child must wear a safety belt. Basically, the law recognizes that it is the size of the child and not the age that determines when the additional protection of a safety seat system is necessary.

Is it legal for a dog to ride in the back of a pickup truck?
"Unfortunately, yes."

Dear Mr. Alderman:
Is it legal for someone to allow a dog to ride in the back of an open pickup? It seems so dangerous.

Although many people would agree with you that it is dangerous for a dog to ride in the back of a pickup, it is not illegal.

Is it legal for children to ride in the bed of a pickup truck?
"Dogs yes, children no."

Dear Mr. Alderman:
I recently saw a child riding in the back of a pickup truck. This seems very dangerous. Is it legal?

Under the law, it is a misdemeanor to operate a pickup truck with a child younger than eighteen years of age in the bed of the truck. This law does not apply to:

- Operating the vehicle on the beach;
- Operating a vehicle that is the only vehicle owned by the family;
- Operating the vehicle to transport farmworkers from farm to farm;
- Operating the vehicle in a parade;
- Operating the vehicle for a hayride; or
- Operating the vehicle in the case of an emergency.

Can a child use a tanning bed?
"Not without parental consent."

Dear Mr. Alderman:
Our daughter has decided that she is too pale and wants to use a tanning bed. We told her no, but she said it was her money and she would do what she wants. We think these are dangerous for children; what can we do?

Fortunately, the Texas legislature agrees with you. Under a law passed in 2009, minors under the age of sixteen-and-a-half may no longer use a tanning bed. Children between the age of sixteen-and-a-half and eighteen must have parental consent. Tell your daughter it might be her money, but the law applies to everyone.

Doesn't the person who hit my car have to pay for all the damages?
"He does not pay for damages that were your fault."

Dear Mr. Alderman:
I had an accident with a truck. The police said it was his fault. His insurance company says I was 20 percent at fault and will pay only 80 percent of my damages. What can I do? The damage to my car is almost $4,000.

The law supports what the insurance company told you. Under a doctrine known as "proportionate responsibility," the person who caused the accident is liable for only the damages that were his fault. If you were, in fact, partially responsible, you could not collect that portion of damages from him.

If you believe, however, that you were not at fault, I suggest you ask for an explanation of why they disagree. Because the amount of your damages is less than $10,000, justice court may the best place to have an impartial party decide who is right. Let the insurance company know you are considering justice court if you can't work things out. If you don't resolve the matter you should consider filing a claim against the person who hit you. He will bring his insurance company into the dispute.

Can a high school drug test students?
"Yes, in some circumstances."

Dear Mr. Alderman:
My daughter tried out for the high school band. After she was accepted, she was told she had to submit to a drug test. Is this legal?

She told me that all students who participate in extracurricular activities are tested for drugs.

As a general rule, the Constitution of the United States prohibits a school from requiring all students to submit to a drug test. In some cases, however, the courts have recognized that drug testing may be done in a constitutionally permissible manner, and may be required. For example, in the 1990s the United States Supreme Court recognized that athletes could be required to submit to drug testing. In 2002, the court extended this ruling and held that a school has the authority to require testing for all students who participate in extracurricular activities. I should point out that the court also noted that reasonable efforts must be made to ensure a student's privacy both in the taking of the sample and in the use of the information. A positive test is not to be turned over to authorities but can only be used in connection with the enforcement of school rules.

Am I entitled to a copy of my medical records?
"Yes, but you may have to pay a reasonable fee."

Dear Mr. Alderman:
My insurance company no longer covers my primary care physician so I had to switch doctors. I asked my former doctor to send a copy of my medical records to my new doctor. The office told me that they would send them but I would have to pay $1 a page. This seems ridiculous. They are my records, why should I have to pay?

Under the law, hospital records are confidential and generally may not be disclosed to anyone without the consent of the patient. The patient has the right to a copy of his or her records, or to ask that a copy be sent to a new physician. The law, however, allows the physician to charge a "reasonable fee." A reasonable fee is defined as no more than $25 for the first twenty pages and $.50 per page for every copy thereafter. For X-rays, the reasonable fee is no more than $8 per film. In addition, a reasonable fee may include actual costs for mailing, shipping, or delivery. The physician is generally entitled to payment of a reasonable fee prior to release of the information.

Based on what you say, your physician is charging you an unreasonable fee. I suggest you let him know that you will pay a fee, but that by state law the amount they are charging is too high.

CHAPTER 16

Justice Court

Knowing your legal rights is just the beginning. To make this knowledge work for you, you must be able to assert your rights. Justice courts fill this need. Justice courts are inexpensive and simple to use, and can promptly settle disputes. Justice court is where you put your knowledge to work.

Since 2013, however, there is no longer a separate "small claims court" in Texas. Small claims, previously filed in "small claims court," are now filed in justice court. As a practical matter, filing a small claims case in justice court is almost identical to filing in what was known as the small claims court. There are a few significant differences, however—some of which provide additional rights for individuals and expand the power of the justice of the peace hearing the small claims case.

As I said in the introduction to this book, once you know your legal rights, you usually will not have to pursue a legal claim. The other party will try to settle the problem. But sometimes a dispute cannot be settled, and you must resort to the legal system to resolve it.

The decision of whether to sue must be made by you, based on the amount of money involved, the importance of the issues, and how much time and expense you are willing to spend to pursue your claim. Don't let emotion reign over common sense. You are always better off trying to settle with the other party before you go to court. But if you cannot settle, justice court gives you a chance to appear before a judge or jury and have an impartial tribunal decide who is correct.

As you will see from the following letters, justice court is relatively easy to use and very inexpensive. Also, if you are successful, you will be awarded the costs of the lawsuit in addition to your other damages. Many people ask me, "Is justice court in Texas like *The People's Court* on TV?" The best answer I can give to that question is what a justice of the peace told me when I asked him how his court compared with the TV court. His answer: "We are a lot like *The People's Court*—just much less formal."

How much can I sue for in justice court?
"Up to $10,000!"

Dear Mr. Alderman:
I heard that there was a change in the law and that I can now sue for
more than $5,000 in justice court.

Good news. The limit on small claims in Texas was $5,000. The legisla-
ture amended the law, and now the limit for a small claim in justice court
is $10,000.

How do I sue in justice court?
"It's easy."

Dear Mr. Alderman:
My laundry man is incompetent! The other day I brought in a brand-
new shirt that I had only worn once, and he ruined it. It has grease
all over it, and even though I had only worn it once, he said it must
have been my fault. Having worn it only to the movies, there was no
way I could have gotten grease all over it. My friend who was with
me saw that the shirt was clean when I left the movies. Now I am
mad! I want to sue, but I am afraid the cleaners will have a big-time
lawyer, and I will lose. Do I need an attorney? The shirt only cost
$50. Is it worth it?

This is the type of small claim that should be filed in justice court. Your
claim can be quickly decided by the court based on the information you
give the judge. You will not need a lawyer. If you can prove the shirt did
not have grease stains on it when you brought it to the laundry, and that
the laundry stained it, you will be entitled to the value of the shirt, plus the
amount it costs you to bring the suit.

Suing in justice court is easy. However, in order to sue in this court,
you must be asking for no more than $10,000. You can sue any person
who is in Texas, has a permanent home in Texas, or is doing business
here. To sue a sole proprietorship, the proprietor must be in Texas; to sue
a partnership, the partners must be here; and to sue a corporation, it must
do business in the state. For more information on what it means to do
business in one of these forms, read Chapter 17.

There are many justice courts, so after you decide to go to justice court,
you must find the proper location for your complaint. Generally, you must
sue in the court that covers the area where the person you are suing lives,
where the business operates, or where the transaction took place. You can

find the local justice court by looking in the phone book or online for the justice of the peace where you want to file suit. If you have any questions about which court to sue in, or whom you can sue, call and ask the clerk of the court. The clerk usually will be able to answer your questions.

Once you know which court to go to, you need to file your "petition." You will need to go to the court to file the petition, but you may be able to obtain copies of the forms beforehand, either online or by calling the court clerk. *To sue, you must have the correct name and address of the laundry and, if you can find it, the name of a person at the laundry who can be served with the legal papers.* If the laundry is a corporation, you can call the secretary of state in Austin and find out who the laundry's "agent for service" is. An agent for service is the person the company has designated to accept legal papers for the corporation.

When you get to the court, the clerk will give you a "petition" to fill out (or if you have already done so at home, take the document from you). If you have any questions about the forms, ask the clerk. The clerk usually will help with simple questions.

You, the person suing, are called the "plaintiff." You start the lawsuit by filing a petition. (Most justice courts have a copy of a petition online.) After you file the petition and pay your fees (about $100), the court will have the constable or sheriff serve the "defendant"—the person or business being sued—with the papers. The defendant will then either answer your claim (that is, state why he thinks he is not responsible) or default (that is, not respond to the petition). If the defendant does not respond to the petition, you will schedule a hearing before the judge and tell him or her your claim. If you have a case, you will win. The judge will award you the amount of your suit plus what it cost for you to sue. *Make sure you ask for all the costs of bringing the suit in your petition.*

If the defendant answers your claim, he will be present in the courtroom on the date set for the trial. Unless either party asks for a jury, the case will be heard by the judge alone. In most cases, the hearing is very informal. The judge lets both sides tell their stories and listens to any other witnesses who may appear. For example, if your friend knows the shirt was not stained when you brought it in, you may want to bring him with you to court to tell this to the judge. Also, if you have any pictures or other records that support your case, you should bring them with you. The sales receipt showing that the shirt was new will also be important. And, of course, bring the shirt to show the judge the damage.

If the other side has a lawyer, I don't believe you should worry about being intimidated. Most judges will limit what a lawyer may do, and will make sure you have a chance to tell your story. A justice court hearing a small claims dispute really is a people's court. Most judges want you to feel that you are treated fairly and have a chance to tell your side of the story.

After hearing all the evidence, the judge usually will make a prompt ruling and state who wins. In most cases, this is the end of the matter. If you win, the other side often pays you the money. But as the following letters show, sometimes the other side may appeal or may not pay. In such cases, it can be difficult to collect your judgment.

Can my son help me in justice court?
"The court may allow it."

Dear Mr. Alderman:
I am sixty years old and my English is not very good. I get very nervous speaking to a group or to people I don't know. I want to file a claim in justice court, but I am afraid I will not be able to communicate well with the judge. I know I could have a lawyer, but I cannot afford one. I have a grown son who has said he will assist me, but I don't know if that will be allowed. Can he help me in court?

Ordinarily, the only person who can assist another person in court is an attorney. Since 2013, however, the rules in justice court are a little more lenient. Although a person may always be represented by an attorney, in an eviction suit an individual may also be represented by an authorized agent. Also, a corporation or other entity may be represented by an employee, owner, officer, or partner. Perhaps the most substantial change in the rules is one that allows an individual to be represented by a person who is not an attorney or agent. The court may, for good cause, allow an individual to be represented by a family member or other individual who is not being compensated.

This means that your son will be allowed to assist you in court, if the judge approves it. Not speaking English well and being nervous seem to be a "good cause."

Can I have a jury trial in justice court?
"Yes, but it will cost a little more."

Dear Mr. Alderman:
I want to file a claim in justice court. I think I have a very sympathetic case, and I would like a jury trial. Am I entitled to a jury trial in justice court?

Yes. When you file your claim you may request a jury trial. The only negative consequences of asking for a jury trial are that the filing fees will be a little higher and it may take a little longer for your case to come to trial.

What happens if I sue for more than $10,000 in justice court?
"You will be thrown out of court."

Dear Mr. Alderman:
I did contracting work for some people. They asked me to do a small job first, and then another, and then another. They now owe me $11,500. I have tried to get them to pay, but it looks like I am going to have to sue. I read that you can only sue for $10,000 in justice court. I would be satisfied to get this much out of them, and I don't want to have to get a lawyer to sue for more. Can I just take the $10,000 and call it even?

If you file a suit in justice court asking for more than $10,000, the court does not have jurisdiction. This means that it does not have legal authority to hear your case and will have to dismiss it. You are not allowed to simply take less to get into court. If you want to sue for more than $10,000, you will have to file in district or county court. This will probably mean hiring an attorney. But there is another alternative for you.

Although you cannot sue for a total of more than $10,000, when there are several contracts you can sue separately for each. For example, you said that you did more than one job. As far as the law is concerned, each job may be a separate contract, and you can file a separate suit for each. As long as each job was less than $10,000, the court has jurisdiction to hear the case. This will cost you a little more in filing fees, but you recover these fees if you win.

One final point: Do not try to get into justice court by reducing your damages. If you are owed $11,500, you cannot just sue for $10,000 to get into justice court. The amount in controversy is over $10,000, and the court will dismiss the case.

Can I use the Deceptive Trade Practices Act in justice court?
"Yes, as long as the amount is less than $10,000."

Dear Mr. Alderman:
You have written about the Texas Deceptive Trade Practices Act. Can I file a claim under this law in justice court? If I win can I recover treble damages?

You may file a claim in justice court for money damages under any legal theory recognized in Texas. The only limitation is that your claim must be less than $10,000. Justice court, just like any other court, may award you additional damages under this law when you prove that the person you sued acted "knowingly." (See Chapter 10 for more information about the Texas Deceptive Trade Practices Act.)

Can I take less to get into justice court?
"No!"

Dear Mr. Alderman:
I am owed $12,000 on a debt. I know you can only sue for up to $10,000 in justice court. Can I sue in justice court if I am willing to accept $10,000 for what I am owed?

As you correctly state, justice court jurisdiction is $10,000. This means that it cannot hear cases involving disputes in excess of that amount. In your case your dispute involves $12,000. Even though you are willing to accept $10,000, you have no legal basis to sue for anything less than $12,000. This means that justice court would not have jurisdiction to hear your case. You should consider a suit in either county or district court. You will probably need an attorney to assist you with this claim.

If I win in justice court, can the other side appeal?
"Yes."

Dear Mr. Alderman:
I am suing someone in justice court for a violation of the Deceptive Trade Practices Act. He offered me a settlement that I think is too low. He told me that if I didn't accept his offer, he would "appeal any justice court judgment and force me to hire an attorney." This seems like coercion. Is it legal?

It sounds like he is trying to induce a favorable settlement by pointing out the possible costs of going to court. Although he is correct about the law, he may be wrong about the effect. Under the law, either side to a justice court dispute has the right to appeal the decision to county court. Appeal in such cases involves retrying the case in the higher court. County court is much more formal than justice court, and the assistance of an attorney is advisable.

I don't think, however, this should deter you from pursuing what you see as a valid claim or force you to settle for an unreasonable amount.

Because you are suing under the Texas Deceptive Trade Practices Act, you will recover your attorney's fees if you prevail. (You are also permitted to recover your attorney's fees if you sue for breach of contract.) Remember that if you have to hire an attorney, the other side must do so as well. Appealing costs both parties. Additionally, if the loser appeals, he may have to post a bond to ensure that you are paid if you prevail.

The costs of a lawsuit, as well as the possibility that you may not win, are always factors that enter into the decision of how much to settle for. I suggest you weigh these factors, as well as the strength of your claim, and make the decision you think is best.

What do I do after I've won?
"Enforce your judgment."

Dear Mr. Alderman:

You may remember me: I am the person who wrote to you about a problem with my cleaner. Well, I took your advice and went to justice court—and I won! Now what do I do? He won't pay, and I still don't have my money.

If you win in justice court, the person you sued usually will immediately pay you the money he or she owes you. However, if you have difficulty collecting your judgment, the law can help you.

The first thing you should do is write or email the defendant and remind him that you have been awarded a judgment. Ask him to pay you the money he owes you, or to let you know when he plans on paying. If he still refuses to pay, there are some things you can do with the law's help.

There are two legal devices you can use to force payment of your judgment. One is called an "abstract of judgment"; the other is a "writ of execution." An abstract of judgment is a legal paper you can file that will give you a lien on any real estate, except for a homestead, owned by the defendant. To do this, you must go back to the court where you sued. The clerk will help you get the abstract of judgment. Then you must file it in every county where you think the defendant may own real property. There will be a small charge to do this, but you will be entitled to collect this amount from the defendant. Once you file the abstract, you will have a lien against the defendant's nonexempt real property. This means the defendant will probably not be able to sell the property without first paying you. You also will have the right to force him to sell the property to satisfy your judgment. Most people do not like to have liens on their property and will pay you to get the lien released.

The other method to force payment is called a writ of execution. This also is issued by the court where you received your judgment. It is an order to the sheriff or constable directing him or her to go to the defendant and collect the judgment. If the defendant still does not pay, the sheriff or constable has the right to take the defendant's nonexempt personal property and sell it in order to pay you your money. There may be a small cost for the writ and the services of the law officer, but this is recoverable from the defendant.

Remember, if you are having trouble collecting your judgment, go back to the court clerk and ask for help. The clerk will tell you what legal devices may be available to enforce your judgment.

There is one last thing you should keep in mind. Texas law is very favorable to debtors. It is often difficult to force people to pay their debts if they really do not want to. For an abstract of judgment to be successfully enforced, the defendant must own real estate other than a homestead. To successfully collect your money with a writ of execution, the defendant must own property not exempted from collection by Texas law. The exemption law in Texas allows a person to keep most of his or her property no matter how much he or she owes. *Read the letters in Chapter 6 to see what property is exempt before you try to collect your judgment with a writ of execution.*

Before taking the time to try to collect your judgment, consider whether it will be worth the time and the effort you will have to put in. While you can usually force a business to pay, be aware that it is much more difficult to force individuals to pay a judgment.

What is garnishment?
"Another way to get your money."

Dear Mr. Alderman:

I sued and won in justice court. Now the person I sued is refusing to pay. A friend told me that if I knew where he banked, I could use garnishment. What is this, and how do I use it?

Garnishment is the name given to the proceeding that allows you to get money that is *owed to* the person you sued. It can be used to get money in a bank account, rent owed to landlords, or debts owed to individuals or businesses.

In some cases, garnishment may be used to get a portion of a person's wages. Wage garnishment is permitted in Texas only for the collection of child support, back taxes, and certain government-backed student loans. For debts other than these, wages are protected, and garnishment cannot be used to get money from someone who pays wages to the person you sued. But money owed to people who are self-employed, such as independent contractors, builders, accountants, or attorneys, is not considered wages. Therefore, you may use garnishment to reach money owed to these individuals.

To use garnishment you should go back to the court and file a "writ of garnishment." To do this, you must have the name and address of the garnishee—the person who is holding the money you want. For example, suppose you know where the person you sued has a bank account. Under the law, the bank technically owes the money to the owner of the account. Therefore, you can use a writ of garnishment to order the bank to pay the money to you to satisfy the debt.

Garnishment is not necessarily a complicated procedure; however, you may want to consult an attorney to help you with it. If you were to make a mistake, it could result in liability to you.

Can bankruptcy defeat recovery if I win in justice court? "Unfortunately, bankruptcy usually means no recovery."

Dear Mr. Alderman:
I followed your instructions on how to file a justice court lawsuit. I won my case and the judge entered a judgment against the defendant. I recently received a notice in the mail that the defendant is now filing Chapter 7 bankruptcy. The letter states that he has no assets from which any distribution can be paid to creditors. Is there anything I can do to ensure that I will receive some of my money, or will the Chapter 7 wipe out the debt he owes me?

Unfortunately for you, this is how bankruptcy works. When people file bankruptcy they give up their nonexempt property in exchange for the release, or discharge, of most of their debts. (Exempt property is discussed in Chapter 6.) The creditors in turn split whatever property there is among them. If there is no property, the creditors do not get any money.

In your case, the debtor apparently has no nonexempt property to give up. This means he will be discharged from his debts (including his debt to you), and the creditors (including you) will get nothing. The fact that you have sued and won does not change this result. You should file a proof of claim form in the bankruptcy proceeding, however, to ensure that if any assets are found, you will share in their distribution.

Justice court is usually a good way to resolve your disputes. Most people who sue and win collect the money they are entitled to. Our bankruptcy laws, however, are designed to give a debtor a fresh start, and this often means that people who are entitled to be paid are not.

Can someone garnish an independent contractor's wages?
"An independent contractor does not work for wages."

Dear Mr. Alderman:
I have been working as an independent contractor for a company since 2006. I was an employee with them prior to that. The company was just served with a garnishment notice for a credit card debt I owe. Since I am not an employee of the company, how can they garnish my wages? I thought wage garnishment was illegal in Texas.

If you were an employee, there could not be any wage garnishment. The Texas Constitution prohibits wage garnishment for debts like credit card debts. Unfortunately for you, you are not an employee.

A writ of garnishment is an order from the court to a person who owes the debtor money to withhold the money and pay it to the creditor. Wage garnishment is a type of garnishment. In your case, they are not garnishing your wages; they are garnishing the money you are owed for doing the work. This is a debt subject to garnishment, and not within the prohibition against wage garnishment. The only way I know to avoid the garnishment is to make arrangements to pay the creditor.

Does a corporation have to have an attorney to go to justice court?
"No."

Dear Mr. Alderman:
I am the president of a small corporation. We are owed money by several of our customers, and I want to go to justice court. A friend told me that a corporation can only go to court if it is represented by an attorney. Is this true? It will cost me more to hire an attorney than the amount of the claims.

Generally, your friend is correct. A corporation can only appear in court or file legal papers through an attorney. This is because the law treats a corporation as a separate legal entity, and as a separate entity, it must act through a representative. The only type of representative who can go to court is an attorney. If someone else went to court, he or she would be guilty of practicing law without a license.

But there is one important exception. A corporation may be represented in *justice court* by any authorized agent. The legislature recognized that much of what goes on in justice court is too simple to require the additional expense of an attorney. Therefore, you, as president of the corporation, may file the claim on behalf of the corporation.

What determines where I am sued?
"You may be sued in a number of places."

Dear Mr. Alderman:
I am being sued in justice court in the precinct where the plaintiff lives. The judge is one of his best friends. I thought I had the right to be sued where I live. What can I do?

Generally, a defendant in a small claims case is entitled to be sued in one of the following venues:

- In the county and precinct where the defendant resides;
- In the county and precinct where the incident, or the majority of incidents, that gave rise to the cause of action occurred;
- In the county and precinct where the contract or agreement, if any, that gave rise to the cause of action was to be performed; or
- In the county and precinct where the property is located, in a suit to recover personal property.

If the problem arose where you live, you have the right to be sued there. I suggest you speak with the clerk of the court about a "change of venue" to get the proceeding moved to the proper precinct.

How much time do I have to sue someone who ran into my car?
"Two years."

Dear Mr. Alderman:
About ten months ago I had an automobile accident. It was the other person's fault, and he keeps saying he is going to pay to have my car repaired. I am getting concerned that if I wait too long to try to settle this matter I will not be able to sue. How much time do I have to file a lawsuit?

You are correct in thinking that if you wait too long you will be unable to sue. The law puts limitations on how long you have to sue based on the nature of the lawsuit. A lawsuit arising out of a car accident is called a "tort," usually based on negligence. For most tort cases, including those based on negligence, you have two years from the date of the accident to file a claim. In your case, you can continue to negotiate for at least another year.

Why can't I use the Deceptive Trade Practices Act in justice court?
"You can."

Dear Mr. Alderman:
I just filed a suit in justice court trying to collect under the Texas
Deceptive Trade Practices Act. The judge ruled in favor of the defen-
dant and said she did not have jurisdiction to hear suits under this
law. She told me I had to go to county court with an attorney. What
good is this law if everyday people can't use it in justice court?

You either misunderstood the judge or she is wrong. A justice of the peace, the judge in justice court, has the same jurisdiction over claims under the Deceptive Trade Practices Act as does any other judge.

As long as your claim is within the jurisdictional limit of $10,000 and you are seeking money damages, justice court has jurisdiction to hear disputes under the Deceptive Trade Practices Act. My guess is that your dispute was for more than the maximum amount and that is why the judge said she did not have jurisdiction.

I am being sued by someone I think owes me money. What can I do?
"File a 'counterclaim.'"

Dear Mr. Alderman:
I was about to sue a contractor in justice court for doing faulty work.
Before I had a chance to do anything, he filed suit against me for not
paying. Do I still have the right to file my claim?

Yes. You do not file your claim, however, as a separate lawsuit. You file what is called a "counterclaim" in the contractor's lawsuit. The court then hears both claims and rules on them at the same time.

How do I collect?
"It can be difficult."

Dear Mr. Alderman:
It is a delight to read your responses to legal questions. So here goes
another one. How can I collect on a justice court case I won? I have
filed the abstract of judgment. Yet it seems there is no real power to
collect unless I find where the person banks and then file for garnish-
ment. What good is my judgment?

Unfortunately, it can be hard to collect after you receive a judgment. In Texas, much of a person's property is exempt, and that means it cannot be taken to satisfy the judgment. (You should review the material in Chapter 6 to see what property is exempt.)

In most cases, however, the person you sued will pay if you win. This is in part because most people pay their debts, and in part because having a judgment filed against you can make getting credit more difficult and expensive.

If you are not paid, however, you can garnish money in a bank account if you know where the person banks. If you ever gave the person a check, look on the back to see where it was deposited. If you do not know where the person banks, try a little detective work or even hire a private detective to assist you.

Also, although there is no wage garnishment in Texas, you can garnish money the person is owed if he is self-employed. For example, if he is an independent contractor, you can garnish money he is owed from his customers.

Remember, your judgment will remain on his credit report until it is paid. In many cases, this is enough to get you the money you are owed.

CHAPTER 17

Starting a Business

Each year, thousands of brave entrepreneurs venture out into the world of business. Some achieve a measure of fame and fortune, while most discover the harsh reality of the small business: Few are successful. When you start a new business you suddenly find more and more unexpected legal disputes. To protect yourself it is important to know all the laws that govern your business and to make sure you comply with them. But no matter how diligent and conscientious you may be, things can still go wrong, and you may find yourself being sued by one of your customers. For example, if you do not promptly clean up the spill on the floor, you may incur substantial liability when someone slips and falls. And even though the product you sold was manufactured by someone else, you may be responsible when it breaks and injures someone.

There are three ways to avoid liability when you operate a business:

- Make sure you comply with the law.

- Purchase enough insurance to cover any unexpected liability, such as the patron who slips on a banana peel and falls.

- Consider incorporating. A business may be run as a sole proprietorship, a partnership, or a corporation. As you will see from the next few letters, the legal form your business assumes can determine the extent of *your* liability.

What is a sole proprietorship?
"The same thing as yourself."

Dear Mr. Alderman:
I just opened up a little fix-it shop in my garage. I put up a sign that reads Sam's Fix-It. So far I am not getting rich, but I am making enough extra money to make it worthwhile. The other day someone brought in a toaster that needed to be repaired. I fixed it and returned it. Today the person came back. The toaster had caught on fire. I had apparently crossed two wires that shouldn't be crossed. The owner

*was pretty nice about it and told me I was lucky his house hadn't
burned down. Then I started thinking. . . . What if the house had
caught on fire because of my mistake? Who is responsible for things
from my shop that go wrong?*

The simple answer to your question is: You are. When you run a business as
a sole proprietorship, you are the business. Whatever debts or obligations
are incurred by the business are actually incurred by you. The business is
not a separate entity. This is referred to as DBA ("doing business as").

Many people start a business by simply assuming a name and opening
shop. While this is legal (of course you should file the assumed name with
the county clerk), it may not be the best form for you. For example, if you
didn't properly repair the toaster and it caught the house on fire, you may
have had a substantial lawsuit to contend with. Even though you were acting as a business when you repaired the toaster, you would have personal
liability for the damages caused. This means that you could lose personal
and business assets to pay the debt.

As you will see from the next few letters, you may want to consider
incorporating. A corporation is a separate entity. You are usually not personally liable for the obligation of the corporation. *Of course, no matter
what form your business takes, you should make sure you have adequate
liability insurance.*

Who is responsible for partnership debts?
"Each of the partners."

Dear Mr. Alderman:
*I have two partners in a small restaurant. One of them has gone
crazy. He thinks we're the Ritz and has started buying caviar and
all sorts of expensive junk. Most of the food goes bad because no
one orders it. The other day, we got the bills for all this stuff, and we
were shocked. There is no way we can pay for all the stuff he bought
and still stay in business. We are now talking about splitting up and
closing the restaurant, but I am worried about what my share of the
bills might be. Do I have to pay a third of everything we owe?*

I have some bad news for you. You are not liable for one-third of the debts
your partners have incurred. *You are responsible for all of the debts if they
are not paid by the partnership.* Basically, each partner has full liability for
all the partnership debts. Each partner, however, has the right to recover
from the others his fair share.

Here is how the law works:

Suppose A, B, and C form the ABC partnership. Each partner contributes $5,000. The business then incurs $21,000 in debts. The partnership assets, $15,000, will first be used to pay the debt. The remaining $6,000 is now owed by the partners. Each is responsible for $2,000, but if one doesn't pay, the others must pay his share. For example, if a creditor sues all the partners, but only A has any money, A will have to pay the entire $6,000. He will be responsible for getting $2,000 each from B and C. Remember, a partnership is not a separate legal entity when it comes to liability. It is simply a way for more than one person to do business jointly. As far as the law is concerned, each partner is usually liable for whatever the partnership does. This can even include wrongful acts of the other partners, such as an automobile injury not fully covered by insurance that occurs while making a delivery.

If you are concerned with your individual liability for the debts of the business, don't use a partnership. Read the following letters and set up a limited partnership or a corporation. But first, consider the partnership's liability for the personal debts of the partners.

Can my partner's creditors take partnership property for his private debts?
"No, partnerships generally are not liable for personal debts of the partners."

Dear Mr. Alderman:
I set up a partnership with my friend Bob. We have a small business with about $5,000 in parts. Recently, the bank that loaned Bob money to build a pool at his house told us if Bob didn't pay, it would sue and take the property of the partnership. Can the bank do this? The business didn't borrow the money. Bob borrowed it himself. Our business is going along OK, and I wouldn't want to have to end it.

It is tempting here to go into a lot of law about liability and partnerships. But the simple answer is that your partner's creditors cannot force you to sell the partnership, or take partnership assets. The partnership is not responsible for the personal debts of the individual partners. Of course, your partner's creditors can take your partner's interest in the business— and receive his share of the profits—to pay off the debt, but this should not affect the running of the business.

Partners are responsible for partnership debts, and personal assets may be taken to pay them off, but the reverse is not true. A creditor of an individual partner may not take partnership property.

What is a limited partnership?
"A cross between a partnership and a corporation."

Dear Mr. Alderman:

I am about to start a business with some friends. We have considered a partnership and a corporation, but someone told us there is such a thing as a limited partnership. We were told this is just like a partnership but without the liability. Because we are worried about our individual liability if we start a partnership, this sounds like a good idea. How does it work? Would you suggest we start one?

You are right. A limited partnership is like a partnership but with limited liability. For example, if you start a partnership, you and each of the partners are responsible for all the debts of the partnership. As I said in an answer to an earlier letter, you, as a partner, could end up losing your personal property to pay off the partnership debts.

In a limited partnership, the limited partners are only responsible for an amount equal to their investments in the business. For example, if you were a limited partner with a $5,000 investment, the most you could lose would be the $5,000 you put in.

But there are two big drawbacks to a limited partnership: There must be at least one general partner, who has individual liability for all the partnership debts; and as a limited partner, you cannot be directly involved in the day-to-day running of the business. A limited partner is really a silent partner. He invests in the business and then hopes it succeeds so he can share in the profits. From your letter it doesn't sound like a limited partnership is what you are looking for. You seem to want to be actively involved in the business, and a limited partner cannot be.

But just in case you do decide to start a limited partnership, I should tell you that unlike a regular partnership, which can be started with only a handshake, a limited partnership is created by law and needs a formal agreement to be valid. To start a limited partnership you should consult with an attorney and have him or her draw up the papers.

Is there a way to avoid liability?
"Form a corporation."

Dear Mr. Alderman:

I am going to open a small fruit stand/cheese shop. I just read about a restaurant owner who was sued for over $100,000 by someone who slipped on a banana peel in his store. I am worried about

this happening to me. I know my insurance will cover most dam-
age claims, but I really don't want to be held responsible for all the
obligations of the business. Is there some way the business can be
responsible for its own debts?

One way for an individual to avoid liability for debts incurred by his
business is to incorporate. Under the law a corporation is a separate legal
being. It sues and is sued in its own name. The individuals involved in a
corporation can only lose their investments in the business.

For example, suppose you start your business as a sole proprietorship,
and a customer is injured slipping on your floor. She sues for $150,000,
not an unusually high amount these days. You lose, and your insurance
pays $100,000. *You are personally responsible for the remaining $50,000.*

The same result would occur if the business were a partnership. But
if you had incorporated, then the business—not you—would owe the
remaining $50,000. If the business didn't have enough money to pay the
debt, the customer could not collect from you. If the business were to stop
doing business or file bankruptcy, that would be the end of the matter. *One*
of the most important benefits of a corporation is that it shields the shareholders and officers from personal liability for business debts.

If you are worried about liability from your business I strongly recommend that you incorporate or consider a new business form called a
"limited liability company." The limited liability company offers many
of the same benefits as the corporation. It may be a good idea to talk with
an attorney about which form is best for you. Many attorneys are able to
handle either business form. Shop around and get a fair price before you
hire one.

I own a gas station. Someone told me I have to pump gas
for handicapped drivers at no extra charge. Is this the law?
"Yes."

Dear Mr. Alderman:
I own a small gas station. I sell both full-service and self-service gas.
Of course, there is a substantial difference in price. The other day a
customer with a handicapped person license plate drove up to the
self-service pump and told me I had to fill her tank for the self-service
price. I told her if she wanted full service to pull up to the full-service
pump. She said there was a law that required me to fill her tank at the
self-service price. I did it this time, but now I want to know—is there
really such a law?

Yes. The Texas Legislature passed a law in 1989 that requires a gas station that has both self- and full-service options to pump gas for a handicapped person at the self-serve price. It is important to emphasize that this law only applies when you have both self- and full-service options. A station that sells only self-serve gas does not have to pump for a handicapped person, and a full-service-only station does not have to charge a different price. As you see, you did the right thing and the legal thing by pumping the gas.

Can I tow cars parked in my spaces?
"Not without a proper sign."

Dear Mr. Alderman:
I own a small store in a strip mall. The management has given each store some parking spaces that we can limit to our customers. I have put up a small sign saying the parking is for my customers and others may be towed. So far I have not had any problems. I am wondering, however, whether I really have the right to tow them. Do I? I am also considering booting those parked illegally.

Although you have the contractual right to tow or boot cars wrongfully parked, based on what you say you have not provided the proper signs required by law to either tow or boot. Under state law, parking lot owners generally may only tow or boot cars if they have very specific signs. The law provides in part that the signs must be:

1. Conspicuously visible to and facing the driver of a vehicle that enters the lot;

2. Located on the right-hand or left-hand side of each driveway through which a vehicle can enter the lot;

3. Permanently mounted on a pole, post, wall, or barrier;

4. Installed on the lot; and

5. Installed so that the bottom edge of the sign is no lower than five feet and no higher than eight feet above ground level.

The law also provides details about the sign itself. The sign must:

1. Be made of weather-resistant material;

2. Be at least 18 inches wide and 24 inches tall;

3. Contain the international symbol for towing vehicles;

4. Contain a statement describing who may and who may not park;

5. Bear the words Unauthorized Vehicles Will Be Towed or Booted at Owner's or Operator's Expense;

6. Contain a statement of the days and hours towing and booting is enforced; and

7. Contain a current telephone number, including the area code, that is answered twenty-four hours a day to enable the owner of the towed or booted car to locate it.

The bottom line is that it is unlawful to tow or boot any vehicle from your lot unless you have signs as discussed above. Towing without the proper signage could result in a lawsuit.

What is the ADA?
"A law you should know about."

Dear Mr. Alderman:
I operate a small strip-mall shopping area. At a chamber of commerce meeting, a speaker told us about the ADA. He stressed the importance of this law and told us we should immediately take steps to comply with it. The only specific thing I remember him saying, however, is that we should have ramps for people in wheelchairs to get in and out. I know there must be much more to this law. Exactly what does it cover, and what do I have to do to comply?

The ADA, or **Americans with Disabilities Act,** is generally referred to as the bill of rights for the disabled. Basically, this law prohibits discrimination against an individual with a disability and requires that public transportation and public accommodations, such as a strip shopping center, must be accessible. This is a rather complex law; however, I will give you a brief overview. I strongly suggest you speak with your attorney to get more details.

A person with a disability is defined by the ADA as anyone with a physical or mental handicap that is a substantial impairment of a major life activity. The law also applies to people who do not have such an impairment but are still considered impaired. For example, the law covers people who have hearing or speech impairments and anyone who does not have the physical ability to walk or see. The law also covers a cancer patient who is cured, if that person is considered by others to still be impaired. It is estimated that more than 43 million Americans have disabilities covered by the ADA.

Under the ADA, an employer with fifteen or more employees may not discriminate against an otherwise qualified individual because of a disability. A qualified individual is one who, with or without a reasonable accommodation, is able to perform the job. For example, a person in a wheelchair who is able to perform a job would be considered qualified for the purposes of the ADA even if the employer had to build a special desk to accommodate the employee. Employment discrimination claims under the ADA should be filed with the Equal Employment Opportunity Commission (EEOC).

The ADA also covers most forms of public transportation and requires that new buses, trains, and other vehicles be made accessible. This means they must be equipped with lifts, ramps, and wheelchair spaces or seats. The law also prohibits discrimination based on a disability. For example, a taxi driver may not refuse to pick up a person using a wheelchair.

Finally, the ADA prohibits discrimination against persons with disabilities in their use of public accommodations, such as restaurants, hotels, theaters, doctors' offices, pharmacies, grocery stores, shopping centers, museums, schools, parks, and other similar establishments. Basically, the law requires that existing barriers be removed, provided this can be done without much difficulty or expense, and that new construction be accessible.

For more information, contact the EEOC at www.eeoc.gov.

Can I just copy cartoon characters?
"Not under our copyright laws."

Dear Mr. Alderman:
I design T-shirts. I sometimes draw freehand images of cartoon characters I have seen. I do not copy them out of a book. I draw them from memory. I have been told this is illegal. Is it?

Copying the image of a cartoon character is probably a violation of our copyright laws whether you do it from memory or directly from a book. Under federal law, the person who creates a work of art, such as a cartoon character, may "copyright" the image. This gives that person the exclusive right to reproduce it. If the characters you are drawing are copyrighted, you are in violation of the law and could be liable for damages.

Can a business ask for a social security number?
"Yes, but you don't have to give it."

Dear Mr. Alderman:
It seems like every person I do business with wants my Social Security number. Can businesses require this information?

Basically, you don't have to give businesses any information you don't want to. And they don't have to deal with you if they don't want to. In my opinion, many businesses ask for information they either don't need or shouldn't be allowed to have. As a legal matter, however, they can ask for it. Because of the importance of a Social Security number, I suggest you refuse to provide it, unless the person asking can demonstrate a need for the information, such as an IRS requirement. In most cases, however, the law says the business cannot refuse to deal with you if you do not provide the number.

I should point out that the law regarding use of a Social Security number is undergoing some changes. New laws are being proposed to help keep your number private. To keep current with these laws, visit my website, www.peopleslawyer.net.

CHAPTER 18

Warranties

When you buy something, you expect to get what you pay for—this is what warranty law is all about. A warranty is any promise by a seller or manufacturer to stand behind its product. To have a warranty, there is no need to use special words such as "warranty," "guarantee," or "promise." Anything said about a product that you rely on when you purchase it is usually sufficient to give rise to a warranty that the product will do what it is supposed to do. An advertisement, the salesman's promises, a written document that came with the product, and even a sample or a model of the product can give rise to a warranty. These warranties that arise due to the seller's words or conduct are called "express" warranties.

A warranty may also arise by "implication," based on the nature of the product, without the need for any action by the seller. For example, if you buy a shovel and nothing is said about its qualities, there is a warranty that the shovel will be fit for its ordinary purpose, and will be able to dig a hole. These warranties are called "implied" warranties.

Warranty law is governed by two statutes: a state law called the **Uniform Commercial Code** and a federal law called the **Magnuson-Moss Warranty Act.** Both of these laws protect you by making a seller or a manufacturer responsible whenever a product does not live up to your expectations. As you will see from the letters in this chapter, a few formalities must be followed to establish a warranty. Often, a consumer has more than adequate warranty protection, even though nothing was ever said about a warranty. To review a copy of these laws, as well as all other consumer laws, check out my website at www.peopleslawyer.net.

What is a warranty?
"More than just a tag."

Dear Mr. Alderman:
I have been shopping for a new lawn mower. I found one I liked and was waiting for it to go on sale when my neighbor told me that I shouldn't buy it because it had a bad warranty. I never really thought

about warranties before—they have always been just a tag hanging on the product that I never bothered to read. Just what is a warranty? And how important is it?

Your friend is right. One of the most important parts of any purchase is the warranty you receive. In simple terms, the warranty is the obligation, or promise, of the seller of the goods as to the quality of the goods being sold.

Warranties can arise by agreement or automatically by operation of law. For example, most products come with written warranties, which give you specific rights, and implied warranties, which the law imposes in most sales. *But the law allows a merchant to contractually change or disclaim his warranty liability, and most written warranties are actually taking away some of the rights you would otherwise have.*

For example, if you buy a lawn mower and nothing is said about warranties, you have an implied warranty that the mower will cut grass, and if it doesn't, the dealer is responsible. But a dealer can sell a lawn mower with no warranties at all by contractually disclaiming them, for example, selling it "as is." If this was done you would have no right to return it if you got the mower home and it only ran for one hour. In fact, the dealer doesn't even promise you it will run. When you buy without a warranty, you basically accept all the risks that the product is defective.

In your case, consider the warranty as part of what you are buying. For instance, let's assume a store has a lawn mower that sells for $150 but has only a limited thirty-day warranty covering replacement of parts, but not labor. Another store is selling a similar mower for $175, but this one has a two-year warranty that covers parts and labor. Which is the better deal? Well, the ultimate decision is up to you, but if the mower breaks down during the first two years and repairs are more than $25, you would be much better off with the "more expensive" mower.

Remember, your legal rights against a seller are based on the warranty you receive. If you have a good remedy, you will be well protected if something goes wrong. You should shop around for warranties, just like you shop for color or price.

What is the difference between a full warranty
and a limited warranty?
"Read the small print."

Dear Mr. Alderman:
Whenever I shop around for a good warranty, I notice most of them say they are "limited" warranties. What does this mean? What is limited? If I don't want a limited warranty, what other choice do I have? Is there such a thing as an unlimited warranty?

Congress found so many problems with warranty law that it passed the Magnuson-Moss Warranty Act. This law requires that warranties be written in simple and readily understandable language. It also requires that all warranties be labeled either "full" or "limited." Under the law a warranty can only be called full if it meets these requirements:

1. The warrantor (the person making the warranty) must repair or replace the product, or give the consumer a refund within a reasonable time and at no charge, if the product does not conform with the warranty.

2. The warrantor may not impose any limitation on the duration of any implied warranty (those warranties that arise by operation of law and are discussed in the next letter).

3. The warrantor may not exclude or limit consequential damages (those caused by the defective product) unless the exclusion is conspicuously written on the face of the warranty.

4. If the product can't be repaired after a reasonable number of attempts, the consumer must be permitted to elect to receive a refund or a replacement.

5. The warranty is good for anyone who owns the product during the warranty period.

Under the law any warranty that does not live up to all these requirements must be labeled "limited." When you see the word "limited," the company is telling you it has not given you all the protection it could have. *A full warranty is always better than a limited one.* For example, here are some "full" warranties.

A full warranty.

MAXELL FULL LIFETIME WARRANTY

Maxell warrants this product to be free from manufacturing defects in materials and workmanship for the lifetime of the original purchaser. *This warranty does not apply to normal wear or to damage resulting from accident, abnormal use, misuse, abuse or neglect.* Any defective product will be replaced at no charge if it is returned to an authorized Maxell dealer or to Maxell. HOWEVER, MAXELL SHALL NOT BE LIABLE FOR ANY COMMERCIAL DAMAGES, WHETHER INCIDENTAL, CONSEQUENTIAL OR OTHERWISE.

Full warranties offer the most protection.

THIS WARRANTY SUPERSEDES ALL OTHER PRODUCT WARRANTIES
INCLUDING ANY WARRANTY WHICH MAY BE FOUND IN THE USE
AND CARE BOOKLET

FULL ONE YEAR WARRANTY

This appliance is warranted against defects in materials or workmanship for a full one year from the date of purchase.

During the warranty period this product will be repaired or replaced, at Hamilton Beach's option, at no cost to you.

In event of a [warranted] product defect, please deliver the product to the nearest authorized service station, listed on the reverse side of this warranty [or look in your local yellow pages for your nearest authorized Hamilton Beach Service Station].

This warranty does not apply in cases of abuse, mishandling, unauthorized repair or commercial use.

In using your new appliance, as directed in the Use and Care Booklet, we are confident it will serve you faithfully. Should you ever feel our products or services do not meet our high standards, please direct your comments to:

PRINTED IN U.S.A.
3-266-223-00-00

Manager, Consumer Relations
P.O. Box 2028
Washington, N. C. 27889

Hamilton Beach Division

Scovill

Reading these warranties tells you what rights you have if the product does not work. As you can see, the company tells you in simple language that if anything is wrong with the product, you or any other owner can get it replaced at no charge. In capital letters, the first warranty also tells you what damages it is not responsible for: commercial damages. The companies are responsible for all other damages—for example, if the product caused damage to another piece of equipment or if the cooler damaged your food.

Following this answer is a limited warranty. Can you see what the company has not given you? If the company can't fix the product, do you have to keep taking it back? What damages is the company liable for if the goods are defective? Who pays for labor, insurance? Can someone else use the warranty or is it limited to the original purchaser?

The Magnuson-Moss Warranty Act applies to any consumer product costing more than $10. Under the law, warranties must be available before the sale. Take advantage of the law and read the warranty before you buy.

You should shop for warranties the same way you shop for price and quality. For more information about the Magnuson-Moss Warranty Act, check out the Federal Trade Commission (FTC) website, www.ftc.gov.

A limited warranty leaves out some protection. Read it carefully.

SONY®

> DVD Recorder
> BD Player

LIMITED WARRANTY (U.S. Only)

Sony Electronics Inc. ("Sony") warrants this product against defects in material or workmanship for the time periods and as set forth below. Pursuant to this Limited Warranty, Sony will, at its option, (i) repair the product using new or refurbished parts or (ii) replace the product with a new or refurbished product. For purposes of this Limited Warranty, "refurbished" means a product or part that has been returned to its original specifications. **In the event of a defect, these are your exclusive remedies.**

Term: For a period of one year from the original date of purchase of the product, Sony will, at its option, repair or replace with new or refurbished product or parts, any product or parts determined to be defective.

This Limited Warranty covers only the hardware components packaged with the Product. It does not cover technical assistance for hardware or software usage and it does not cover any software products whether or not contained in the Product; any such software is provided "AS IS" unless expressly provided for in any enclosed software Limited Warranty. Please refer to the End User License Agreements included with the Product for your rights and obligations with respect to the software.

Instructions: To obtain warranty service, you must deliver the product, freight prepaid, in either its original packaging or packaging affording an equal degree of protection to the Sony authorized service facility specified. **It is your responsibility to backup any data, software or other materials you may have stored or preserved on your unit. It is likely that such data, software, or other materials will be lost or reformatted during service and Sony will not be responsible for any such damage or loss.** A dated purchase receipt is required. For specific instructions on how to obtain warranty service for your product,

Visit Sony's Web Site:
www.sony.com/service

Or call the **Sony Customer Information Service Center**
1-800-222-7669

For an accessory or part not available from your authorized dealer, call:

1-800-488-SONY (7669)

Repair / Replacement Warranty: This Limited Warranty shall apply to any repair, replacement part or replacement product for the remainder of the original Limited Warranty period or for ninety (90) days, whichever is longer. Any parts or product replaced under this Limited Warranty will become the property of Sony.

This Limited Warranty only covers product issues caused by defects in material or workmanship during ordinary consumer use; it does not cover product issues caused by any other reason, including but not limited to product issues due to commercial use, acts of God, misuse, limitations of technology, or modification of or to any part of the Sony product. This Limited Warranty does not cover Sony products sold AS IS or WITH ALL FAULTS or consumables (such as fuses or batteries). This Limited Warranty is invalid if the factory-applied serial number has been altered or removed from the product. This Limited Warranty is valid only in the United States.

LIMITATION ON DAMAGES: SONY SHALL NOT BE LIABLE FOR ANY INCIDENTAL OR CONSEQUENTIAL DAMAGES FOR BREACH OF ANY EXPRESS OR IMPLIED WARRANTY ON THIS PRODUCT.

DURATION OF IMPLIED WARRANTIES: EXCEPT TO THE EXTENT PROHIBITED BY APPLICABLE LAW, ANY IMPLIED WARRANTY OF MERCHANTABILITY OR FITNESS FOR A PARTICULAR PURPOSE ON THIS PRODUCT IS LIMITED IN DURATION TO THE DURATION OF THIS WARRANTY.

Some states do not allow the exclusion or limitation of incidental or consequential damages, or allow limitations on how long an implied warranty lasts, so the above limitations or exclusions may not apply to you. This Limited Warranty gives you specific legal rights and you may have other rights which vary from state to state.

What if nothing is said about a warranty? Am I out of luck?
"No, just the opposite."

Dear Mr. Alderman:
The other day I went into the hardware store to buy a shovel to plant
some bushes. The store had six or seven different models of pointed
shovels, so I picked out the one that seemed best. After coming home,
I went out back to dig a hole to plant a small bush, and after the first
shovelful, the shovel bent. I couldn't believe it. The metal part actu-
ally bent in half. I went right back to the store clerk and told him I
wanted my money back. He said I must have done something wrong
with the shovel. He also said, "Tough luck. You bought it; it's your
problem." My wife told me I should take the store to justice court,
but I want to know the law first. What do you think? I am worried
because I didn't get any warranty, and I always thought that when
this happened it was "tough luck, buyer."

If the store still refuses to give you your money back, let it know the next
step may be justice court. The law is on your side. Under the law, whenever a merchant sells you something, you automatically get what is called
a "warranty of merchantability." This warranty arises automatically; nothing has to be said or done. This warranty is in addition to any other warranties you may be given.

Under the warranty of merchantability, a merchant guarantees that any
product it sells you is fit for its "ordinary purposes" and will "pass without objection in the trade." What this means is that whenever you buy
something, the merchant promises you the merchandise will do what a
reasonable person thinks it will do. In your case, the merchant automatically made a warranty that the shovel is fit for its ordinary purpose—that
is, digging holes. When the shovel bent, the warranty was breached, and
you are entitled to damages.

In other words, *when nothing is said about a warranty, the law gives*
you a substantial one. The law gives you a guarantee that what you bought
will do what it is designed to do, the way it is supposed to do it, and for as
long as a reasonable person would think it would do it.

I suggest you go back to the store and try again to settle the problem.
Let the store know that you know about warranty law. Also remember that
any breach of warranty automatically violates the Deceptive Trade Practices Act. As the next letter shows, this gives you added leverage when
dealing with a merchant.

My laundry ruined my shirt. Is there a service warranty?
"There is a service warranty."

Dear Mr. Alderman:
I took a new shirt to the laundry to have it cleaned. When I picked it up I noticed several small holes in it. I know they were not there when I took it in because it was the first time I had worn it. The manager said, "Tough luck. Sometimes the machines do that. It is not our fault." He agreed to give me a few dollars, but the shirt cost $50. I want to take him to justice court. Do you think I have a case?

Whenever someone performs a service for you, there is an "implied warranty" that he will do it in a "good and workmanlike" manner. This means that he will maintain the same standards as others in the business and will perform as a reasonable competent person in the same business would expect. In my opinion, putting holes in a shirt would breach this warranty. It is not good and workmanlike cleaning to ruin the clothes.

You should also know that any time a warranty is breached, this also constitutes a violation of the Deceptive Trade Practices Act. In other words, the cleaners could be responsible for as much as $150 if you took it to justice court. Reread the material in Chapter 10 to find out how to use this law.

What can I do if the food made me sick?
"There may be a warranty."

Dear Mr. Alderman:
The other night my friends and I went to a restaurant for dinner. After my appetizer I felt a little nauseated. By the time I got home, I was very sick. I went to the hospital and was told it was food poisoning. I was sick for two days and spent nearly $200 on doctor bills. I went back to the restaurant, and management refused to help pay for my expenses. Do I have any legal rights?

Under the law, whenever a restaurant sells you food, it makes what is known as a warranty of merchantability. This, basically, is a guarantee that the food is fit for its ordinary purpose: consumption. Selling tainted food would breach this warranty and give you a claim for damages.

I should point out that this is what is known as an implied warranty, and it arises even though nothing is said about the food. Therefore, if you were to eat in a restaurant and get sick because of tainted food, the restaurant would be liable. As the next letter indicates, this could result in substantial damages.

Is it really worth suing for breach of warranty?
"In Texas you may get three times your damages."

Dear Mr. Alderman:

My husband and I bought a plant-light lamp. It came with a written guarantee that said it would be suitable for special "plant light-bulbs." The store assured us it was "just right for us." When we got it home we set it up in front of our plants and put in a new bulb. After a few hours we smelled something burning and realized the lamp casing was melting from the heat of the bulb. Luckily there wasn't a fire, but it did burn our favorite plant and curtains.

When we went back to the store, we were told it was the manufacturer's fault and the store would not stand by the warranty. The manufacturer is in El Paso, and we are in Dallas. We wrote, but the manufacturer hasn't responded. The light cost $69, our plant was worth at least $20 and the curtains cost $250. My husband says for $339 we should just forget it; no lawyer would take it, and justice court takes a lot of time. It seems like the person with the little claim is just out of luck. Can't something be done?

Ask your husband if he would go to justice court if he could receive $1,017 plus court costs, because under the law that is how much you may recover if you are successful. According to Texas law, any breach of warranty automatically violates the Deceptive Trade Practices Act. If you show the person acted "knowingly," that is "knew or should have known" about the defect, you are entitled to up to three times your damages plus court costs and attorney's fees.

Based on what you say in your letter, you clearly have a claim against the manufacturer for breach of an express warranty, and you probably also have a claim against the seller for breach of the warranty of merchantability and fitness. I suggest you read Chapter 10 and find out how to use the Deceptive Trade Practices Act. My guess is once you contact the store and the manufacturer, and let them know you know your rights, they will quickly settle the matter.

Texas warranty law is very favorable to consumers. Under the law you are always entitled to your attorney's fees plus court costs and up to three times your damages if you have to sue. Merchants know the law. Let them know you know it too, and see how quickly problems are resolved.

I just bought a lemon. Can you help?
"Texas lemon-aid."

Dear Mr. Alderman:
I just bought a new car. It stinks! Ever since the day I got it, I have
had nothing but problems: first the brakes, then the transmission,
now the air conditioning. The car has been in the shop for over two
months, and I have only owned it for three. I need help. Is there any-
thing I can do?

Fortunately for you, the law has changed. Historically, when you bought
a car you lived by the old maxim "caveat emptor" (let the buyer beware).
Once you took the car off the lot, it was yours, and if it was a lemon, you
were just out of luck. But not so today. Now, when you buy a car, the law is
"caveat vendor" (let the seller beware). If you buy a lemon, the law places
a burden on the seller to promptly take care of the problem, and you have
strong remedies if he doesn't.

There are three separate laws a consumer can rely on after buying what
turns out to be a lemon:

1. The Texas Deceptive Trade Practices Act
2. The Uniform Commercial Code
3. The Texas Lemon Law

The Texas Deceptive Trade Practices Act, discussed in Chapter 10, simply states that if the seller deceives you as to the nature of the automobile,
or if there is a breach of warranty, you may be entitled to three times
your damages, plus your attorney's fees. You should read over Chapter 10,
but I want to emphasize one thing here: *If you are having a problem get-*
ting your car repaired properly, let the dealer know that you know about
the Deceptive Trade Practices Act. You may be amazed at how fast the
mechanics improve.

Another law that can help you with a lemon is the **Uniform Commer-**
cial Code. This law can be somewhat complicated, so I will just give a
brief summary of what it does. If you think it applies to your problem, you
will probably have to get an attorney to help you.

The Uniform Commercial Code lets a person "revoke his acceptance."
In simple, nonlegal terms, this means you can change your mind and not
keep the car after you have taken it. You are allowed to revoke your acceptance whenever there is a defect in the car that substantially impairs its
value to you, and you took the car without knowing about this defect and
without having a reasonable opportunity to discover it. After you revoke

your acceptance, you can give the car back to the seller, and he must give you back your money. It is as if you never took the car.

For example, if you buy a new car and, as soon as you get it home, you discover it won't go into reverse, you can return the car and revoke your acceptance. In other words, the law gives you a chance to make sure what you bought does what it was supposed to do. If it does not, you don't have to keep it.

If you buy a car that quickly turns out to be a lemon, you may have the right to revoke your acceptance and retrieve your money. But you must show that the defects in the car substantially impair its value to you and that you didn't know about them when you bought the car. *The application of this law can be affected by your contract with the seller. Before thinking you can revoke your acceptance and return your lemon, read your contract and see an attorney!*

The final law that may help you with your lemon is the **Texas Lemon Law.** This law applies only to new vehicles and provides that if you buy a lemon, the *manufacturer* must either return your money or give you a new car. Before you get your new auto, though, two things must happen.

1. Your car must meet the statutory definition of a lemon.
2. You must have an administrative hearing regarding your dispute and give the manufacturer a chance to fix things.

Under the law, a lemon is defined as a car that has a serious defect that has been reported within the warranty term and has not been repaired in a reasonable number of attempts. A dealer or manufacturer has a reasonable number of attempts to fix the car:

1. When you have taken the car to be repaired two times for the same problem within the first 12 months or 12,000 miles, whichever occurs first, and twice more during the 12 months or 12,000 miles after the second repair attempt; or
2. A serious safety defect is subject to repair once during the first 12 months or 12,000 miles, whichever occurs first, and once more during the 12 months or 12,000 miles following the first repair; or
3. The car has been out of service for a total of 30 days or more during the first 24 months or 24,000 miles, whichever occurs first, and there were two repair attempts during the first 12 months or 12,000 miles, and a substantial problem still exists. Any time for which you were provided a free loaner car does not count toward the 30 days.

In other words, if your car has a defect that substantially affects the use or value of the car and that defect is not repaired within the above time limits, it meets the definition of a legal lemon.

To make certain you protect yourself under the lemon law, or for that matter any time you have a lemon, be sure that the dealer documents your problem each time you bring your car in. Also, tell him your problem in general terms. Under the law you must have had the car in to be fixed four times for the same defect. If your engine stalls out, just tell him that, and make sure that is how it is written up on the service order. If you complain about the carburetor and then bring it back saying it is the fuel pump, and then the fuel line, you will have three different problems, not one problem repaired three times. *It is the dealer's job to pinpoint the exact nature of your problem. Describe the problem in general, nonmechanical terms and let the dealer worry about the exact nature of the defect.*

Once you think you have met the test for a lemon, you should contact the Texas Department of Motor Vehicles and file a complaint, requesting a hearing to resolve the dispute with the manufacturer. The department will contact the dealer and manufacturer, which may then repair or replace your vehicle. If the matter is not resolved, a hearing examiner will schedule a hearing to determine the validity of your complaint. The examiner will listen to evidence of your complaint and has the power to order the manufacturer to repair the car, refund your money, or give you a new car. The department has much more information about this law on its website.

For more information about the lemon law or to file a complaint, contact the Texas Department of Motor Vehicles at www.txdmv.gov, (888) DMV-GOTX or (888) 368-4689.

**Here is a sample letter you can send to the manufacturer
if you believe you have a lemon law complaint.**

Your Name
Your Address
Your City, State, Zip Code
Your Area Code and Daytime Phone
Date

Manufacturer's Name
Address from Manufacturer's Warranty Manual
City, State, Zip Code

To Whom It May Concern:
I am writing to notify you of the problems I am experiencing with my
(insert year, make, model, and VIN number of your vehicle) and to
request that you correct this problem within thirty (30) days of your
receipt of this letter.

   I purchased my vehicle from (insert name and location of selling dealership) on or about (insert date of purchase). Approximately
(insert amount of time after purchase) I began having trouble with
(insert description of problem). I took my vehicle back to the dealer
for repairs on (insert dates of repair attempts) but, to date, the dealer
has been unable to correct the problem. Attached are copies of the
repair orders, which document the dealership's attempts to repair my
vehicle. This problem (choose one or both of the following statements) (substantially impairs the use or value of my vehicle) or (creates a serious safety hazard). Therefore, if you and/or your dealer are
unable to correct this problem, I will expect you to (insert "replace"
or "repurchase") the vehicle pursuant to the Texas Lemon Law.

   Please contact me on receipt of this letter at the above address or
telephone number to arrange a mutually convenient date and time
for you to have an opportunity to inspect my vehicle and make any
necessary repairs.

Sincerely,
(insert your name)

Enclosures
Certified Mail
Return Receipt Requested (insert certified receipt number)

Does the Texas Lemon Law apply to motorcycles?
"It applies to most types of vehicles."

Dear Mr. Alderman:
I bought a motorcycle that keeps breaking down. I know there is a
"lemon law" for cars, but what about a motorcycle?

As discussed in the above letter, the Texas Lemon Law can provide relief
when you purchase a defective automobile. But the lemon law applies to
most new "vehicles," including cars, trucks, vans, motorcycles, all-terrain
vehicles, motor homes, and towable recreational vehicles (TRVs), that
develop problems covered by a written factory warranty. This means the
lemon law applies to your motorcycle. To learn about this law and how to
use it, review the question and answer above.

Is there a lemon law for manufactured homes?
"No, but there are legal protections."

Dear Mr. Alderman:
I bought a manufactured home. Since the day it was delivered, I have
had problems. At first the manufacturer was very helpful but it now
refuses to talk to me. Is there a lemon law for manufactured homes?
Do I have any legal protections when I am sold a defective home?

There is no "lemon law" that covers manufactured homes, but Texas
does have a Manufactured Housing Standards Act that protects consumers. I suggest that you start by contacting the Texas Department of
Housing and Consumer Affairs. It administers the Texas Manufactured
Housing Standards Act and has a website that provides information on
manufactured housing complaints: www.tdhca.state.tx.us/mh. You also
may review the entire text of the Texas Manufactured Housing Standards
Act on this site.

The Manufactured Housing Division (MHD) of the Texas Department
of Housing and Community Affairs administers the Texas Manufactured
Housing Standards Act. Because of its regulatory nature, MHD has its own
board and executive director. MHD licenses and regulates those who man-
ufacture, sell, broker, and install manufactured homes. MHD issues and
maintains records on manufactured home ownership and location, inspects
manufactured home installations, and investigates and oversees the resolution of consumer complaints. It maintains offices in Austin, Dallas/Fort
Worth, Houston, San Antonio, Lubbock, Tyler, Waco, and Edinburg.

Our house leveler won't live up to its warranty. What can I do?
"The Deceptive Trade Practices Act may help."

Dear Mr. Alderman:
Last year we had our house leveled. The company gave us a fifteen-year guarantee it would fix any problems. This year the house had major settling problems with the foundation. The company won't return our calls and refuses to talk to us. I sent a certified letter and still have not received a reply. I don't want to sue. What can I do?

Unfortunately, you may have to sue to get your problem solved. Knowing a little bit about the law, however, may help solve the matter without litigation.

As discussed in Chapter 10, the Texas Deceptive Trade Practices Act is our state's consumer protection law. One of the things actionable under this law is a breach of warranty. In your case, the refusal to honor the warranty violates this law.

The Deceptive Trade Practices Act allows you to recover your economic damages plus attorney's fees. Additionally, if you can show the breach was done knowingly, which appears true in your case, you can recover up to three times your damages plus mental anguish.

Because of the amount of money involved, you probably will need an attorney to assist you with your claim under the Deceptive Trade Practices Act. As a first step, however, you should send another certified letter letting the company know that you know about this law and will use it if necessary. Remember, if you are successful with your lawsuit, you can recover your attorney's fees from the other party.

What are my rights when my new puppy dies?
"Puppies may have a warranty."

Dear Mr. Alderman:
I purchased a new pedigree puppy. As soon as I got it home, it became very ill. I immediately brought it to the veterinarian, but after two days and $1,000 in expenses, the puppy died. The vet said that the dog was extremely ill the day I bought it. The seller refuses to help pay the vet bills or even give me my money back. What are my legal rights?

Under the law, unless you bought the dog "as is," you get what is called a warranty of "merchantability." This is a warranty that the law implies in any contract for the sale of "goods." A dog is considered a "good," just like any other product you purchase.

Under this warranty, any merchant who sells a product warrants that it is "fit for its ordinary purpose," and will "pass without objection in the trade." In my opinion, this basically means that you have a guarantee that the dog is healthy at the time of the sale. If you can show that the dog had the medical problem at the time you purchased it, my opinion is that the seller has breached the warranty of merchantability, and should be liable for damages.

If there is a breach of warranty, you will be entitled to all of the damages you suffered as a result of the breach. That includes the cost of the puppy, as well as your veterinarian bills. You also would have a claim under the Deceptive Trade Practices Act, which entitles you to attorney's fees, and up to three times your damage if the seller knew the puppy was sick when it was sold.

I suggest you let the seller know that you know your rights, that you expect your money back or a new puppy, and that you expect to be compensated for some or all of the vet bills. If you cannot settle the matter, consider a claim in justice court.

CHAPTER 19

Wills & Probate

One of the most common questions asked is: "Do I need a will?" Well, frankly, no; you don't need a will. It really isn't going to matter to you. But on the other hand, it may be extremely important to your family, because the only way you can ensure they receive your property with a minimum of time and expense is to make out a will.

When you die without a will, you are said to have died "intestate." If you die intestate, the state decides which of your heirs gets your property; it does not go to the state. Also, when you die intestate, the process of distributing your property and seeing that all your bills are paid is usually closely supervised by the court.

But if you die with a will, you can give your property to whomever you wish, and you can also appoint an "executor" to handle the distribution of the property. Usually the executor can act without the supervision of the court. In other words, *having a will is the most effective way to make certain your property goes where you want—and that your estate is not tied up with the additional time and expense of court supervision.*

What is a living will?
"Death with dignity."

Dear Mr. Alderman:
A friend told me that a law exists in Texas that permits a person to refuse to be kept alive by machine when he is going to die anyway. Should I ever be diagnosed as terminally ill, I would not wish my family to pay for expensive treatment simply to allow me to live a little longer. What can I do to make certain I can refuse such treatment? What if I am in a coma? How, then, can I protect my family?

There is a legal device designed to let you make the choice of whether to be left on a life-sustaining machine after you have been found to be terminally ill. The document is called an "advance directive" or a "directive." The common name given to this document is "living will."

273

If you are being kept alive by a machine, a physician may not disconnect you or turn the machine off without your consent, even if your family requests it. This is because of the potential liability to the doctor. The Texas Legislature, however, has passed a law that lets you decide in advance whether to be kept alive by a machine. If you execute a directive under this law, the physician can follow your wishes without worrying about liability to your estate or your heirs. Although a doctor is not obligated to comply with a living will, most do. If a physician refuses to comply with your directive, he must transfer you to an institution or physician willing to comply.

Under the **Advance Directive Law,** you can fill out a written directive at any time, or you may make an oral directive in front of two witnesses and your doctor. Because you may not be competent to make such a decision when you need to, it is a good idea to make out a directive now and keep it in a safe place.

An advance directive, or living will, does not have to be in any special form, but the form on pages 312 to 316 is suggested by the legislature.

The directive to physicians gives you the choice to die with dignity and avoid costly medical bills for your family. The choice is up to you. If you want to make that choice, simply fill in the form and keep it in a safe place where your family can find it.

Is a living will from another state valid in Texas?
"Yes, but only to the extent permitted by Texas law."

Dear Mr. Alderman:
I just moved here from another state. I have a living will I prepared about a year ago. Is this document still effective in Texas?

Under Texas law a living will or other directive validly executed in another state is given the same effect in Texas as a properly prepared Texas directive. If, however, the document authorizes conduct not permitted in Texas, that part of the document will not be effective.

Even though your living will is probably valid in Texas, it is still a good idea to prepare a new Texas directive. This will remove any question as to the document's validity or scope.

What can I do to ensure that I am not resuscitated
at my home by an emergency medical team?
"Complete an Out-of-Hospital DNR Order."

Dear Mr. Alderman:

Recently, an elderly friend suffered a serious stroke and heart attack while at home. She had told her family and friends when she was hospitalized that she did want to be resuscitated if her heart stopped beating. Her doctor had issued a DNR (do–not-resuscitate) order. After she was released from the hospital and sent home, she suffered a severe attack. Her family called 911 and an ambulance arrived. The family told them she did not want to be resuscitated, but they still attempted to resuscitate her. They told us she needed a special form if she did not wish to have life-sustaining treatment. What is this form? How do I get one?

The form you are referring to is called an out-of-hospital do-not-resuscitate order (OOH-DNR). The OOH-DNR program allows people to decide that they do not want to be resuscitated. The program allows individuals to declare that certain resuscitative measures will not be used if they suffer respiratory or cardiac arrest while not in a hospital. Those resuscitative measures specifically listed in the OOH-DNR legislation are cardiopulmonary resuscitation (CPR), advanced airway management, defibrillation, artificial ventilations, and transcutaneous cardiac pacing. For more information and to obtain an OOH-DNR form, visit the Texas Department of Health and Human Services website, www.dshs.texas.gov/emstrauma systems/dnr.shtm.

I am going into the hospital for complicated surgery. Can my son make medical decisions for me if I am not competent to do so? "Yes, through a Medical Power of Attorney."

Dear Mr. Alderman:

I am seventy-two years old and just found out I have a tumor that must be removed. The doctors said it is a very serious operation and I may not recover. I am able to face the possibility of death, but I am concerned about being subjected to unwanted medical treatment. For example, I do not want to be kept alive by a feeding tube when all hope for recovery is gone. I know that a living will gives me the right to have life support systems disconnected if I have a terminal condition, but I would like to have some control over the type and extent of treatment I receive. I trust my son's judgment and want to know if there is some way to have him make my medical decisions in the event I cannot.

Texas has enacted the Advance Directives Act, which allows you to pre-pare a **Medical Power of Attorney.** This device permits you to appoint someone to make health-care decisions for you in the event that you are no longer competent to act on your own behalf. The Medical Power of Attor-ney does not take effect until your doctor certifies that you are no longer competent to make your own decisions. If you change your mind about the Medical Power of Attorney, you may change it at any time, or revoke it by giving oral or written notice to the person you appoint or to your physician or health-care provider.

Before you complete a Medical Power of Attorney, the law requires that you read a disclosure statement explaining the document. The disclosure statement may be found on pages 316 to 318. If, after reading the disclo-sure form, you still want to complete the Medical Power of Attorney, the form is on pages 319 to 322. Filling out this form will authorize your son to make medical decisions in the event you are unable to do so.

Is there a difference between a Durable Power of Attorney and a Medical Power of Attorney? "Yes, a big difference."

Dear Mr. Alderman:
I am seriously ill and do not think I will be able to manage my affairs much longer. I want to give my son the authority to make medical decisions for me and to pay all my bills and handle my financial affairs. I filled out a Medical Power of Attorney last year. Now I have been told there is another type of power of attorney I must complete. What is it?

As you already know, a Medical Power of Attorney allows you to desig-nate someone else to make medical decisions regarding your health care in the event that you are unable to. This document does not, however, grant any other authority.

If you want to authorize someone else to make your financial decisions, you must fill out a *Durable* Power of Attorney. If a power of attorney is durable, it remains valid and in effect even if you become incapacitated and unable to make decisions for yourself. If a power of attorney doc-ument does not explicitly say that the power is durable, it ends if you become incapacitated.

A Durable Power of Attorney is a very powerful, legally binding form that gives someone else the power to make decisions regarding your prop-erty and financial matters in the event you become disabled or otherwise incapable of making decisions. For example, the person designated as your agent may write checks on your account to pay your bills and can withdraw money from any of your accounts as needed. This power, however, is very broad. Money can be withdrawn to pay your bills, or it might just be taken and used for a trip to Hawaii. Although such action by your agent would be illegal, the money still would be gone from your account.

Before you sign a Durable Power of Attorney and designate someone as your agent, you must give very serious consideration to what you are doing. You also may want to contact an attorney to make sure you grant only as much power as you have to.

I have included a Statutory Durable Power of Attorney form on page 323. This is the form suggested by the legislature. Any document in substantially the same form is effective. As you can tell, the law lets you determine the extent of the powers you grant to your agent. Once you sign the document, however, anyone who in good faith relies on it is protected, even if your agent doesn't do what you wanted.

What is community property?
"Part yours . . . part your spouse's."

Dear Mr. Alderman:
I have married, and my friends tell me that, henceforth, all my property is considered "community property" and that I should keep track of the property I owned prior to the marriage. Why does it matter?

When people get married, all their property is either community or separate. This distinction is important because it determines who gets what upon death or divorce. Basically, community property is everything people acquire after they get married. Separate property is everything you owned before you were married and gifts or inheritances acquired after you were married. *Community property is considered to be owned in part by each spouse. Separate property belongs solely to the spouse who owned or acquired it.* Why is this important? Because when the marriage ends, either by death or divorce, community property is split between the parties or the heirs, while separate property goes to just one spouse or his or her heirs. Let me give you an example.

Suppose you are about to get married. You own a car, some clothes, and furniture, and you have about $5,000 in the bank. Your wife-to-be has about the same property. You marry and both open bank accounts in your own names. After a few years you buy a house with money you saved after you were married, and you also buy a car. During the marriage your rich aunt dies and leaves you $25,000. If, at this point, one of you should die, or if you divorce, the house and car would be community property. This means if you were to divorce you would split them (or the money obtained from their sale), and if one of you died, his or her heirs would acquire an interest in the house and car. On the other hand, the money you put in the bank saved from your premarriage earnings, and the money received from your aunt, are separate property. This means that upon divorce it would be exclusively yours, and if you died, all of it would go to your heirs. You should be aware, though, that the interest earned on your separate property is community property, and your spouse is entitled to one-half that amount.

In Texas, people usually do not pay alimony upon divorce. Property is split according to community property laws, and that is the end of it. Remember, once you get married nearly everything you acquire will be considered community property and will be owned by both spouses.

If you are concerned about the community property law—for example, you are an older person getting married for a second time, and you want to make sure your first family is taken care of—you can enter into a contract to change the community property laws. Texas law now allows people to decide how their property will be designated. If you think this is something you may be interested in, you should consult a family law attorney.

What if I don't have a will?
"The state writes one for you."

Dear Mr. Alderman:
I have remarried. My wife and I both have children from our prior marriages and now want to have children together. We own a house we purchased after we got married. My friends have told me it is important to have a will if I want to ensure that the children of my first marriage are taken care of. I am going to have a will prepared, but I am curious: What happens if I die without a will?

If you die without a will, the state, in effect, writes one for you. There are very specific laws that determine to whom your property passes after your death. This determination is based on the type of property, whether it is separate or community, and who survives you—for example, is your spouse living? Are your children living? If you are interested in a general idea of what happens in a specific case, you should first read the previous letter to find out what property is separate and what property is community.

As a general rule, community property is divided between spouses. If one member of a married couple dies, that person's share of the community property goes to the spouse. But things get much more complicated if the property is separate property, or if the deceased has children by another marriage. There also are different rules if the deceased is no longer married. As you can tell, the process of distributing property after death can get very complicated. The best advice I can give you is to prepare a will.

Remember: If you have a will, your property is divided as you direct, regardless of how the law would otherwise distribute it. If you want your property to go to someone other than the person(s) it would go to according to the law, you must have a will. Your case is a good example of how complicated it can get without a will. If you died without a will, the house you bought with your second wife would go half to your second wife (she already owns half as community property) and half (your half of the community property) to the children of your first marriage. This may not be what you would choose to do in a will. You always have a choice of where your property goes after your death—simply write a will.

Married Man or Woman With No Child or Children (Father and Mother Surviving)

A. SEPARATE PROPERTY

Real Estate

¼ father
½ to surviving spouse
¼ mother

All Other Property

all to surviving spouse

If only one parent survives, he or she takes ¼ of the real estate in the separate property, and ¼ is equally divided between brothers and sisters of the deceased and their descendants. If there are no surviving brothers and sisters, then the surviving parent takes ½ of real estate. If neither parent survives, then ½ of real estate is equally taken by brothers and sisters of the deceased and their descendants. If no parents, no brothers or sisters, or their descendants survive the deceased—then all the real estate is taken by the surviving husband or wife.

B. COMMUNITY PROPERTY

All community property—real or personal—is taken by surviving husband or wife.

Married Man or Woman With Child or Children

A. Separate Property

Real Estate

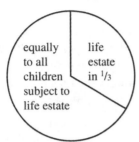

All Other Property

Surviving husband or wife only inherits an estate for life in ⅓ of the land of the deceased. When such surviving husband or wife dies, all the real estate is owned by the deceased's child or children.

B. Community Property

Real Estate

All Other Property

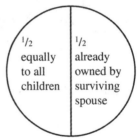

IF all surviving children are also children of the surviving spouse.

IF a surviving child is not also a child of the surviving spouse. Descendants of deceased children take their parent's share.

Unmarried Man or Woman or Widower or Widow With No Child or Children

(Father and Mother Surviving)

Entire Estate

| ½ father | ½ mother |

(Father or Mother & Brother or Sisters Surviving)

Entire Estate

| ½ father or mother | ½ brothers and sisters |

If only father or mother survives, then that parent takes ½, and the other ½ goes equally to all brothers and sisters. If there are no surviving brothers or sisters or their descendants, then all the estate goes to such surviving father or mother.

Widower or Widow With Child or Children

Real Estate

equally to all children

All Other Property

equally to all children

Children of deceased children take their parent's share.

Can I leave my property to just one person?
"You can leave property to whomever you want."

Dear Mr. Alderman:
I have a granddaughter and a great-granddaughter. I want to leave all my property to my great-granddaughter. I have been told I cannot cut my granddaughter out of my will. Is this possible?

Under the law, you may leave your property to whomever you want. In Texas, there is no requirement that a spouse, child, or grandchild take any specific share of what you own.

I suggest you speak with an attorney about preparing your will in a manner that clearly spells out your intentions. This way you can ensure the will is not challenged as ambiguous or unclear. Shop around for an attorney who charges what you believe is a fair price. A few phone calls could save you a lot of money.

Can I donate my body to science?
"Yes, just include a request in your will or fill out a document."

Dear Mr. Alderman:
I want to donate my body to a medical school to be used for teaching purposes. How do I ensure that my desires are given effect after my death?

Texas law authorizes a person over eighteen years of age to donate all or part of his or her body to a hospital or medical school, to be used for medical education or research. You may make such a gift either in your will or through a separate document. The donation is effective on the death of the donor.

If you use a separate document, it must be signed in the presence of two witnesses. The witnesses must also sign the document in your presence. No "formal" document is required and you may even use a card of your own design. The important thing is to make your intentions clear. If you wish to make the donation to a particular institution, the document should specify the name of the institution. If you change your mind, you may cancel your bequest at any time. Many medical schools have more information and forms on their websites.

Who decides where and how my remains
will be handled after death?
"You can decide."

Dear Mr. Alderman:
I recently prepared my will. That got me thinking about what hap-
pens to my body after I die. Who decides whether I will be buried or
cremated, and where?

The simple answer is that you can determine how your remains will be
handled after your death. Many people know exactly what they want
to happen to their bodies when they die. You can leave detailed written
instructions for your family, or appoint an agent, such as your spouse, to
make the decisions for you.

You may include a statement of your wishes in your will or in a separate
writing, such as a prepaid funeral contract. You may state whether and
where you choose to be buried, or that you wish to be cremated and have
your ashes scattered in a specific manner.

If you do not indicate how you wish your remains to be handled, the
decision in made by the following people, in order:

1. your surviving spouse;
2. any one of your surviving adult children;
3. either one of your surviving parents;
4. any one of your adult siblings;
5. one or more of the duly qualified executors or administrators of your
   estate.

Although the law will determine who makes the decision if you do not
leave instructions or an agent, the best way to makes things easy and less
costly for your family is to make this decision yourself, in advance.

Can I say whether I will be buried or cremated?
"Yes, the law lets you designate how your remains
will be disposed of after death."

Dear Mr. Alderman:
I want to be cremated after I die. I also would like my ashes destroyed.
I am concerned that my family will not follow my wishes. What can I
do to ensure that my remains are disposed of the way I want?

Texas law permits a person to direct, in writing, how his or her remains
should be disposed of following death. You may do this in your will or

in a separate document. You also have the right to designate an agent to carry out your wishes. This is the best way to ensure that your remains are handled in the manner that you desire.

As discussed in the above answer, if you do not leave directions for the disposition of your remains, the law determines who makes the decision. In most cases it is the surviving spouse, or, if there is no spouse, the children.

What happens to a joint bank account after death?
"It belongs to the survivor."

Dear Mr. Alderman:
My mother passed away a few months ago. She had a joint bank account with my sister. My mother's will says my sister and I split everything. My sister says she is entitled to all the money in the bank account and that we split everything else. I say we split everything. Who is right?

Your sister is right. Your mother had a joint bank account with a right of survivorship. What this means is that the account is owned jointly by the two parties, and when one dies, the other automatically owns the entire account.

A will provides how the estate of the deceased will be distributed after her death. The estate, however, includes only property owned at the time of death. By operation of the bank agreement, the bank account was no longer owned by your mother and was the property of your sister.

Can I write my own will?
"Sure, but you may not want to."

Dear Mr. Alderman:
I have read a lot about how important it is to have a will. I have decided that I should have one, and I would like to write it myself. Is this legal? How should I do it?

It is perfectly legal for anyone to write his or her own will. If the will meets the requirements of the law, it will be just as valid as a will prepared by an attorney. But if you are going to write your own will, you must be careful. One small mistake can invalidate the entire will and cause real problems for your family. *For this reason, I strongly urge you to see a lawyer.*

There are two basic kinds of wills in Texas: a holographic will, which is written entirely in your own handwriting and signed; and a formal will, which can be handwritten, printed, or typed, and which must be signed and witnessed by two people.

If you write a holographic will, it is valid so long as it is completely handwritten and signed. It is not a valid holographic will if you type part of it or if you fill in blanks on a form. It also should be dated, and it should state that it replaces all other wills you may have written. A holographic will must clearly indicate it was intended as a will and should not have any printing, typing, or obliterations. For example, the document on page 286 would serve as a holographic will.

Holographic wills should be used only in emergency situations. Best advice: Don't rely on a holographic will. It must be letter-perfect, and it is too easy to make a mistake. If you feel you must write your own will, consider a formal will.

A formal will must be signed by the testator and witnessed by at least two witnesses. It can be written, typed, or part of a preprinted form. For example, you can buy a form and fill in the proper blanks, or you could type it. You should also date your will, publish it (that is, declare it to be your will), and make sure everyone signs in the presence of everyone else. To give yourself added protection in other states, you should have three witnesses.

In addition to the proper signature, you should have what is known as a "self-proving affidavit." This allows your survivors to probate the will without having to go out and find the witnesses. A self-proving affidavit is simply a notary's statement that he has seen the people sign. At the end of this chapter I have included some sample wills and a self-proving affidavit.

Although the law allows you to prepare your own will, I don't recommend it. One small mistake can totally invalidate the entire will. To be safe, you should have an attorney prepare your will, and you should not have to pay much money to have it done. *Shop around and ask several attorneys what they charge. Most attorneys are competent to draft a simple will, and you may save yourself hundreds of dollars by making a few phone calls.*

A holographic will should be letter-perfect.

Last Will & Testament

I, Jane Smith, a resident of Harris County, Texas, declare this to be my Last Will & Testament. I revoke all prior wills and codicils.

First: I leave my 2004 Buick to my only brother, Jack Smith.

Second: I leave my dog, Shasta, to Nancy Jones, who resides at 1324 West Oaks, Houston, Texas.

Third: I leave the remainder of my estate to my parents, Susan Smith and Joe Smith, in equal shares. If they are not living, I leave the remainder of my property to the Society for the Prevention of Cruelty to Animals, Houston, Texas.

Fourth: I nominate Larry James as independent executor of my will. If he is not living or does not want to be executor, I nominate Keith Long to act in his place. I direct that no bond be required of my executor.

Executed at Houston, Texas, on July 2, 2017.

Jane Smith

Does my will have to be notarized?
"No, but it should be."

Dear Mr. Alderman:
I just noticed that my will is not notarized. Is it still valid?

In Texas, a will that is witnessed does not have to be notarized to be valid. A will that is notarized, however, will be easier and less costly to probate. The form that the notary signs is called a "self-proving affidavit." Using this form eliminates the requirement that you prove the people who signed as a witness actually witnessed and signed the document.

I suggest you consider having a new will prepared with a self-proving affidavit. It should not be too expensive to prepare a simple will, and it will save your loved ones a lot of time and money in the future.

Does a will control property given away right before death?
"Probably not. A will deals with only property
owned at the time of death."

Dear Mr. Alderman:
My father gave away much of his property right before he died. His will left everything to me. Do I have any right to the property he gave away?

If your father was competent at the time of the gifts, you probably have no right to the property. A person has the right to dispose of his or her property in whatever way he or she feels is reasonable. A will deals only with what is left in the person's estate after death.

On the other hand, if you feel that your father was not competent when he made the gifts, or was coerced or tricked into giving his property away, you may have the right to challenge them. If that is the case, you should speak with an attorney.

What is an executor?
"The person in charge."

Dear Mr. Alderman:
My sister just passed away, and I was told I am the executor of her will. What does this mean? Does this mean that I won't inherit anything? Will it cost me any money? I don't want to sound cheap, but I am not a wealthy man.

When you die it is necessary for someone to gather up all your property, close your bank accounts, transfer title to your house, and then make sure everything is given to the people you designated in your will. This person is called an "executor" if it is a man, and an "executrix" if it is a woman. Usually you appoint someone you trust, and who you believe is competent to do what must be done, as executor or executrix. By appointing you as executor, your sister was saying she believed you would be the best person to make sure her wishes are fulfilled. Depending on the terms of the will, you also may receive a fee for serving as the executor.

There is no reason why the executor or executrix cannot also receive property under a will, and if the will provides, he or she does not have to post a bond, or pay any money, to serve.

But in order to put the will into effect, it has to be probated. Probate is a legal proceeding that gives the executor the power to act. To probate the will, you probably need the assistance of an attorney. But probate is usually a routine matter, and you should shop around for an attorney. Be sure to compare prices and ask how the fee is computed. Some lawyers charge a percentage while others charge a flat fee or by the hour. You may be better off paying by the hour, but discuss this with the attorney. I should also point out that the attorney's fees are paid by the estate, not you, so you don't have to worry about being responsible for this cost.

How can I avoid probating a will?
"You can't."

Dear Mr. Alderman:
I am getting on in years, and I want to leave my children property in my will without them having to go through probate. I don't have much property, and it seems a waste to spend a lot of money on probate costs. How can I make sure my will doesn't have to be probated?

As I said in the previous letter, "probate" is the legal term used to describe the process by which the terms of a will are given legal effect. Any property left to someone through a will has to go through some form of probate. Probate does not, however, have to be a long, expensive process. In fact, there is a new form of probate called "informal probate" that is designed for small estates. Informal probate should be very inexpensive.

If you wish to avoid any form of probate, you must either give the property outright, as a gift, have beneficiaries or joint holders on your accounts, or place it in trust before you die. You may want to speak with an attorney to find out what would be best for you in light of your concerns about probate and tax law. There are many forms of trusts, and before giving any gift you must consider the consequences of the gift tax law. You should still, however, have a will to cover any property you were not able to deal with outside of probate.

Does the executor have to pay if there is no money in the estate?
"No, the executor is not responsible."

Dear Mr. Alderman:
I am the executor of my mother's will. In the will, she left $7,000 to her grandchild. There is no money in her estate. Do I have to pay the $7,000?

No. The executor merely puts the will into effect and distributes the assets of the deceased. If there are no assets, the exccutor is not responsible for fulfilling the terms of the will.

Do creditors get proceeds of life insurance?
"No, life insurance proceeds are exempt."

Dear Mr. Alderman:
My father passed away. I know the assets in his estate are subject to the claims of his creditors. There is not enough money in my father's estate, however, to pay all of his bills. Do his creditors have the right to the proceeds of his life insurance?

Life insurance proceeds are exempt and will pass to the policy beneficiary free of the claims of your father's creditors.

Which takes priority: a life insurance policy or a will?
"The life insurance policy controls."

Dear Mr. Alderman:
I have a life insurance policy. I also have a will. Who will get the money from the life insurance policy? Is it the person I designated as the beneficiary in the life insurance policy or the person named in the will?

The beneficiary named in the life insurance policy will receive the property regardless of who is named the beneficiary in your will. The will deals with only the property in your estate. The proceeds of your life insurance policy do not become part of your estate, unless you make your estate the beneficiary of the policy.

What are payable-on-death and survivorship accounts?
"A good way to avoid probate."

Dear Mr. Alderman:
I am opening a bank account and want my wife to get the money in
the account if anything happen to me. What is the difference between
an account payable on death and one with a right of survivorship?

A payable-on-death (POD) account is one where the funds are paid to the named beneficiary when the account holder dies. This is similar to the way life insurance works.

A joint tenancy with a right of survivorship account automatically passes to the surviving account holder when the other holder dies.

The most important aspect of both these accounts is that the funds in the account pass outside of a will and the terms of the account supersede any term in the will. This means that there is no court involvement to transfer the funds in the account. I should point out, however, that although the property in the account is not considered part of your estate for purposes of probating your will, it is considered when determining the value of your estate for estate taxes.

Do I have to list all of my property in my will?
"You can leave either specific bequests or general designations."

Dear Mr. Alderman:
My husband and I both have grown children from a previous mar-
riage. After we made our wills, we purchased some rental property
in both our names. The property is not specifically mentioned in the
will. If one of us were to die, how will this property be distributed?

Based on what you say, the property is community property. Basically, this means you own half and your husband owns half. If either of you were to die, his or her half would be distributed according to the will. Generally, a will has some specific provisions stating who gets certain property, as well as some general designations regarding the remainder, or "residuary" estate. If the property is not specifically mentioned in the will, it will be considered part of the "residuary estate," and will be distributed along with all of your other property. I should emphasize that the surviving spouse will continue to have a one-half interest in the property.

How do I change my will?
"With a codicil."

Dear Mr. Alderman:
I want to change a gift I made in my will. I left someone $5,000 and
want to give him $10,000. Can I just change the amount?

If you just take a pen and make changes to your will, the changes are not valid, and may invalidate the entire will. To change the terms of your will you must prepare what is called a codicil.

You may prepare a codicil yourself. If it is in your own handwriting, it is valid without a witness or notary. If you type it or use a form, you need two witnesses, and should have a notarized self-proving affidavit. All that it is necessary for you to do is say something to the effect that, "This is a codicil to my will that I signed on [date]. I am completely changing [state article and section numbers identifying what you are changing], to read as follows: [Copy the language of your will with the change you want.]" Then say "In all other respects, I hereby affirm and republish my existing will." You should date and sign the codicil at the end.

You also may use software designed to prepare wills or codicils, or, any one of the many books that are available. Most of the products available carefully explain how to prepare a codicil.

Although a codicil is not a complicated legal document, I do not recommend you do it yourself, unless you are making minor changes. Any change to a will could have ramifications you were not aware of. In my opinion, it is often a good idea to get the advice of an attorney to make sure that your codicil is prepared correctly and you fully understand its legal ramifications.

Does my spouse have an interest in my IRA?
"Your IRA is community property."

Dear Mr. Alderman:
My wife passed away. We had been married for ten years. I have an
IRA in my name that I began right after we were married. Is my IRA
a part of her estate?

The IRA, like any other property you acquired after you were married, is community property. This means that your wife has a half interest in the IRA, no matter whose name it is in. If your wife had a will, the IRA will be distributed according to the provisions of the will. If she did not have a will, and did not have any children by a prior marriage, the IRA will pass to you. If she has children by a prior marriage and no will, the children will inherit her half of the IRA. Finally, I should point out that the IRA is community property because all of the money in it came after you were married. If you had the IRA before you were married it would be separate property.

If I win the lottery, does my spouse own any of the winnings?
"Lottery winnings are usually community property."

Dear Mr. Alderman:
I buy a lottery ticket each week on payday. I was wondering, if I win, will the winnings be community property? If so, does that mean my wife owns half?

Assuming you buy the lottery with money you have earned while you were married, the lottery winnings would be community property. The only exception would be if you and your spouse have signed a prenuptial agreement saying otherwise. Because the winnings are community property they would be considered jointly owned by you and your wife.

Who can be an executor?
"Nearly anyone."

Dear Mr. Alderman:
I am making out a will. A friend told me I couldn't make my son the executor of the will because he was going to inherit my property. I don't know who else to use. Can I name a bank?

The simple answer is to name your son. A person can be an executor of a will even if he is going to inherit under the will. The only people who may not serve as executors of a will are minors, incompetents, convicted felons, and others the court finds unsuitable. There are also some restrictions on when a nonresident or a corporation may act as an executor. A nonresident may only serve if he appoints a resident agent to accept service of process. A corporation may only serve if it is authorized to act as a fiduciary in this state.

The bottom line is that in most cases the executor is also a family member who will inherit some property under the will. Tell your friend he was misinformed.

Do I have to pay estate taxes?
"Check the current law."

Dear Mr. Alderman:
I am eighty-three, and I have been told I should begin to give some
of my property away to avoid paying estate taxes. I am married, and
we don't have much money. We own a house worth about $375,000
and maybe another $450,000 in other property. In my will I leave
everything to my wife, and if she dies before me, to our children. Will
my heirs have to pay much in estate taxes?

First, I must make one thing clear: Estate taxes, which are collected by
state and federal governments, are not paid by the heirs. They are paid out
of the estate. In other words, the money is taken out before your estate is
distributed to your heirs. Also, very few people actually owe any estate
taxes. Texas has no estate tax. Federal estate taxes are imposed at a very
high rate, but only for very large estates. In 2017, for example, estate taxes
were imposed at the maximum rate of 40 percent, but they were imposed
only on estates valued in excess of $5.49 million.

Currently, Congress is considering completely eliminating the estate
tax. It is impossible to predict what Congress will do, but most believe that
the tax will be eliminated.

The bottom line is that if you have a substantial estate, worth in excess
if $5.49 million, you should seek the assistance of an estate-planning attor-
ney to make sure you protect yourself, until Congress acts.

What is the difference between a tax exemption and a deferment?
"One you don't pay, the other you pay later."

Dear Mr. Alderman:
I am sixty-seven years old. I don't pay property taxes because of my
exemptions. Someone just told me that when I die, my children will
have to pay all the back taxes, plus interest. Is this true?

Your question points out the difference between a tax exemption and a tax
deferment. At age sixty-five, you are entitled to additional property tax
exemptions, or you may defer taxes you owe. An exemption means that
you do not owe the taxes. In your case, there are no taxes owed because
of the exemption.

On the other hand, if your property is valued at more than your exemption, and you owe taxes, at age sixty-five you have the right to defer the
taxes. This means that you do not have to pay when the taxes are assessed.

The taxes, however, are still owed. Taxes, plus interest, must be paid when you die or sell the property.

What is a life estate?
"Another type of ownership."

Dear Mr. Alderman:
Recently my father died. The lawyer in charge of things told me that my father left me his house but that he left a "life estate" to my stepmother, so I can't have it until she dies. I don't understand. If it is my house, why do I have to let her live there? I live in a small house, and it would be really nice to have a big place to live in. I don't want to sound cold, but my father had only been married to my stepmother for less than a year, and it doesn't seem fair. Is there anything I can do?

What the lawyer told you is right. If your stepmother has a life estate in the house, it is hers to do with as she pleases until she dies. It then becomes yours.

When you transfer property, there are many different ways of doing it. For example, you can give it outright, as in the case of a gift or the standard provision in a will. But this is not the only way to transfer property. *When you transfer property, you do not have to make an absolute transfer. The law allows you to transfer less than an unlimited full interest.* A common example would be when you rent an apartment. The landlord has transferred an interest in the property to you, but as a lessee your interest is limited by the terms of the lease. A life estate is another way to transfer property. When you get a life estate you get full rights in the property, but only for as long as you live. When you die, the property automatically goes to someone else.

So what rights does your stepmother have? Basically, she can do whatever she wants with the property—as if she owned it. But when she dies, it is yours. For instance, let's say she sold the property. All she has legal power to sell is her life estate, and, therefore, when she died, whoever bought the property would no longer have title to it. It would be yours. The purchaser only has the same rights as your stepmother.

A life estate is a useful way of providing for one person during his or her lifetime, while making sure that ultimate title goes to someone else. Your father probably wanted to make sure your stepmother was comfortable for the rest of her life but that you ultimately got the house. That is exactly the result that will occur through the use of a life estate.

I just moved to Texas. Is my will still good?
"Maybe, maybe not."

Dear Mr. Alderman:
My wife and I have lived in Arkansas for over twenty years. We just
moved to Texas to be near our grandchildren. We both have wills
written by an Arkansas lawyer. Are they valid in Texas? We really
would rather not have to spend the money to have new wills written.

The simple answer is, I don't know. To give you an answer I would have
to be an expert on Arkansas law and see the will.

Even though this is the United States of America, every state has its
own laws and is free to regulate its citizens as it sees fit. For example,
although you can gamble in Nevada, gambling generally is illegal in most
states.

The same thing is true with respect to wills. Every state has its own
requirements for what must be included in a will and what happens if you
don't have one or if you have one that is not valid. Although in most cases
the requirements are similar, there is no guarantee that a will valid in one
state is valid in another. *A will made up in another state is valid in Texas if*
it meets the requirements of Texas law. The will is not valid, regardless of
whether it is valid in the other state, if it does not comply with Texas law.

For example, Texas law requires that a will be witnessed by two people.
If a will was made up in a state that required only one witness, and you had
only one witness, it would not be valid when you moved to Texas. But if
you make out a will in a state that requires three witnesses, it will satisfy
Texas law as well.

Also, Texas is a community property state and most states are not.
Therefore, even an out-of-state will valid in Texas may have a different
result under Texas law. In other words, the only way to tell if the will is
valid is to examine it to see if it complies with Texas law and achieves the
result you desire.

To determine the validity of your will and how it distributes property
in Texas, a Texas attorney would have to review it. As I said earlier, you
should shop around for an attorney before you hire one. Wills are considered routine legal matters, and most attorneys are competent to handle
them. It may even be easier to prepare a new will than to carefully examine
your will from Arkansas. You may save a lot of money with a few phone
calls.

What happens to lottery winnings after I die?
"They go to your heirs."

Dear Mr. Alderman:
I have heard different reports about what happens to my lottery win-
nings if I die before they are paid out. Do my heirs collect the money,
or does the state just get to keep the unpaid installments?

Every state with a lottery handles this problem in its own way. In some
states, the money is paid only as long as the winner is alive. In others,
including Texas, the money is considered an asset that will pass to your
heirs as any other asset would.

State law dictates to whom your estate, including lottery winnings, goes
after your death. If you want to ensure that your lottery winnings go to the
person you want with the least time and expense, make sure you have a will.

Can I abandon my property?
"Not if it is land."

Dear Mr. Alderman:
We own a lot in a vacation "estate" that we bought as an "invest-
ment." Unfortunately, it is now almost worthless. We have tried for
years to sell it and cannot. Do we have to keep paying maintenance
fees and taxes? Can we stop paying and let the county take the
property?

Unfortunately, as long as you own the property you are responsible for
the taxes. If you don't pay, the taxing authority has the right to go against
either the property or you. You cannot force them to take the property as
payment for back taxes, and you can't simply relinquish your ownership
by abandoning the property.

The best thing to do is either sell the property or give it to another person or entity. Until then, you will be responsible for the taxes and fees. Of
course, you should also try to get your property reappraised in an effort to
reduce your taxes.

What happens when I inherit half of a house that I don't want?
"You can force a sale."

Dear Mr. Alderman:
My father passed away. He left the family house to my brother and
me. My brother loves the old house and would like to live in it. I

never want to see it again. I told my brother he could buy out my share. He refused. Can I force him to buy my share?

As a legal matter you cannot force your brother to buy your interest in the house. As a practical matter you may be able to convince him that it is the best thing to do. Under the law, either you or your brother have the right to go to court and get an order that the house be sold and the proceeds divided in equal shares. If this occurs, the matter must go to court, and in addition to the costs of selling the house you will also have to pay attorney's fees.

Once your brother understands that you have the right to demand a partition of the property and that this will be costly, he probably will realize that the best thing to do is simply to purchase your interest in the home.

What happens to my homestead after I die?
"Your heirs inherit it."

Dear Mr. Alderman:
Can a creditor take a person's homestead after his death? Are the heirs liable for any judgment against the deceased? I have a young daughter that I would like to have my house after my death.

As you know, a person's homestead generally may not be taken by his creditors, even if they sue and win. The same rule generally applies after a person's death. The homestead will pass to your daughter free of the claims of your creditors. Of course, the homestead will still be subject to any mortgage on the property.

What is a living trust?
"A way to avoid probate."

Dear Mr. Alderman:
I receive numerous advertisements from people offering to sell me a living trust. It seems like a good way to avoid probate. Just what is a living trust? Can I use it to avoid estate taxes? How do I know if this is right for me?

A living trust is an alternative way of disposing of your property after your death. Instead of using a will, you use a trust agreement to transfer title to your property. You can name the same beneficiaries in the living trust as you would in a will.

To set up a living trust, it is necessary that you transfer all your property into the trust before you die. While you are alive you have the right to control the property in the trust and do whatever you want with it. Setting up the trust does not interfere with your use of the property while you are alive.

After your death, however, the property in the trust automatically passes to the beneficiaries named in the trust. There is no need for a will or any form of probate. Because there is no probate, your assets are kept private. You will still need to have a pour-over will prepared, however, to protect against the possibility that some of your property may not have been included in the trust.

One of the primary benefits of a living trust is that it avoids the expense and hassle of probating a will. In Texas, however, probating a will is usually not that time-consuming or expensive. In fact, the cost of a properly prepared living trust and pour-over will is probably no more than the cost of preparing and probating a will.

Also, a living trust cannot be used as a way of avoiding estate taxes. If that is your concern you will need a different type of trust.

I suggest you speak with an attorney who prepares both living trusts and wills, and discuss all of your alternatives. Be sure to discuss a will, a living trust, and the other forms of trusts. That way you can determine which is best for you. I think you will find that for most Texans a standard will, and some simple planning, is the best alternative.

Can I avoid estate taxes by using a living trust?
"No, a living trust does not eliminate estate taxes."

Dear Mr. Alderman:
Someone trying to sell us a living trust approached my wife and me. He said that we would save a lot of money on probate and estate taxes. Our estate is worth a total of about $900,000. The living trust would cost us over $1,500. We already have a will. Is it worth it?

Based on what you say, you will not owe any estate taxes at your death. For 2017, the estate tax does not kick in until your estate is worth over $5.49 million. More important, a living trust does not eliminate liability for estate taxes.

In my opinion, most people in Texas do not need a living trust. As explained in the previous question, a living trust does avoid probate, but in Texas probate is not that expensive. I suggest you speak with another attorney who prepares both wills and living trusts and have him or her compare the benefits and costs of a living trust and a will. In many cases, a will and some simple estate planning are all you need.

Are adopted children treated the same?
"Yes."

Dear Mr. Alderman:
Do adopted children inherit if a parent dies without a will?

Under Texas law, adopted children are treated the same as natural-born children for purposes of inheritance rights. This means they may inherit some or all of their parent's estate if the parent dies without a will and with no living spouse.

Do I have to leave property to my children in equal shares?
"You do not have to leave your property to anyone."

Dear Mr. Alderman:
My husband adopted my children in 1999. Does he have to leave the adopted children anything in his will? I am afraid he will leave more to his natural child.

As discussed above, for purposes of a will, the word "children" includes biological and adopted children. If your husband were to divide his property among his "children," all would share equally.

In Texas, however, you do not have to leave anyone anything in your will. It is your property and you can leave it to whomever you want. This means your husband can leave his property to none of the children, some of the children, or all of your children in different shares.

Is a stepchild treated the same as any other child?
"A stepchild is not a 'child' for purposes of inheritance."

Dear Mr. Alderman:
My stepmother died without a will. Am I entitled to any of her property?

When a person dies without a will, the law determines who inherits his or her property. A stepchild is not considered a "child," and is not included within the list of people to whom property passes after death.

How do I transfer title to a car?
"Use an 'Affidavit of Heirship for a Motor Vehicle.'"

Dear Mr. Alderman:
When my father passed away he owned very little property but had
a car in his name. How do I transfer title to my name? I am his only
living heir.

Transferring title to his car should not be difficult. You use a form available from the Texas Department of Transportation called an "Affidavit of Heirship for a Motor Vehicle." Attached to the form are instructions for using it. The form is available in the "Death and Dying" section of my website, www.peopleslawyer.net.

SAMPLE WILLS

As I said before, there is no one will that is right for everyone. You must consider who you want your property to go to after your death, and how you want that property to be transferred. For example, you may want property given to minors to be put in a trust until they reach a certain age.

The samples that follow are just three examples of a will. One is for a single person, one is for a married person without children, and the last is for a married person with children. Read them carefully. If the model form does what you want to do with your property, then you should consider using it. You also can make changes to fit your needs. But I still urge you to contact a lawyer to draw up a will tailored to your special needs, or to look at some online will providers, such as LegalZoom. These forms should be thought of as merely an emergency measure until you have a chance to see a lawyer. Many lawyers charge a very reasonable fee for a simple will, and a small amount of money spent now may save your loved ones a great deal of time and money in the future.

Instructions

A "testator" is a man who makes out a will, and a "testatrix" is a woman. If you use these model wills, make sure you use the proper designation. Also, "executor" is used for a man, and "executrix" for a woman. Be sure to read the will carefully, and when you write yours *make sure you sign each page at the bottom and at the end of the will.* You should sign in the presence of three witnesses and a notary, and you should declare it to be your will before you sign. You also should have all the witnesses sign in the presence of each other and the notary. *Be sure to attach and complete the self-proving affidavit.*

Model will for single person.

LAST WILL AND TESTAMENT

OF

JANET GRANT

THE STATE OF TEXAS

COUNTY OF HARRIS

KNOW ALL MEN BY THESE PRESENTS

THAT, I, JANET GRANT, a resident of HARRIS County, Texas, being of sound mind and disposing memory and more than eighteen years of age, do hereby make, publish and declare this to be my Last Will and Testament, hereby revoking all Wills and Codicils heretofore made by me.

ARTICLE I.

Declarations

Section 1.1 I declare that I am not now married.

Section 1.2 No children have ever been born to or adopted by me.

Section 1.3 It is my intention to dispose of all real and personal property which I have the right to dispose of by will.

ARTICLE II.

Executorship

Section 2.1 I appoint my father, FRED GRANT of HOUSTON, Texas, Independent Executor of this my Last Will and Testament and of my Estate. Should FRED GRANT, for any reason or at any time be unable or unwilling to qualify, or for any reason fail to qualify, or, after qualifying, for any reason fail to continue to act, I designate my friend TOM POST of HOUSTON, Texas, as successor or substitute Independent Executor under this will.

As used herein the term "Executor" shall mean the person then acting under either of the foregoing appointments.

Section 2.2 I direct that no bond or other security shall be required of my Executor and any Executor hereunder shall be independent of the supervision and direction of the Probate Court to the fullest extent permitted by law. I further direct that no action shall be had in any court of probate jurisdiction in connection with this Will or in the administration or settlement of my Estate other than the probating

_____

TESTATRIX

(continued on next page)

(continued from previous page)

of this Will and the return of any inventory, appraisement and list of claims due by or owing to my Estate.

Section 2.3 My Executor shall have, and may exercise without first obtaining the approval of any court, all of the powers of Independent Executors under the laws of the State of Texas.

ARTICLE III.
Bequests and Devises

Section 3.1 I give my diamond bracelet to my sister SUSAN GRANT, if she survives me by 30 days; if she does not, the gift shall lapse and become part of my estate.

Section 3.2 I hereby give, devise and bequeath the remainder of my estate, whether real, personal or mixed, and wherever situated, to my parents, FRED GRANT and MARTHA GRANT, of HOUSTON, Texas, to share and share alike.

Section 3.3 In the event that either FRED GRANT or MARTHA GRANT does not survive me, I give, devise, and bequeath the remainder of my property of every kind, character and description, wherever situated, whether the same is real, personal or mixed, to the survivor.

Section 3.4 In the event that FRED GRANT and MARTHA GRANT do not survive me, I give, devise and bequeath the remainder of my property to TOM POST of HOUSTON, Texas.

Section 3.5 In the event that none of the persons designated herein survive me, then I direct that my estate pass to my heirs at law.

Section 3.6 No one shall be deemed to have survived me unless that person survives at least 30 days after the date of my death.

IN WITNESS WHEREOF, I, JANET GRANT, testatrix, do hereby subscribe my name this the _____ day of _____, 20__, to this instrument and declare the same to be my Last Will and Testament, in the presence of _____ ,

_____

and _____

attesting witnesses at my request and in my presence and in the presence of each other.

_____

TESTATRIX

(continued on next page)

(continued from previous page)

The foregoing instrument was now here published as the Last Will and Testament of JANET GRANT, and signed and subscribed by her, the Testatrix, in our presence, and we, at her request and in her presence and in the presence of each other, signed and subscribed our names hereto as attesting witnesses.

Address: _____   _____

_____   Witness

Address: _____   _____

_____   Witness

Address: _____   _____

_____   Witness

(ADD SELF-PROVING AFFIDAVIT)

Model will for married person with no children.

LAST WILL AND TESTAMENT
OF
CATHY NAN SIMES

STATE OF TEXAS
COUNTY OF TRAVIS
KNOW ALL MEN BY THESE PRESENTS:

THAT I, CATHY NAN SIMES, of TRAVIS County, Texas, and being of sound mind and disposing memory and above the age of eighteen (18) years, do make, publish and declare this my Last Will and Testament, hereby revoking all other wills and codicils heretofore made by me.

I.

I declare that I am married to THOMAS SIMES and that all references in this Will to my spouse are references to him. I have no child or children, living or dead, born to me or adopted, at the date of the execution of this Will.

II.

I hereby nominate and appoint my spouse, THOMAS SIMES, as Independent Executor of the Will, and I direct that no bond shall be required of him. If my spouse, THOMAS SIMES, should predecease me, or for any reason fail to qualify or decline to act as executor, then I nominate and appoint JOHN TAPER, of AUSTIN, TEXAS, as Independent Executor of this Will, to serve without bond or compensation. If my spouse and JOHN TAPER both fail to qualify or decline to act as executor, I nominate and appoint ALICE BRADLEY of AUSTIN, TEXAS, as Independent Executrix of this Will, to serve without bond or compensation.

My executor/executrix shall have and possess all of the rights and powers and be subject to all of the duties and responsibilities conferred and imposed on an independent executor by the Texas Probate Code as the Code now provides or as it may be hereafter amended.

I direct that no action shall be taken in any court in relation to the settlement of my estate other than the probating and recording of the Will and the return of a statutory inventory and appraisement and list of claims of my estate.

_____
TESTATRIX

(continued on next page)

(continued from previous page)

III.

I give, devise, and bequeath to my beloved spouse, THOMAS SIMES, all of my property, real, personal, and mixed, and wheresoever located, of every sort and description of which I may die possessed, or to which I may be entitled at the time of my death, to have and to hold as his property absolutely.

IV.

If my spouse, THOMAS SIMES, should predecease me, or if he and I die as a result of a common disaster or under such circumstances that there is not sufficient evidence to determine the order of our deaths, or if my spouse, THOMAS SIMES, shall die within a period of 30 days after the date of my death, then all bequests, devises, and provisions made herein to or for his benefit shall be void and my estate shall be administered and distributed in all respects as though my spouse, THOMAS SIMES, had not survived me.

V.

If my spouse, THOMAS SIMES, does not survive me, I give the sum of ten thousand dollars ($10,000) to SANDY WRIGHT of HOUSTON, TEXAS, if she survives me, and I give, devise, and bequeath my Hammond organ, automobile, jewelry, and the residue of my estate to JOHN TAPER of AUSTIN, TEXAS, if he survives me.

VI.

In the event that JOHN TAPER does not survive me, then I direct that my estate pass to my heirs at law.

VII.

No one shall be deemed to have survived me unless that person survives at least 30 days after the date of my death.

VIII.

If any beneficiary under this will in any manner, directly or indirectly, contests or attacks this will or any of its provisions, any share or interest in my estate given to the contesting beneficiary under this will is revoked and shall be disposed of in the same manner provided herein as if that contesting beneficiary had predeceased me without issue.

_____

TESTATRIX

(continued on next page)

(continued from previous page)

IX.

I declare that I have made and paid for funeral arrangements with PLEASANT VALLEY REST, AUSTIN, TEXAS, and I direct my executor/executrix to take all steps necessary to carry out such arrangements.

IN WITNESS WHEREOF, I, CATHY NAN SIMES, testatrix, do hereby subscribe my name this the _____ day of _____, 20__, to this instrument and declare the same to be my Last Will and Testament, in the presence of _____

_____

and _____ attesting witnesses at my request and in my presence and in the presence of each other.

_____

TESTATRIX

The foregoing instrument was now here published as the Last Will and Testament of CATHY NAN SIMES, and signed and subscribed by her, the Testatrix, in our presence, and we, at her request and in her presence and in the presence of each other, signed and subscribed our names hereto as attesting witnesses.

Address: _____   _____

_____   Witness

Address: _____   _____

_____   Witness

Address: _____   _____

_____   Witness

(ADD SELF-PROVING AFFIDAVIT)

Model will for married person with children.

LAST WILL AND TESTAMENT
OF
JOSEPH RALPH SMITH

STATE OF TEXAS
COUNTY OF HIDALGO
KNOW ALL MEN BY THESE PRESENTS:

THAT I, JOSEPH RALPH SMITH of HIDALGO County, Texas, and being of sound mind and disposing memory and above the age of eighteen (18) years, do make, publish and declare this my Last Will and Testament, hereby revoking all other wills and codicils heretofore made by me.

I.

I declare that I am married to ROSIE JONNA SMITH, and that all references in this Will to my spouse are references to her. I have TWO children, now living, namely,

EMERSON SMITH	FEB. 18, 1989
	date of birth
BARBARA SMITH	OCT. 27, 1987
	date of birth

No other child or children, except as named above, were born to me at the date of execution of this Will and no child or children were adopted by me at the date of execution of this Will. All references in this Will to "my children" are to said named children and to any children hereafter born to or adopted by me.

II.

I hereby appoint my spouse, ROSIE JONNA SMITH, as Independent Executrix of my Will, and I direct that no bond shall be required of her. If for any reason she cannot, or refuses to act as Executrix, then I appoint GEORGE JAMES of DONNA, TEXAS, as Independent Executor of my Will, to serve without bond. If my spouse and GEORGE JAMES both fail or refuse to qualify, I appoint FIRST BANK OF DONNA as Independent Executor of my Will, to serve without bond. I direct that no action shall be had in any court in relation to the settlement of my estate other than the probating and

_____
TESTATOR

(continued on next page)

(continued from previous page)

recording of this Will and the return of a statutory inventory and appraisement and list of claims of my estate.

III.

I give, devise, and bequeath to my beloved spouse, ROSIE JONNA SMITH, all of my property, real, personal, and mixed and wheresoever located of every sort and description of which I may die possessed, or to which I may be entitled at the time of my death to have and to hold as her property absolutely.

IV.

If my spouse, ROSIE JONNA SMITH, should predecease me, or if she and I die as a result of a common disaster or under such circumstances that there is not sufficient evidence to determine the order of our deaths, or if my spouse, ROSIE JONNA SMITH, shall die within a period of 30 days after the date of my death, then all bequests, devises, and provisions made herein to or for her benefit shall be void and my estate shall be administered and distributed in all respects as though my spouse, ROSIE JONNA SMITH, had not survived me.

V.

If my spouse does not survive me, I direct that my entire estate go to my surviving children, EMERSON SMITH and BARBARA SMITH, to share and share alike. If any child of mine is a minor at the time of my death, then I hereby deliver his/her estate to GEORGE JAMES as guardian of the estate of my child, to serve without bond. If for any reason GEORGE JAMES cannot act in such capacity, then I appoint LEE EARL, of DONNA, TEXAS, to act as guardian of the estate of my child and to serve without bond.

VI.

In the event that at any time it may be necessary to appoint a guardian for the person of any child of mine, then I nominate and appoint as such guardian GEORGE JAMES, and if for any reason he shall fail or cease so to serve I nominate and appoint in his place LEE EARL as guardian hereunder, and I direct that no guardian shall be required to furnish any bond.

_____

TESTATOR

(continued on next page)

(continued from previous page)

VII.

In the event that any of my children shall predecease me or if he/she and I die as a result of a common disaster or under such circumstances that there is not sufficient evidence to determine the order of our deaths, then all bequests, devises, and provisions made herein to or for his/her benefit shall be void and my estate shall be administered and distributed in all respects as though my child/children had not survived me.

VIII.

In the event that none of the persons designated herein survive me, then I direct that my estate pass to my heirs at law.

IX.

No one shall be deemed to have survived me unless that person survives at least 30 days after the date of my death.

IN WITNESS WHEREOF, I, JOSEPH RALPH SMITH, testator, do hereby subscribe my name this the day of _____, 20__, to this instrument and declare the same to be my Last Will and Testament, in the presence of _____, _____, and _____ attesting witnesses at my request and in my presence and in the presence of each other.

_____
TESTATOR

The foregoing instrument was now here published as the Last Will and Testament of JOSEPH RALPH SMITH, and signed and subscribed by him, the Testator, in our presence, and we, at his request and in his presence and in the presence of each other, signed and subscribed our names hereto as attesting witnesses.

Address:

_____   _____

_____   Witness

Address:

_____   _____

_____   Witness

Address:

_____   _____

_____   Witness

(ADD SELF-PROVING AFFIDAVIT)

The Self-Proving Affidavit should be added at the end of any will.

SELF-PROVING AFFIDAVIT
For Will

STATE OF TEXAS

COUNTY OF _____

Before me, the undersigned authority, on this day personally appeared _____,

_____,

_____,

and _____,

known to me to be testator/testatrix and the witnesses, respectively, whose names are subscribed to the annexed or foregoing instrument in their respective capacities, and all of said persons being by me duly sworn, the said _____, testator/testatrix, declared to me and to the said witnesses in my presence that said instrument is his/her last will and testament, and that he/she had willingly made and executed it as his/her free act and deed for the purposes therein expressed; and the said witnesses, each on their oath, stated to me, in the presence and hearing of the said testator/testatrix, that the said testator/testatrix had declared to them that said instrument is his/her last will and testament, and that he/she executed same as such and wanted each of them to sign as a witness; and upon their oaths each witness stated further that they did sign the same as witnesses in the presence of the said testator/testatrix and at his/her request; that he/she was at the time eighteen years of age or over and was of sound mind, and that each of said witnesses was then at least fourteen years of age.

_____

Testator/Testatrix

Address:

_____   _____

Witness

Address:

_____   _____

Witness

Address:

_____   _____

Witness

(continued on next page)

(continued from previous page)

SUBSCRIBED AND ACKNOWLEDGED before me by the said testator/testatrix, _____,
and subscribed and sworn to before me by the said _____
_____, and_____,
witnesses, this _____ day of _____, 20___.

_____
Notary Public

_____
My commission expires:

The Texas Legislature's suggested form for an Advanced Directive, or living will. A free copy of a living will form may also be found at http://livingwillforms.org/tx and other online sites.

DIRECTIVE TO PHYSICIANS AND FAMILY OR SURROGATE

Instructions for completing this document:

This is an important legal document known as an advance directive. It is designed to help you communicate your wishes about medical treatment at some time in the future when you are unable to make your wishes known because of illness or injury. These wishes are usually based on personal values. In particular, you may want to consider what burdens or hardships of treatment you would be willing to accept for a particular amount of benefit obtained if you were seriously ill.

You are encouraged to discuss your values and wishes with your family or chosen spokesperson, as well as your physician. Your physician, other health care provider, or medical institution may provide you with various resources to assist you in completing your advance directive. Brief definitions are listed below and may aid you in your discussions and advance planning. Initial the treatment choices that best reflect your personal preferences. Provide a copy of your directive to your physician, usual hospital, and family or spokesperson. Consider a periodic review of this document. By periodic review, you can best assure that the directive reflects your preferences.

In addition to this advance directive, Texas law provides for two other types of directives that can be important during a serious illness. These are the Medical Power of Attorney and the Out-of-Hospital Do-Not-Resuscitate Order. You may wish to discuss these with your physician, family, hospital representative, or other advisers. You may also wish to complete a directive related to the donation of organs and tissues.

DIRECTIVE

I, _____, recognize that the best health care is based upon a partnership of trust and communication with my physician. My physician and I will make health care decisions together as long as I am of sound mind and able to make

(continued on next page)

(continued from previous page)

my wishes known. If there comes a time that I am unable to make medical decisions about myself because of illness or injury, I direct that the following treatment preferences be honored:

If, in the judgment of my physician, I am suffering with a terminal condition from which I am expected to die within six months, even with available life-sustaining treatment provided in accordance with prevailing standards of medical care:

_____ I request that all treatments other than those needed to keep me comfortable be discontinued or withheld and my physician allow me to die as gently as possible; OR

_____ I request that I be kept alive in this terminal condition using available life-sustaining treatment. (THIS SELECTION DOES NOT APPLY TO HOSPICE CARE.)

If, in the judgment of my physician, I am suffering with an irreversible condition so that I cannot care for myself or make decisions for myself and am expected to die without life-sustaining treatment provided in accordance with prevailing standards of care:

_____ I request that all treatments other than those needed to keep me comfortable be discontinued or withheld and my physician allow me to die as gently as possible; OR

_____ I request that I be kept alive in this irreversible condition using available life-sustaining treatment. (THIS SELECTION DOES NOT APPLY TO HOSPICE CARE.)

Additional requests: (After discussion with your physician, you may wish to consider listing particular treatments in this space that you do or do not want in specific circumstances, such as artificial nutrition and fluids, intravenous antibiotics, etc. Be sure to state whether you do or do not want the particular treatment.)

_____

_____

_____

After signing this directive, if my representative or I elect hospice care, I understand and agree that only those treatments needed to keep me comfortable would be provided and I would not be given available life-sustaining treatments.

(continued on next page)

(continued from previous page)

If I do not have a Medical Power of Attorney, and I am unable to make my wishes known, I designate the following person(s) to make treatment decisions with my physician compatible with my personal values. (Name of person and second person)

1. _____

2. _____

(IF A MEDICAL POWER OF ATTORNEY HAS BEEN EXECUTED, THEN AN AGENT HAS BEEN NAMED AND YOU SHOULD NOT LIST ADDITIONAL NAMES IN THIS PART.)

If the above persons are not available, or if I have not designated a spokesperson, I understand that a spokesperson will be chosen for me following standards specified in the laws of Texas. If, in the judgment of my physician, my death is imminent within minutes to hours, even with the use of all available medical treatment provided within the prevailing standard of care, I acknowledge that all treatments may be withheld or removed except those needed to maintain my comfort. I understand that under Texas law this directive has no effect if I have been diagnosed as pregnant. This directive will remain in effect until I revoke it. No other person may do so.

Signed_____ Date_____

City, County, State of Residence _____

Two competent adult witnesses must sign below, acknowledging the signature of the declarant. The witness designated as Witness 1 may not be a person designated to make a treatment decision for the patient and may not be related to the patient by blood or marriage. This witness may not be entitled to any part of the estate and may not have a claim against the estate of the patient. This witness may not be the attending physician or an employee of the attending physician. If this witness is an employee of a health care facility in which the patient is being cared for, this witness may not be involved in providing direct patient care to the patient. This witness may not be an officer, director, partner, or business office employee of a health care facility in which the patient is being cared for or of any parent organization of the health care facility.

(continued on next page)

(continued from previous page)

Witness 1 _____   Witness 2 _____

DEFINITIONS

"Artificial nutrition and hydration" means the provision of nutrients or fluids by a tube inserted in a vein, under the skin in the subcutaneous tissues, or in the stomach (gastrointestinal tract).

"Irreversible condition" means a condition, injury, or illness:

1. that may be treated, but is never cured or eliminated;
2. that leaves a person unable to care for or make decisions for the person's own self; and
3. that, without life-sustaining treatment provided in accordance with the prevailing standard of medical care, is fatal.

Explanation: Many serious illnesses such as cancer, failure of major organs (kidney, heart, liver, or lung), and serious brain disease such as Alzheimer's dementia, may be considered irreversible early on. There is no cure, but the patient may be kept alive for prolonged periods of time if the patient receives life-sustaining treatments. Late in the course of the same illness, the disease may be considered terminal when, even with treatment, the patient is expected to die. You may wish to consider which burdens of treatment you will be willing to accept in an effort to achieve a particular outcome. This is a very personal decision that you may wish to discuss with your physician, family, or other important persons in your life.

"Life-sustaining treatment" means treatment that, based on reasonable medical judgment, sustains the life of a patient and without which the patient will die. The term includes both life-sustaining medications and artificial life support such as mechanical breathing machines, kidney dialysis treatment, and artificial hydration and nutrition. The term does not include the administration of pain management medication, the performance of a medical procedure necessary to provide comfort care, or any other medical care provided to alleviate a patient's pain.

"Terminal condition" means an incurable condition caused by injury, disease, or illness that, according to reasonable medical judgment, will produce death within six months, even with available

(continued on next page)

(continued from previous page)

life-sustaining treatment provided in accordance with the prevailing standard of medical care.

Explanation: Many serious illnesses may be considered irreversible early in the course of the illness, but they may not be considered terminal until the disease is fairly advanced. In thinking about terminal illness and its treatment, you again may wish to consider the relative benefits and burdens of treatment and discuss your wishes with your physician, family, or other important persons in your life.

INFORMATION CONCERNING
THE MEDICAL POWER OF ATTORNEY

THIS IS AN IMPORTANT LEGAL DOCUMENT.
BEFORE SIGNING THIS DOCUMENT,
YOU SHOULD KNOW THESE IMPORTANT FACTS:

Except to the extent you state otherwise, this document gives the person you name as your agent the authority to make any and all health care decisions for you in accordance with your wishes, including your religious and moral beliefs, when you are no longer capable of making them yourself. Because "health care" means any treatment, service, or procedure to maintain, diagnose, or treat your physical or mental condition, your agent has the power to make a broad range of health care decisions for you. Your agent may consent, refuse to consent, or withdraw consent for medical treatment and may make decisions about withdrawing or withholding life-sustaining treatment. Your agent may not consent to voluntary inpatient mental health services, convulsive treatment, psychosurgery, or abortion. A physician must comply with your agent's instructions or allow you to be transferred to another physician.

Your agent's authority begins when your doctor certifies that you lack the competence to make health care decisions.

Your agent is obligated to follow your instructions when making decisions on your behalf. Unless you state otherwise, your agent has

(continued on next page)

(continued from previous page)

the same authority to make decisions about your health care as you would have had.

It is important that you discuss this document with your physician or other health care provider before you sign it to make sure that you understand the nature and range of decisions that may be made on your behalf. If you do not have a physician, you should talk with someone else who is knowledgeable about these issues and can answer your questions. You do not need a lawyer's assistance to complete this document, but if there is anything in this document that you do not understand, you should ask a lawyer to explain it to you.

The person you appoint as agent should be someone you know and trust. The person must be 18 years of age or older or a person under 18 years of age who has the disabilities of minority removed. If you appoint your health or residential care provider (e.g., your physician or an employee of a home health agency, hospital, nursing home, or residential care home, other than a relative), that person has to choose between acting as your agent or as your health or residential care provider; the law does not permit a person to do both at the same time.

You should inform the person you appoint that you want the person to be your health care agent. You should discuss this document with your agent and your physician and give each a signed copy. You should indicate on the document itself the people and institutions who have signed copies. Your agent is not liable for health care decisions made in good faith on your behalf.

Even after you have signed this document, you have the right to make health care decisions for yourself as long as you are able to do so and treatment cannot be given to you or stopped over your objection. You have the right to revoke the authority granted to your agent by informing your agent or your health or residential care provider orally or in writing or by your execution of a subsequent medical power of attorney. Unless you state otherwise, your appointment of a spouse dissolves on divorce.

This document may not be changed or modified. If you want to make changes in the document, you must make an entirely new one.

(continued on next page)

(continued from previous page)

You may wish to designate an alternate agent in the event that your agent is unwilling, unable, or ineligible to act as your agent. Any alternate agent you designate has the same authority to make health care decisions for you.

THIS POWER OF ATTORNEY IS NOT VALID UNLESS IT IS SIGNED IN THE PRESENCE OF A NOTARY OR TWO COMPETENT ADULT WITNESSES. THE FOLLOWING PERSONS MAY NOT ACT AS ONE OF THE WITNESSES: [It is also available at file:///Users/richard/Downloads/Medical_Power_of_Attorney.pdf]

1. the person you have designated as your agent;
2. a person related to you by blood or marriage;
3. a person entitled to any part of your estate after your death under a will or codicil executed by you or by operation of law;
4. your attending physician;
5. an employee of your attending physician;
6. an employee of a health care facility in which you are a patient if the employee is providing direct patient care to you or is an officer, director, partner, or business office employee of the health care facility or of any parent organization of the health care facility; or
7. a person who, at the time this power of attorney is executed, has a claim against any part of your estate after your death.

MEDICAL POWER OF ATTORNEY
DESIGNATION OF HEALTH CARE AGENT

I, _____ (insert your name),
Appoint:

Name:_____

Address:_____

Phone: _____

As my agent to make any and all health care decisions for me, except to the extent I state otherwise in this document. This medical power of attorney takes effect if I become unable to make my own health care decisions and this fact is certified in writing by my physician.

LIMITATIONS ON THE DECISION-MAKING AUTHORITY OF MY AGENT ARE AS FOLLOWS: _____
_____
_____

DESIGNATION OF ALTERNATE AGENT.
(You are not required to designate an alternate agent but you may do so. An alternate agent may make the same health care decisions as the designated agent if the designated agent is unable or unwilling to act as your agent. If the agent designated is your spouse, the designation is automatically revoked by law if your marriage is dissolved.)

If the person designated as my agent is unable or unwilling to make health care decisions for me, I designate the following persons to serve as my agent to make health care decisions for me as authorized by this document, who serve in the following order:

A. First Alternate Agent

Name:_____

Address:_____

Phone: _____

(continued on next page)

(continued from previous page)

B. Second Alternate Agent

Name:_____

Address:_____

Phone: _____

The original of this document is kept at:

_____

_____

The following individuals or institutions have signed copies:

Name:_____

Address:_____

Phone: _____

Name:_____

Address:_____

Phone: _____

DURATION.
I understand that this power of attorney exists indefinitely from the date I execute this document unless I establish a shorter time or revoke the power of attorney. If I am unable to make health care decisions for myself when this power of attorney expires, the authority I have granted my agent continues to exist until the time I become able to make health care decisions for myself.

(IF APPLICABLE) This power of attorney ends on the following date: _____

PRIOR DESIGNATIONS REVOKED.
I revoke any prior medical power of attorney.

ACKNOWLEDGMENT OF DISCLOSURE STATEMENT.
I have been provided with a disclosure statement explaining the effect of this document. I have read and understand that information contained in the disclosure statement.

(continued on next page)

(continued from previous page)

(YOU MUST DATE AND SIGN THIS POWER OF ATTORNEY. You may sign it and have your signature acknowledged before a notary public or you may sign it in the presence of two competent adult witnesses.)

I sign my name to this medical power of attorney on

_____ (Day, month, year)

At

_____ (City and State)

_____ (Signature)

_____ (Print Name)

SIGNATURE ACKNOWLEDGED BEFORE NOTARY

I sign my name to this medical power of attorney on

_____ (Day, month, year)

At

_____ (City and State)

_____ (Signature)

_____ (Print Name)

State of Texas, County of _____.

This instrument was acknowledged before me on _____ (date)

by _____ (name of person acknowledging).

NOTARY PUBLIC, State of Texas

Notary's printed name:_____

My commission expires: _____

OR

STATEMENT OF FIRST WITNESS

I am not the person appointed as agent by this document. I am not related to the principal by blood or marriage. I would not be entitled to any portion of the principal's estate on the principal's death. I am not the attending physician of the principal or an employee of

(continued on next page)

(continued from previous page)

the attending physician. I have no claim against any portion of the principal's estate on the principal's death. Furthermore, if I am an employee of a health care facility in which the principal is a patient, I am not involved in providing direct patient care to the principal and am not an officer, director, partner, or business office employee of the health care facility or of any parent organization of the health care facility.

Signature: _____

Print Name: _____ Date: _____

Address: _____

SIGNATURE OF SECOND WITNESS

Signature: _____

Print Name: _____ Date: _____

Address: _____

The Statutory Durable Power of Attorney gives your designated agent the power to make decisions regarding your property and financial matters in the event that you are unable to do so. The form below is suggested, but not mandated, by the Texas Legislature. It was amended by the Texas Legislature to go into effect in September 2017. Copies of the form should be available on the Internet shortly after that date.

STATUTORY DURABLE POWER OF ATTORNEY

NOTICE: THE POWERS GRANTED BY THIS DOCUMENT ARE BROAD AND SWEEPING. THEY ARE EXPLAINED IN THE DURABLE POWER OF ATTORNEY ACT, SUBTITLE P, TITLE 2, ESTATES CODE. IF YOU HAVE ANY QUESTIONS ABOUT THESE POWERS, OBTAIN COMPETENT LEGAL ADVICE. THIS DOCUMENT DOES NOT AUTHORIZE ANYONE TO MAKE MEDICAL AND OTHER HEALTH-CARE DECISIONS FOR YOU. YOU MAY REVOKE THIS POWER OF ATTORNEY IF YOU LATER WISH TO DO SO. IF YOU WANT YOUR AGENT TO HAVE THE AUTHORITY TO SIGN HOME EQUITY LOAN DOCUMENTS ON YOUR BEHALF, THIS POWER OF ATTORNEY MUST BE SIGNED BY YOU AT THE OFFICE OF THE LENDER, AN ATTORNEY AT LAW, OR A TITLE COMPANY.

You should select someone you trust to serve as your agent. Unless you specify otherwise, generally the agent's authority will continue until:

1. you die or revoke the power of attorney;
2. your agent resigns or is unable to act for you; or
3. a guardian is appointed for your estate.

I, _____ ,
(insert your name and address)

appoint _____
(insert the name and address of the person appointed)

as my agent to act for me in any lawful way with respect to all of the following powers that I have initialed below. (YOU MAY APPOINT CO-AGENTS. UNLESS YOU PROVIDE OTHERWISE, CO-AGENTS MAY ACT INDEPENDENTLY.)

TO GRANT ALL OF THE FOLLOWING POWERS, INITIAL THE LINE IN FRONT OF (N) AND IGNORE THE LINES IN FRONT OF THE OTHER POWERS LISTED IN (A) THROUGH (M).

(continued on next page)

(continued from previous page)

TO GRANT A POWER, YOU MUST INITIAL THE LINE IN FRONT OF THE POWER YOU ARE GRANTING.

TO WITHHOLD A POWER, DO NOT INITIAL THE LINE IN FRONT OF THE POWER. YOU MAY, BUT DO NOT NEED TO, CROSS OUT EACH POWER WITHHELD.

_____ (A) Real property transactions;

_____ (B) Tangible personal property transactions;

_____ (C) Stock and bond transactions;

_____ (D) Commodity and option transactions;

_____ (E) Banking and other financial institution transactions;

_____ (F) Business operating transactions;

_____ (G) Insurance and annuity transactions;

_____ (H) Estate, trust, and other beneficiary transactions;

_____ (I) Claims and litigation;

_____ (J) Personal and family maintenance;

_____ (K) Benefits from Social Security, Medicare, Medicaid, or other governmental programs or civil or military service;

_____ (L) Retirement plan transactions;

_____ (M) Tax matters;

_____ (N) Digital assets and the content of an electronic communication;

_____ (O) ALL OF THE POWERS LISTED IN (A) THROUGH (N). YOU DO NOT HAVE TO INITIAL THE LINE IN FRONT OF ANY OTHER POWER IF YOU INITIAL LINE (O).

SPECIAL INSTRUCTIONS:

Special instructions applicable to agent compensation (initial in front of one of the following sentences to have it apply; if no selection is made, each agent will be entitled to compensation that is reasonable under the circumstances):

_____ My agent is entitled to reimbursement of reasonable expenses incurred on my behalf and to compensation that is reasonable under the circumstances.

_____ My agent is entitled to reimbursement of reasonable expenses incurred on my behalf but shall receive no compensation for serving as my agent.

(continued on next page)

(continued from previous page)

Special instructions applicable to co-agents (if you have appointed co-agents to act, initial in front of one of the following sentences to have it apply; if no selection is made, each agent will be entitled to act independently):

____ Each of my co-agents may act independently for me.

____ My co-agents may act for me only if the co-agents act jointly.

____ My co-agents may act for me only if a majority of the co-agents act jointly.

Special instructions applicable to gifts (initial in front of the following sentence to have it apply):

____ I grant my agent the power to apply my property to make gifts outright to or for the benefit of a person, including by the exercise of a presently exercisable general power of appointment held by me, except that the amount of a gift to an individual may not exceed the amount of annual exclusions allowed from the federal gift tax for the calendar year of the gift.

ON THE FOLLOWING LINES YOU MAY GIVE SPECIAL INSTRUCTIONS LIMITING OR EXTENDING THE POWERS GRANTED TO YOUR AGENT.

_____

_____

_____

_____

_____

_____

_____

_____

_____

_____

_____

UNLESS YOU DIRECT OTHERWISE BELOW, THIS POWER OF ATTORNEY IS EFFECTIVE IMMEDIATELY AND WILL CONTINUE UNTIL IT TERMINATES.

(continued on next page)

(continued from previous page)

CHOOSE ONE OF THE FOLLOWING ALTERNATIVES BY CROSSING OUT THE ALTERNATIVE NOT CHOSEN:
(A) This power of attorney is not affected by my subsequent disability or incapacity.
(B) This power of attorney becomes effective upon my disability or incapacity.

YOU SHOULD CHOOSE ALTERNATIVE (A) IF THIS POWER OF ATTORNEY IS TO BECOME EFFECTIVE ON THE DATE IT IS EXECUTED.

IF NEITHER (A) NOR (B) IS CROSSED OUT, IT WILL BE ASSUMED THAT YOU CHOSE ALTERNATIVE (A).

If Alternative (B) is chosen and a definition of my disability or incapacity is not contained in this power of attorney, I shall be considered disabled or incapacitated for purposes of this power of attorney if a physician certifies in writing at a date later than the date this power of attorney is executed that, based on the physician's medical examination of me, I am mentally incapable of managing my financial affairs. I authorize the physician who examines me for this purpose to disclose my physical or mental condition to another person for purposes of this power of attorney. A third party who accepts this power of attorney is fully protected from any action taken under this power of attorney that is based on the determination made by a physician of my disability or incapacity.

I agree that any third party who receives a copy of this document may act under it. Termination of this durable power of attorney is not effective as to a third party until the third party has actual notice of the termination. I agree to indemnify the third party for any claims that arise against the third party because of reliance on this power of attorney.

The meaning and effect of this durable power of attorney is determined by Texas law.

If any agent named by me dies, becomes incapacitated, resigns, or refuses to act, or if my marriage to an agent named by me is dissolved by a court decree of divorce or annulment or is declared void by a court (unless I provided in this document that the dissolution

(continued on next page)

(continued from previous page)

or declaration does not terminate the agent's authority to act under this power of attorney), I name the following (each to act alone and successively, in the order named) as successor(s) to that agent:

_____.

Signed this _____ day of _____, 20____

_____
(your signature)

State of _____

County of _____

This document was acknowledged before me on _____ by
                                                                    (date)

_____
(name of principal)

                              _____
                              (signature of notarial officer)

(Seal, if any, of notary)   _____
                              (printed name)

                              My commission expires: _____

IMPORTANT INFORMATION FOR AGENT
Agent's Duties

When you accept the authority granted under this power of attorney, you establish a "fiduciary" relationship with the principal. This is a special legal relationship that imposes on you legal duties that continue until you resign or the power of attorney is terminated or revoked by the principal or by operation of law. A fiduciary duty generally includes the duty to:

(1) act in good faith;

(2) do nothing beyond the authority granted in this power of attorney;

(3) act loyally for the principal's benefit;

(4) avoid conflicts that would impair your ability to act in the principal's best interest; and

(5) disclose your identity as an agent or attorney in fact when you act for the principal by writing or printing the name of the principal and signing your own name as "agent" in the following manner: (Principal's Name) by (Your Signature) as Agent (or as Attorney in Fact).

In addition, the Durable Power of Attorney Act (Subtitle P, Title 2, Estates Code) requires you to:

(1) maintain records of each action taken or decision made on behalf of the principal;

(2) maintain all records until delivered to the principal, released by the principal, or discharged by a court; and

(3) if requested by the principal, provide an accounting to the principal that, unless otherwise directed by the principal or otherwise provided in the Special Instructions, must include:

(A) the property belonging to the principal that has come to your knowledge or into your possession;

(B) each action taken or decision made by you as agent or attorney in fact;

(C) a complete account of receipts, disbursements, and other actions of you as agent or attorney in fact that includes the source and nature of each receipt, disbursement, or action, with receipts of principal and income shown separately;

(D) a listing of all property over which you have exercised control that includes an adequate description of each asset and the asset's current value, if known to you;

(E) the cash balance on hand and the name and location of the depository at which the cash balance is kept;

(F) each known liability;

(G any other information and facts known to you as necessary for a full and definite understanding of the exact condition of the property belonging to the principal; and

(H) all documentation regarding the principal's property.

Termination of Agent's Authority

You must stop acting on behalf of the principal if you learn of any event that terminates this power of attorney or your authority under this power of attorney. An event that terminates this power of attorney or your authority to act under this power of attorney includes:

(1) the principal's death;

(2) the principal's revocation of this power of attorney or your authority;

(3) the occurrence of a termination event stated in this power of attorney;

(4) if you are married to the principal, the dissolution of your marriage by court decree of divorce or annulment; or declaration that your marriage is void, unless otherwise provided in this power of attorney;

(5) the appointment and qualification of a permanent guardian of the principal's estate unless a court orders otherwise; or

(6) if ordered by a court, the suspension of this power of attorney on the appointment and qualification of a temporary guardian until the date the term of the temporary guardian expires.

Liability of Agent

The authority granted to you under this power of attorney is specified in the Durable Power of Attorney Act (Subtitle P, Title 2, Estates Code). If you violate the Durable Power of Attorney Act or act beyond the authority granted, you may be liable for any damages caused by the violation or subject to prosecution for misapplication of property by a fiduciary under Chapter 32 of the Texas Penal Code.

THE AGENT, BY ACCEPTING OR ACTING UNDER THE APPOINTMENT, ASSUMES THE FIDUCIARY AND OTHER LEGAL RESPONSIBILITIES OF AN AGENT.

INDEX

ABOUT THE AUTHOR

Richard M. Alderman, B.A., J.D., LL.M., is a Professor Emeritus and Director of the Center for Consumer Law at the University of Houston Law Center. Since 1980, he has been known as "The People's Lawyer," and appeared regularly in newspapers and on radio. To learn more about your legal rights you can visit his website, www.peopleslawyer.net. You also can subscribe to his free Consumer Alert Newsletter, delivered three times a week to your email address.